DRAMA FROM IBSEN TO ELIOT

DRAMA
From Ibsen to Eliot

Raymond Williams

1953

OXFORD UNIVERSITY PRESS

NEW YORK

PRINTED IN GREAT BRITAIN BY

T. & A. Constable Ltd.
Edinburgh

Foreword

THE greater part of this book was written between September 1947 and April 1948, but it has since been revised, and, in certain cases, brought up to date. The Introduction includes material from my *Dialogue on Actors*, published in *The Critic*, Spring 1947; and parts of it were summarised in the chapter on Drama in my *Reading and Criticism*, published in May 1950. Two sections of the essay on Ibsen were adapted and broadcast as talks in the B.B.C. Third Programme in December 1949 and May 1950. *Ibsen's Non-Theatrical Plays* was published in *The Listener* of December 23, 1949. The essay on Yeats was commissioned for a volume of *Focus* which has not yet appeared. The essay *Criticism into Drama* was rewritten for publication in *Essays in Criticism*, in April 1951; I have used it here in part in its rewritten form, since, although it repeats certain points made elsewhere in the book, it seems to me to serve as a coherent summary and conclusion. To the editors and similar authorities through whom these parts of the book have been previously published, I make grateful acknowledgment.

I have received much personal help in my work on the book as a whole; from Mr. Wolf Mankowitz and Mr. Clifford Collins, especially in its earlier stages; from Dr. B. L. Joseph; from my wife; and, in the essay on Ibsen, from Mr. R. E. Keen. I am grateful also to Mr. Bernard Miles, Mr. Nevill Coghill, Mr. Martin Browne, and Mrs. Doris Krook, who all kindly discussed my account of contemporary acting, in a very full and interesting correspondence. I have tried to take notice of those of their points with which I could agree, and am much indebted to them. The help which I have received from published sources is very wide; I have tried to make all such obligations plain in my text.

R. W.

For

J. M. W.

Contents

AN OUTLINE OF DATES

1850	IBSEN	*Catilina*
1867	IBSEN	*Peer Gynt*
1867	ROBERTSON	*Caste*
1872	STRINDBERG	*Master Olof*
1881	IBSEN	*Ghosts*
1887	STRINDBERG	*The Father*
1892	YEATS	*The Countess Cathleen*
1892	SHAW	*Widowers' Houses*
1892	HAUPTMANN	*The Weavers*
1894	CHEKHOV	*The Seagull*
1895	WILDE	*An Ideal Husband*
1898	STRINDBERG	*The Road to Damascus*
1899	IBSEN	*When We Dead Awaken*
1902	SHAW	*Man and Superman*
1902	BRIEUX	*Damaged Goods*
1903	CHEKHOV	*The Cherry Orchard*
1907	STRINDBERG	*Ghost Sonata*
1907	SYNGE	*The Playboy of the Western World*
1914	JOYCE	*Exiles*
1914	LAWRENCE	*The Widowing of Mrs. Holroyd*
1916	PIRANDELLO	*Right You Are*
1917	YEATS	*At the Hawk's Well*
1921	PIRANDELLO	*Six Characters in Search of an Author*
1923	SHAW	*Saint Joan*
1924	O'CASEY	*Juno and The Paycock*
1927	TOLLER	*Hoppla!*
1928	ELIOT	*Sweeney Agonistes*
1935	ELIOT	*Murder in the Cathedral*
1936	AUDEN and ISHERWOOD	*The Ascent of F6*
1939	YEATS	*The Death of Cuchulain*
1939	ELIOT	*The Family Reunion*
1944	ANOUILH	*Antigone*
1948	FRY	*The Lady's not for Burning*
1950	ELIOT	*The Cocktail Party*

ix

A *

Introduction

(i)

IN 1850, a play named *Catilina*, advertised as by Brynjolf Bjarme, was published in Christiania. It was the first play, a three-act tragedy in verse, of Henrik Ibsen. In 1950, in London, there appeared another verse play, a comedy: T. S. Eliot's *The Cocktail Party*. The hundred years which passed between those plays were very eventful in European drama. When *Catilina* appeared, the drama, in most European countries other than France, was at perhaps its lowest ebb in six centuries. In England, no writer of importance was even attempting to write plays for the theatre, although poets, from time to time, were producing long dramatic works in verse: works intended, not for performance, but for private reading. The theatres themselves were filled with farces, melodramas, and huge archaeological productions of the great drama of the past. From France, the intrigue plays of a decadent romantic drama went out to all the leading theatres of Europe, providing the only serious contemporary standard. In the succeeding hundred years, and particularly in the last sixty of them, a whole new dramatic movement—the naturalist prose drama— spread and grew to maturity. It gave us the prose plays of Ibsen, the early plays of Strindberg, the plays of Chekhov, of Synge, of Pirandello, of Hauptmann, of Shaw. The prose play, also, was the basis of another dramatic movement in these years; what we now call expressionism. From this we have the later plays of Strindberg, and the work of a school of German dramatists of our own century. Verse drama, which had come to an isolated greatness in Ibsen's *Peer Gynt*, came in the twentieth century, in Ireland and in England, back into the popular theatre. Further, as a necessary part of these developments in the drama itself, the whole art of the theatre was radically reconsidered and revised.

My purpose in this book is to give, not so much a history of the drama of these hundred years, as a critical account and revaluation of it. It seems to me that this has never been adequately done. Of the movement which bulks largest in the period, naturalism, we have no real critical record. I have

11

tried, in my studies of the relevant work of Ibsen, Strindberg, Chekhov, Synge, Shaw, Pirandello, and certain other drama- tists, to meet this deficiency; to offer an account of modern naturalist drama which is supported by detailed analysis of several naturalist plays. In my study of Strindberg, I have tried also to provide a critical account of the early stages of expressionism. Finally, in my studies of the plays of W. B. Yeats and T. S. Eliot, and of some of the younger English verse dramatists, I have attempted a critical examination of the main revolt against naturalism, in the revival of contemporary verse drama.

My criticism is, or is intended to be, literary criticism. It is literary criticism, also, which in its major part is of the kind based on demonstrated judgments from texts, rather than on historical survey or generalised impressions: of the kind, that is to say, which is known in England as practical criticism. Practical criticism began, in the work of Eliot, Richards, Leavis, Empson, and Murry, mainly in relation to poetry. It has since been developed, notably by both F. R. and Q. D. Leavis, in relation to the novel. In the drama, apart from the work of Eliot on Elizabethan dramatists and of other critics on Shakespeare, the usefulness of practical criticism remains to be tested. This book, in addition to its main objects, is intended, therefore, as a working experiment in the application of practi- cal criticism methods to modern dramatic literature.

I have tried to make my critical position clear at the outset, because I am very much aware of the prejudices which it is likely to involve. I am thinking not only of those general prejudices against critical analysis (prejudices which normally involve some such phrase as "murdering to dissect"), but also of the special prejudices inherent in any contemporary criti- cism of the drama. With the general prejudices I am prepared to take my chance; in trials for murder there is, after all, a jury as well as counsel for the prosecution. But the special prejudices involve a more considerable difficulty. Drama, I shall be told (I have been told it already), is a "practical art." It is, the argument goes, something quite different from literature; in the theatre the writ of the literary critic does not run. Any purely literary account of the drama, it is argued, is bound to be both partial and unreal. On this point, I would say at once that it is impossible to reach a critical understanding of the drama of the last hundred years without an understanding of the methods of the theatre in the same period. In all my studies of particular dramatists I have tried to keep closely in mind, and in most cases have discussed, the kind of theatre for which they wrote. But this, I am sure, will not be sufficient to allay the very widespread doubt as to whether literary criticism of the drama is appropriate. Accordingly, because I believe that this uncertainty of the relation between drama and literature is in fact one of the major critical problems of the modern drama, I wish, before continuing with my particular studies of dramatists, to consider as an issue in itself the general question of the relation between drama and literature. An understanding of my conception of this relation is certainly necessary if the particular critical studies which follow are to be of use.

(ii)

It is a popular habit, in contemporary English, for the terms "drama" and "literature" to be sharply distinguished, while the terms "drama" and "acting" are often virtually interchangeable. Few people see any need for literary criticism of the drama; it is the reviewers of performances who are dramatic critics. It is assumed, very widely, that the value of a play has not necessarily anything to do with its literary value; it is held, and firmly asserted, that a play can quite commonly be good, without at the same time being good literature.

This prejudice between drama and literature is, it seems to me, a symptom of a particular stage in the development of the drama. It is inherent, primarily, in the practices of modern naturalist drama, which as a form is only a phase in the drama's long and varied history. But today, the great majority of people who are interested in drama rarely read plays; they only see performances. And most performances seen by the average playgoer will be of contemporary work, which will almost always be based on the assumptions of naturalism (assumptions that we shall need to define). Other performances, of older plays, will usually display a fundamentally naturalist attitude in production (a practice of which we shall look at certain examples). It is not surprising, in this situation, if the average playgoer assumes that the attitudes and practices of the contemporary theatre are things necessary and permanent in drama itself.

Criticism which succeeds in broadening judgment, by overcoming the limits of the purely contemporary view, is always potentially useful, but it is both necessary and urgent in a period in which there is considerable dissatisfaction with contemporary practice. In our own day, the phase of naturalism, in the opinion of several critics and dramatists, has, so far as serious original work is concerned, already ended. Even if this is not yet true, there is at least considerable rejection of the form, and much experiment with alternatives. In other periods, for example the Elizabethan, the fact that plays were more seen than read was no limitation. The critical difference between 1600 and 1950, in this respect, is that the Elizabethans had a more satisfactory—and a more literary—drama.

Literature, in its most general definition, is a means of communication of imaginative experience through certain written organisations of words. And drama, since it has existed in written plays, is clearly to be included under this general definition. A play, as a means of communication of imaginative experience, is as clearly the controlled product of an author— the control being exerted in the finalised organisation of words —as any other literary form. But, in the drama, when the actual and specific means of communication are considered, what is essentially a singular literary statement becomes, in performance, apparently plural.

> Now after all the efforts of that ingenious person (the dramatist) a Play will still be supposed to be a Composition of several persons speaking *ex tempore*.[1]

Howard, in this definition, comes very near to the implicit attitude of a contemporary theatre audience, although few perhaps of that same audience would admit to the attitude in this explicit form. Mr. Sykes-Davies has pointed out,[2] for example, that a theatre audience is less disturbed by an actor fumbling for his words, or speaking them badly (either of which might happen if the words were his own) than by hearing what it takes to be the interfering voice of the prompter, who is the representative of the author's control. Similarly, such general critical assumptions as the right of an actor to "interpret" his part, or as the quasi-human existence of characters and persons in literature, are tenable only if some such illusion is maintained. But it is idle to complain against the tendency to this illusion as such, since it is an integral part of the conditions of performance. What is necessary to emphasise is that it is this

[1] *The Duke of Lerma: To the Reader.*
[2] *Realism in the Drama*, pp. 74-5 (C.U.P., 1934).

element of drama which has often misled criticism. Critical statement and discussion demand, inevitably, certain abstract terms. Such terms in the drama are "plot", "action", "incident", "situation", "character", "personality", "relationship", "unspoken thought", and so on. These terms are abstract in the sense that they are not primary responses to the written or spoken words of a play, but subsequent formulations of parts of the total response. Mr. C. H. Rickword has put the point well with reference to the novel:

> Schematic plot is a construction of the reader's that corresponds to an aspect of the response and stands in merely diagrammatic relation to the source. Only as precipitates from the memory are plot and character tangible; yet only in solution have either any emotive valency.[1]

The danger is always that the abstractions tend to become absolutes, so that a critical enquiry often begins with them: this is particularly the case both in drama and in the novel, where two of these abstractions—"character" and "plot"— are normally given a virtually absolute existence.

When the challenge is directly put, few readers will admit to the belief that characters and actions in a novel have any independent existence, that they are in any sense "real creations" outside the particular sequence of words which conveys an experience of which they are a part.[2] But, by the fact of performance, it is less easy to see this question clearly in the drama, for there the character abstractions are given flesh by the presence of actors, and much of the action is directly

---

[1] *The Calendar of Modern Letters*, October 1926.

[2] The most notable example of this assumption that characters act on their own volition is a comment by Mr. J. B. Priestley, in his Introduction to *They Came to a City*:

'The criticism that the City appears to offer nothing but hearty communal activities is really rather stupid, because obviously it is the communal activities that casual visitors, there for a few hours only, would notice, and, furthermore, my characters naturally single out what attracts them.'

But the visitors are, after all, 'casual', because Mr. Priestley made them so; they are there 'for a few hours only' because that was the time Mr. Priestley decided on. What the characters single out is what Mr. Priestley wants them to single out, because he invented them as he wanted them. If he had wanted anything else singled-out he could have invented other and different characters.

It is something of a surprise to find a controversialist of Mr. Priestley's calibre hiding behind this kind of abstraction.

shown, so that the opportunity for illusion is both practical and substantial.

Yet performance is an essential condition of drama, and there is a danger of so insisting on the existence of a play in a settled verbal organisation (corresponding exactly to the printed novel or poem) that one overlooks the writer's intention that the play should be performed on the stage. And Mr. Eliot has pointed out[1] that to consider plays as existing simply as literature, without reference to their function on the stage, is part of the same fallacy as to say that plays need not be literature at all. No separation of drama and literature is reasonable. What we need to be clear about, however, is the actual function, in the drama as a whole, of those elements of character and action which are emphasised in performance.

Even at the simplest levels of literature, a writer is hardly likely to concern himself with a story or a character unless these have some meaning to him and seem important in his general experience of life. We do not pick our favourite stories, of any kind, any more than we pick our favourite historical personages or our preoccupying abstractions, by chance. We pick them because they represent aspects of experience which, however submerged the connection, are relevant to our own experience. By most people, and by most writers at the simpler levels, this fact goes generally unnoticed; or, if it is noticed, it is only partially understood, and there is little impulse, and insufficient energy, to fix any further attention on the connection, for its greater comprehension. The story, the personage, the abstraction will be accepted, that is to say, at their face value, and it may even be sincerely believed that their capacity to hold one's interest is contained in something intrinsic to them, unconnected with more general experience. A point made by W. B. Yeats on this question is worth quoting:

> My *Countess Cathleen*, for instance, was once the moral question: may a soul sacrifice itself for a good end? But gradually philosophy is eliminated, until at last the only philosophy audible, if there is even that, is *the mere expression of one character or another*. When it is completely life *it seems to the hasty reader a mere story*.

This, of course, is the account of a conscious artist; but the process—not perhaps this exact process, but something like it —is common. Differences on the matter are mainly differences of degree of consciousness.

[1] In 'Four Elizabethan Dramatists', p. 110 of *Selected Essays* (Faber, 1932).

INTRODUCTION

Story, character, idea, seem to have two related uses to the
artist. In one sense, they serve as a formula for the expression
of his experience, in the way defined by T. S. Eliot:

> The only way of expressing emotion in the form of art is by
> finding an "objective correlative", in other words, a set of objects,
> a situation, a chain of events which shall be the formula of that
> *particular* emotion; such that when the external facts, which must
> terminate in sensory experience, are given, the emotion is
> immediately evoked.

In another sense, they may serve as a precipitant to the
artist, in that through their comprehension the artist is able to
find a provisional pattern of experience. By the force of his
grasp on their actuality, the artist is able to release his own,
and their, reality. The only difference in the senses here outlined concerns the placing of these stages in the artistic process.
Mr. Eliot's statement of the matter implies an ordered process,
in which the particular emotion is first understood, and an
objective correlative subsequently found for it. The second
statement suggests that finding the objective correlative may
often be for the artist the final act of evaluation of the particular
experience, which will not have been completely understood
until its mode of expression has been found.

Whichever account may be correct, the place of objective
facts such as story, character, or system of ideas in the artistic
process should be generally clear. They will serve, that is to
say, as general modes of expression for something particular
and unique. Certain series of events, certain lives, certain
beliefs, will be used for this purpose again and again by
different artists for different reasons, because their relevance to
certain central human experiences offers opportunity for
precise expression. Such lives and stories—Faust, Prometheus,
Orestes, Perseus—have the richness of myth. But even here,
and this is the most extreme case, the significance of these
objects in any work of art will not be intrinsic, but will rest
on the adequacy of their function as a mode of particular
expression.

It is necessary to understand the use made of objective and
apparently real events by the artist, in order that the reader or
listener shall not find his response hampered by preconceptions.
The concern of the reader or listener, that is to say, must often
be with what these objects express, rather than with what they
are. The action of a play, for example, is often only incidentally

important in itself. Its interestingness, its truth, cannot be judged as if it were an action in real life. Similarly, with characters, the important dramatist is concerned, not necessarily to simulate "real, live people", but rather to embody in his personages certain aspects of experience. That this will frequently result in the creation of characters which we feel we can accept as "from the life" is certain; but the result will not always be so, and we must be careful that our judgment depends not on whether the characters are lifelike, but on whether they serve to embody experience which the author has shown to be true. All we are obliged to remember, for ordinary purposes, is that character and action, in any good play, are ordered parts of a controlled expression, and that the author's control over their presentation ought to be final. It is the fact that these parts become apparently independent, in the flesh-and-blood illusion of dramatic performance, which has so often misled dramatic criticism. A concern merely with performance is, for this reason, always liable to do a play less than justice. At this point, more than at any other, the literary nature of drama needs re-emphasis.

Now the most important fact about the contemporary theatre is that it is a manifestation, in hard material terms, of certain limiting assumptions about literature, assumptions dictated by a literary decline which has itself been the index of a far-reaching human change. If we name the dominant characteristic of the contemporary theatre as "personality", the change is made clear.

> *Andiamo.* Again the word is yelled out and they set off. At first one is all engaged watching the figures: their brilliance, their blank martial stare, their sudden angular gestures. There is something extremely suggestive in them. How much better they fit the old legend-tales than living people would do. Nay, if we are going to have human beings on the stage, they should be masked and disguised. For in fact drama is enacted by symbolic creatures formed out of human consciousness: puppets if you like: but not human *individuals*. Our stage is all wrong, so boring in its personality.[1]

D. H. Lawrence is here describing a show in a marionette theatre in Palermo, and making a point about the theatre from a single experience which can be supported by many other kinds of evidence. We notice, for example, the relation of

[1] *Sea and Sardinia*, p. 189.

his definition of drama to Mr. Wilson Knight's description of characters in the Elizabethan drama:

> The persons, ultimately, are not human at all, but purely symbols of a poetic vision.[1]

At one level one assents easily: drama, after all, is not life, but, like all art, an abstraction from life. The characters are not, in any biological sense, independent organisms, but, within the limits of the work of art which is the limit of their existence, simply marionettes of the abstraction, symbols of the literary pattern. But it is impossible in this century to make any such statement without a measure of self-consciousness. The very terms—"puppet", "abstraction"—have become associated with limitation. An impression is conveyed of something "wooden", "bloodless" (favourite terms in conventional dramatic criticism).

As one reflects on this situation, one becomes more and more aware of the crucial nature of this question of "character" in literature. Quickly aware, also, that differences of opinion about it are not merely literary questions, but rather symptoms of fundamental differences and changes in whole attitudes of living.

> You mustn't look in my novel for the old stable *ego* of the character. There is another *ego*, according to whose action the individual is unrecognisable, and passes through, as it were, allotropic states which it needs a deeper sense than any we've been used to exercise, to discover are states of the same single radically unchanged element. (Like as diamond and coal are the same pure single element of carbon. The ordinary novel would trace the history of the diamond—but I say, "Diamond, what! This is carbon. And my diamond might be coal or soot, and my theme is carbon.")[2]

This passage from one of D. H. Lawrence's letters, which is of course essential for an understanding of his novels or of related novels like *Wuthering Heights*, is usually taken as simply idiosyncratic. But it is in fact a very general statement, and suggests the whole difference between conventional and naturalist forms of art. It may be set alongside Mr. Eliot's recent definition of a verse play:

> It should remove the surface of things, expose the underneath, or the inside, of the natural surface appearance. It may allow the

[1] *The Wheel of Fire*, p. 16.
[2] Quoted by Huxley, Introduction to *Selected Letters*, p. 16 (Penguin).

characters to behave inconsistently, but only with respect to a deeper consistency. It may use any device to show their real feelings and volitions, instead of just what, in actual life, they would normally profess to be conscious of; it must reveal, underneath the vacillating or infirm character, the indomitable unconscious will, and underneath the resolute purpose of the planning animal, the victim of circumstances, and the doomed or sanctified being.[1]

Mr. Eliot's statement is at once more practical and more limited. There are certain phrases of the formulation with which perhaps one would disagree. If, for instance, one takes the phrases about character as a wish for the "revelation of character"—and Mr. Eliot's words do not seem to exclude this—then this is not simply a definition of a verse play, but of a host of modern plays up to and including the latest West End "psychological drama." Clearly, Mr. Eliot would not admit these others, but if you set up any definition of drama which involves the consideration of characters as absolutes, or which suggests that "characterisation" is the end of drama, then you have, in fact, given away your case to naturalism. Unless the assumption of the absolute existence of characters is firmly dismissed, little to the point is likely to be written about dramatic technique.[2] What one is sure Mr. Eliot means, and what elsewhere he has expressed so admirably, is involved in the phrase:

> it may allow characters to behave inconsistently but only with respect to a deeper consistency.

This deeper consistency is not, of course, a matter of "character" at all, but of the total work of art. It is a consistency which represents—the phrase is blunted but perhaps still capable of accuracy—a radical reading of life. It is the reduction to essentials (perhaps in the way suggested by Lawrence in the

---

[1] Introduction to *Shakespeare and the Popular Dramatic Tradition*, by S. L. Bethell, p. 13 (Faber, 1945).

[2] Miss Ellis-Fermor, for example, in her book *The Frontiers of Drama*, contrives to carry on a seemingly penetrating discussion of technique—in such matters as 'conveying unspoken thought'—without realising that all her argument is simply sleight-of-hand. How, she asks, can a dramatist reveal the significance of atmosphere, or throw sidelights on characters, unless he uses conventions? But this is not the point. There are no characters to have 'unspoken thoughts'; they are simply conventions of expression. The artist needs characters as a convention, and the other conventions he needs are for further communications of the experience, not for amplifying the characters.

diamond and carbon analogy, perhaps in some other) of living experience; the refusal to be distracted by "the natural surface appearance." It is the consistency of art rather than the consistency of representation. The consistency, in fact, is that of the pattern or the structure of experience, as it has been defined above. The relation of characters to this pattern is simply an expressive relation. The "character"—like "action", "relationship", "situation"—is "any device."

<h2 style="text-align:center">(iii)</h2>

I have considered the question of the nature of "character" and "action" in literature in some detail, because the fact that character and action become substantial in dramatic performance is one of the main reasons for the denial of drama as a literary form. Performance is the means of communication of dramatic literature, and these main elements in it—which do not seem to be literary at all—lead to the prejudice which we are considering. And this has been particularly the case in the naturalist drama, because these elements have been heavily emphasised, while at the same time the element of language, in which the literary existence of drama principally resides, has been modified in such a way as to make it appear not to exist at all.

Drama, as a literary form, is an arrangement of words for spoken performance by a group of actors. And where the speech which the dramatist intends is of an everyday, naturalist tone, it is very easy to slip into the illusion mentioned by Howard, and suppose the play to be "a composition of persons speaking *ex tempore*." It is easy, in fact, to forget the author, and to forget, even, that the words which the actors speak are words which have been arranged by him into a deliberate literary form. Yet the difference between naturalism and the most conventional drama is, in this respect, only a matter of degree. Even where the dramatist succeeds in creating a perfect illusion of *ex tempore* conversation, he is still engaged in the arrangement of words into a particular, and conventional, literary form for the communication of a particular kind of experience. It is, after all, a fact equally requiring that consent which is convention, that the people moving on the stage in front of an audience should talk intimately and personally *as if they were not being overheard*.

The principal modification which naturalism effected in the drama was this change of the conventional level of language. The change may be seen clearly in a study of the development of Ibsen, who, after writing all his early plays in verse (and achieving work of the status of *Peer Gynt* and *Brand*), changed deliberately to conversational prose, to

> the very much more difficult art of writing the genuine, plain language spoken in real life . . . My desire was to depict human beings, and therefore I would not make them speak the language of the gods.[1]

Shaw, later, took up this same point about the difficulty of dramatic prose, and put *The Admirable Baskerville* into blank verse because he "had not time to write it in prose." Eliot's comment on this matter is worth quoting:

> Shaw points out that it is easier to write bad verse than good prose—which nobody ever denied; but it is easy for Shaw to write good prose and quite impossible for him to write good verse.[2]

There remains, however, Ibsen's main point. The naturalist dramatists wanted to produce "the illusion of reality." (The unconscious irony of the phrase is perhaps the final critical judgment of naturalism.) In deliberately choosing "everyday contemporary situations" and "everyday, ordinary characters" they felt it necessary to reject the older conventions of dramatic speech. It may be remarked in parenthesis that there is a curious phrase in Ibsen's account of the matter, where he speaks of poetry as "the language of the *gods*." Against this one might set a further comment of Eliot's:

> The *human* soul, in intense emotion, strives to express itself in verse. It is not for me, but for the neurologists, to discover why this is so, and why and how feeling and rhythm are related. The tendency, at any rate, of prose drama is to emphasise the ephemeral and superficial; if we want to get at the permanent and universal we tend to express ourselves in verse.[3]

To explain why the naturalist attitude arose in nineteenth-century Europe is a task, not for the critic, but for the

---

[1] Letter to Edmund Gosse. Quoted in Archer's Introduction to *Emperor and Galilean* (Heinemann).
[2] *A Dialogue on Dramatic Poetry.*
[3] *Ibid.*

historian. We can only deal here with the nature of its manifestation. It was, obviously, in part a product of a new conception of man's relation to the universe, and of his place in
society. It was also—and this is more to our present purpose—
a response to certain changes in *language* and in *feeling*.

In the matter of feeling, Yeats has described one of the
central facts very well, when he speaks of the habit of modern
people, under great emotional stress, of *saying very little*, but
instead of "staring out of the window, or looking into the
drawing-room fire." This was indeed the context of feeling of
the naturalist method, and it had certain important consequences for dramatic speech. Since this was the way people
lived, the naturalists argued, we must, if we are to produce the
"illusion of reality", use language of a natural, conversational kind: our scale is not the forum, but the "small room."

A different position, starting from the same observed facts
of behaviour, might well have been taken up. The fact that
people undergo their emotional crises in silence, or speak of
them inarticulately, might have been granted; and the point
then made that the purpose of drama can as well be described
as "expression" as "representation", with the result that the
dramatist is entitled to articulate the inarticulate, and to
express the silence. Such a convention, in fact, was a necessary
element of the earlier verse drama; and it is to it that our
contemporary verse dramatists have returned.

The naturalists, however, insisted on representation, and
accepted the limitations of normal expression. For those of them
who were concerned merely with surface emotions, these limitations presented no difficulty: conversational resources for the
discussion of food or money or bedrooms remained adequate.
But the more important naturalist writers were fully serious
artists, and wanted to be able to express the whole range of
human experience, even while committed to the limitations of
probable conversation. To meet this difficulty, several dramatic
methods were employed. The most important, perhaps, since
it was used by three of the greatest dramatists—Ibsen, Strindberg, and Chekhov—was what came to be called "symbolism."
The limitations of verbal expression were to be overcome by
the use of visual devices that should bear a large part of the
experience of the play.

Another method was the use of normal conversational speech
for the body of the play, and its intensification into something
more like a literary statement at the point of crisis. This was

used commonly by both Ibsen and Chekhov, and, with certain changes, is the method of the most recent verse plays of Eliot.

A third method, somewhat related to this, was the giving to characters, at certain important points, of unlikely speeches, and then apologising for the improbability. This method, too, appears in Eliot, particularly in *The Family Reunion*, in relation to which it will be discussed in the separate study of his work. But it has mainly appeared in the prose play, and some examples may conveniently be taken here.

What the dramatist is trying to escape from, one must remember, is his own commitment to understatement. He is not convinced, as was William Archer, that the greatest emotions can be dramatically suggested by such words as Pinero had given to the betrayed Letty, learning that her lover was married:

You might have mentioned it. You might have mentioned it.

The dramatic method we are considering allows speech to go beyond the bounds of likely conversation, and then attempts to rally the illusion of naturalism by apology. Here, for example, in Granville-Barker's *Waste*:

TREBELL: . . . I don't care what their beauty or any of their triumphs may be . . . they're unhappy and useless if they can't tell life from death.

CANTELUPE: (*interested in the digression*) Remember that the Church's claim has ever been to know that difference.

TREBELL: My point is this. A man's demand to know the nature of a fly's wing, and his assertion that it degrades any child in the street not to know such a thing, is a religious revival . . . a token of spiritual hunger. What else can it be? And we commercialise our teaching!

CANTELUPE: I wouldn't have it so.

TREBELL: Then I'm offering you the foundation of a New Order of men and women who'll serve God by teaching. His children. Now shall we finish the conversation in prose?

CANTELUPE: (*not to be put down*) What is the prose for God?

TREBELL: (*not to be put down either*) That's what we irreligious people are giving our lives to discover.

The discussion which Granville-Barker felt to be necessary fits badly into conversation; it sounds more like part of a public speech. But he is too good a theatrical craftsman not to realise this, and so he puts his finger into the balance to lull our uneasiness at the mounting rhetoric:

> Now shall we finish the conversation in prose?
> What is the prose for God?

The dramatist is acutely conscious that he has overstepped the limits of his realistic form, and in this way he attempts to restore the illusion. In doing so he has provided a lasting epitaph for self-consciousness—the uneasiness of tone, which is at the heart of this method.

> What is the prose for God?

That, indeed, was the question which naturalism could never answer: how could men speak adequately of experience of that kind in probable conversational terms?

On efurther example will suffice. It is from Denis Johnston's *The Moon in the Yellow River*.

> DOBELLE: . . . I wonder after all do they want to be happy? The trees don't bother, and they're not unhappy. And the flowers too. It's only men who are different, and it's only men who can be really unhappy. And yet isn't it unhappiness that makes men so much greater than the trees and the flowers and all the other things that feel as we do? I used to thank the Devil for that and call him my friend. But there's more to it than that. I suppose the Devil can do nothing for us unless God gives him a chance. Or maybe it's because they're both the same person. Those glittering sorrows, eh? Asleep? Well, here endeth the first lesson.

The statement, we may feel, is naïve. Its prettiness of philosophy is in fact the just retrospective comment on the play. But the important point here is the last sentence:

> Here endeth the first lesson.

The statement has gone beyond the natural probability; and our uneasiness at this mixing of level must be headed off with a laugh. But the defensive irony is again the mark of a fatal self-consciousness.

One further dramatic method, which proceeds from this same realisation of inarticulacy, is the school of Jean-Jacques Bernard, normally called the *Théâtre du Silence*. Silences, its supporters argue, can be as dramatically effective, in the right circumstances, as speech. There is, of course, partial truth in this contention, but of the plays of the *Théâtre du Silence* as a whole one comes to feel that they show no important difference from many other modern plays where the social convention is that of understatement. Compare, for example, M. Bernard's *L'Invitation au Voyage* with Mr. Noel Coward's *Brief Encounter*. The *Théâtre du Silence* is less a solution of the problem of inarticulacy than a symptom of it.

The problem of speech is the central one in contemporary drama: in judging that certain of its attempted solutions have failed, one must be careful not to underestimate the profound central difficulty. For many reasons—and perhaps primarily under the pressure of that complex of forces which we call industrialism—contemporary *spoken* English is rarely capable of exact expression of anything in any degree complex. The effect of this fact on the drama is obviously great. Why, for example, do so many critics who are fully aware of the poverty of contemporary naturalist drama fail to distinguish the substantial elements of naturalism in such a drama as the Elizabethan? Because, surely, the medium of naturalism—the representation of everyday speech—is immeasurably less satisfying in the twentieth century than in the sixteenth.

The Irish drama of the present century provides what is probably the best example of a richness of expression based directly on a common speech. But even here, we must make very definite distinctions: it is a long way from the language of Synge to that of O'Casey. (The reader may be referred to the discussion of this point in the note to the chapter on Synge.)

In a rich, vital, and intensely personal language such as the Elizabethan, the limitations of naturalism, if they do not disappear, are at least disguised. And the representational medium has a close and organic relation to the fully literary language. The common language, in fact, contains the elements of literary precision and complexity. The otherwise startlingly incongruous elements of Elizabethan drama—its lowest naturalism and its highest conventionalism—are given a working unity by this community of expression. Such a community of expression is not today the universally accessible tool but rather the very crown of craftsmanship. Very powerful arguments can be advanced in support of the idea that a fully serious drama is impossible in a society where there is no common system of belief. It seems to me, however, that the condition of a fully serious drama is less the existence of a common faith than the existence of a common language. (I mean, of course, a common language which includes, and is organically related to, the language of contemporary serious literature.) Those critics who insist on the necessity of a common faith are of course right in insisting on the moral element in serious drama, as in all serious literature. And it is clear that the essential moral conventions of drama are more accessible in an age where moral conclusions are shared by the overwhelming majority of the audience. But morality in literature is not necessarily the assumption of certain ethical conclusions as a background against which the immediate experience of the drama is paraded and tested. The moral activity of the artist can also be an individual perception of pattern, or structure, in experience; a process which involves the most intense and conscious response to new elements of substantial living, so that by this very consciousness new patterns of evaluation are created or former patterns reaffirmed. In an age of widespread community of individual belief, the conventions of this process are clearly easier to establish, and full communication is more likely. But at all times, the community between artist and audience which seems to matter is the *community of sensibility*. The artist's sensibility—his capacity for experience, his ways of thinking, feeling, and conjunction—will always be finer and more developed than that of the mean of his audience. But if his sensibility is at least of the same kind, communication is possible. Where his sensibility is of the same kind, his language and the language of his audience will be closely and organically related; the common language will be the expression of the common sensibility. There is no such common sensibility today. The pressure of a mechanical environment has dictated mechanical ways of thought, feeling, and conjunction, which artists, and a few of like temper, reject only by conscious resistance and great labour. That is why all serious literature, in our own period, tends to become minority literature (although the minority is capable of extension and in my view has no social correlative). But within that minority, serious literature, even serious drama, is in fact possible: Mr. Eliot's plays are not the only evidence. And it is surely true that such minority literature does *not* depend on any community of faith, if faith is to be taken as adherence to any formulated system of belief. The community which assures communication is a community of sensibility, a community of process. The artist is no longer the spokesman of the whole society, and he suffers by that fact. But it is not the lack of common beliefs in society which restricts his communication.

It is rather the lack of certain qualities of living, certain capaci-
ties for experience. Thus drama at the present time, if it is to
be serious in the full traditional sense, is inevitably minority
drama. It will never become majority drama if it is to wait on
the spread of universal beliefs. But its communication may be
extended, and its writing made more possible, if developments
in society (the sum of individual developments) make possible
the re-creation of certain modes of living and of language
against which such complexes as industrialism have militated.
On the chances of such development this is not the place to
comment.

(iv)

Drama, as a literary form, is an arrangement of words for
spoken performance; language is the central medium of
communication. But there are in drama other means of communication which are capable of great richness of effect. There
are those elements derivative from the dance, such as movement
and grouping applied by several actors, and movement and
gestures applied by the single actor. There is also design, as it
appears in the construction of sets or scenery, and in all the
related effects of lighting; and there is costume, either integral
to the dance or to the design or to both. There is also, in certain
forms of drama, music.

All these elements are important, and it would be an im-
poverished drama which attempted to dispense with them.
The visual media of movement and design are a necessary
part of the richness of drama (and they have, indeed, in the
drama of our own day, been as essentially neglected as
language). But movement and design have been valuable, in
many of the great periods of drama, precisely when they have
facilitated and enforced the communication of language. In
our own day they have tended consistently towards autonomy.
As richness of speech in drama has declined, so have the visual
elements become more and more elaborated, and have even
attempted individuation. Scenery has become more explicit as
the power of realisation of place through language has declined.
Acting has become more personal as the capacity to communicate experience in language has diminished. The visual
elaboration of drama is related, in fact, not only to the impoverishment of language, but to changes in feeling.

It seems to me that the most valuable drama is achieved

when the technique of performance reserves to the dramatist primary control. It does not greatly matter whether this control is direct or indirect. In an age when it is accepted that the centre of drama is language, such control is reasonably assured. For when the centre of drama is language, the *form* of the play will be essentially literary; the dramatist will adopt certain conventions of language through which to work. And if, in such a case, the technique of performance—methods of speaking, movement, and design—is of such a kind that it will communicate completely the conventions of the dramatist, the full power of the drama is available to be deployed. This, indeed, should be the criterion of performance: that it communicates, fully and exactly, the essential form of the play. The control, that is to say, is the dramatist's arrangement of words for speech, his text.

In the Greek drama, visual elements of performance, whether those of the chorus, engaged in certain formal movements, or those of the actors, whose personality was concealed behind masks and conventional costumes, offered a means of expression to the dramatist which was comparable in precision to the conventional forms of language which he normally employed. In the Elizabethan drama, as the researches of Mr. B. L. Joseph have recently confirmed, not only was there a highly stylised convention for the representation of place, but certain fixed conventions of acting, ranging from the representation of women by boys to an ordered stylisation of gesture and speech for the representation of particular emotions. In the Greek drama, virtually absolute control of performance was assured to the dramatist because he was frequently the leading actor, and usually what we should now call the producer, and all elements of presentation remained under his direction. In the Elizabethan drama, so close a direction was not the rule, but the dramatist was always aware of the conventions of performance, and was able, in this way, to foresee and determine the precise effect, not only of his language, but of the whole acted play.

The most cursory examination of the contemporary theatre reveals a very different state of affairs. The dramatist rarely employs a conventional form of language, but attempts to represent everyday speech. Although similar naturalist representation is the aim of actors, the means employed will vary widely, and the dramatist can have little knowledge of how his words will be spoken, what gestures will accompany them, and what will be the actual spoken effect. Again, the dramatist may indicate certain stage directions, and descriptions of the appearance of his characters, but these will usually be in general terms, and the final appearance on the stage will be the product not only of these indications, but of the ideas of the producer, the stage designer, and of the individual actors. It is true that it is the task of the producer to weld these elements into some integral whole, but this does not alter the fact that the dramatist, whose particular expression is the essence of the play, will not be able to control the exact stage expression in certain of its most powerful elements. He provides words which, since they are rarely cast in any conventional form, can be spoken in a great variety of ways; and over all else, gesture, movement, grouping, and the scenic and lighting elements of atmosphere, he has no effective control whatever. And the fact that the effect of a contemporary play, presentation in the modern theatre being as elaborate as it is, depends almost entirely on these added elements, only emphasises the dramatist's abdication of authority.

It is no surprise that in these circumstances the author's contribution is often merely a script, rather than a self-sufficient work of art. It is a commonplace that the text of a successful modern stage play is usually disappointing, and rarely has any literary merit. For the dramatist is aware of theatrical practice; he knows that he cannot enforce an exact stage presentation. In most cases, then, he will compromise, and will be content to provide a sketch, a "treatment", of a certain theme, which the creative and interpretative talents of others will bring to full expression.

The natural comment on this argument is that it would be wrong to deny these opportunities for creative and interpretative talent on the part of actors, producers, and designers. To meet this point, some closer examination is necessary of what the function of such creation and interpretation should be.

The actor, it is sometimes said, is, like an instrumentalist, a creative-interpretative artist. The analogy is interesting, but no longer very true. In music, the composer commands a means of expression which is highly conventionalised, formal, and exact. The instrumentalist, in translating this expression into sound, is in fact merely expressing a convention. Now in all conventions, intensity, which means in practice tempo and tone, is variable. Expression of a convention, that is to say, is, *within certain defined limits*, open to interpretation. The great instrumentalist, by a personal effort of comprehension such as is necessary with all forms of artistic statement, is able to complete the conventional expression with a maximum of intensity and precision. The activity is, in a sense, creative, in the sense that critical activity is creative; for it is a personal apprehension, and expression of the essential *form* which is immanent in the artist's work. And this further expression will have value, as criticism has value, in the degree of exactly realised understanding of the finalised expression of the original artist. This is only possible by a consistent discipline of attention and loyalty to the central fact; which is the actual expression, in his own medium, of the original artist. Now clearly, just as the instrumentalist expresses a conventional written music in sound, just as the ballet dancer expresses the directions of the choreographer in movement, so can the actor express a sequence of written words in speech. The same degree of creative activity is possible to each, and there will always be great performers and performances. But when we apply this general truth to contemporary plays, we see that the situation has seriously changed. In the first place, the contemporary dramatist is not as a rule concerned to use conventional forms of language; he is more interested in imitating natural speech. And clearly, when natural speech is written down, it is open to the large number of individual, personal variations which it has in life. The actor, as a result, is no longer expressing a convention, but rather taking over certain words into his own personality. And this activity is very different from that of the instrumentalist or dancer. This point is further emphasised when it is remembered that, by its nature, contemporary drama is closer to everyday activity than either dancing or music. What the actor has to do on the contemporary stage is very similar to what he has to do immediately he is off it. The inevitable assertion of his personal habits, or of certain stage habits which he has acquired, combined with the lack of any close guidance by the dramatist, exert irresistible pressure on him to express, not a controlled literary form but rather his own personality or his observations of the personalities of others. The gibe against actors that they are attracted to the profession by a desire to assert their own personalities in a thoroughly favourable atmosphere applies in certain cases. But there are other actors, with a genuine creative interest, to whom the gibe cannot apply. These actors submit to a certain discipline; they attempt to "enter the soul of a character", and work

31

hard at acquiring techniques, from observation of representative personalities, by which they may suppress their own personality and "become the character." This discipline commands a personal respect; but it is far from the essential discipline of drama. It is the sincere attempt at discipline of interpretative artists who have been denied adequate guidance; but it is no substitute for that guidance, it is no substitute, in fact, for a convention.

The form of a play is always a convention, which it is the business of performance to express. It is, moreover, a literary convention, even in the case of the most obvious "realism" or "likeness to life." But today a play is hardly considered to be a literary form, essentially comparable to a novel or a poem. It is considered, instead, as a collection of events and character-parts, which require performance for completion. Often, indeed, the play becomes a mere "vehicle" for a particular actor.

This raises the whole question of the "star" system. With the commercialisation of both drama and society, the most saleable elements are naturally emphasised. And popular interest is certainly much more centred on actors and acting than on dramatic literature. It is not only outside the theatre that this is evident, in the posters where the leading actors' names are printed in larger type than the name of the play, and with a great deal more emphasis than the name of the author.[1] Inside the theatre, also, one quickly becomes aware of the real interest of the audience: the whispered "here he comes" as the star appears; the comments at intervals on actors, and on where they were last seen; and the interesting remark, "Wasn't he *good*!" when an actor has delivered a particularly impressive speech.[2] In this last remark, we see how near we still are to

[1] This happens even when the author is at least as well known as the actor. I remember a bill advertising

the renowned actor ROBERT SPEAIGHT

in very large type, while the name of the author, T. S. Eliot, was given rather less emphasis than the names of the producer and the designer of the scenery. In raising this point, one implies no disrespect to Mr. Speaight, and Mr. Eliot would not, one imagines, trouble himself about this sort of thing. But the tendency is very general, and certainly significant.

[2] One lacks a convention to express the exact tone of this comment, which could be taken as no more than praise of those things which are the province of the actor. But in fact the comment often refers to the substance of the actor's speech, to that which is not personal to him. Yet the fact that it is not personal to him is commonly ignored.

Howard's definition of the attitude of an audience to a play, which we might modify to:

> it will still be supposed to be a Composition of several actors speaking *ex tempore*.

When we consider how much the actor does for himself in a contemporary play, we realise that the statement has in fact a certain intrinsic truth.

Then the emphasis on actors is carried on by the newspaper reviewers, who prefer discussing the acting to the play; and by related forms of publicity. The result is obvious. The audience's response is directed away from the central matter, the words of the play; and, worse, the interest of all but the most tenacious artists among the dramatists will be similarly misdirected. The play will become a mere stalking horse for the star (as has happened completely in the commercial cinema), and while we may then expect a virtuoso act, it is entirely a matter of chance if we get any of the more permanent qualities of dramatic literature.

It might be pointed out, in this connection, that it is very probable that Shakespeare and other Elizabethan dramatists wrote plays with particular actors in mind. This is true, and there is nothing wrong, and perhaps everything right, with the practice. But the Elizabethan dramatist—the evidence is the text—was not concerned merely to exploit an actor's personality, but maintained a sufficient interest in more permanent experience to achieve a work that is self-sufficient as art when the actor's personality is totally forgotten. There is little evidence of such interest in related contemporary practice.

The effect on classic productions of the contemporary emphasis on actors is very unfortunate. Perhaps I may quote a previous comment of mine on this point:

> In every classic season, the emphasis, in reviews as well as in publicity (for the commercial reviewers accept the actors' attitude wholeheartedly), is on interpretation and performance. The play, one feels, is being revived to see what so-and-so can do with it rather than for any reason of an impartial completion of an existing work of art. We are invited to watch Mr. X's Hamlet, Miss Y's Desdemona, Mr. Z's Faustus. When *Dr. Faustus* was performed twice in a week last July (1946) nearly all the critics, after a blushing and rather stolid genuflection to the Mighty Line, went on, with

obvious relief, to talk about performance and interpretation. Now what all this means, if it is not that the plays *Hamlet, Othello,* and *Faustus* are to be presented to us altered, be it ever so slightly, by the impact of X, Y and Z's personality, I cannot even guess. Of course the personality of a leading actor is, by definition, an attractive one, in the broadest sense of the adjective, and it is easy enough to imagine why audiences, already rather self-consciously aware that they are in the presence of a Work of Art, are content to have this attractive personality on which to cling. . . . The bad actor . . . lacks the impersonality of the true artist and finds scope, in his profession, for expressing his personality on the basis of another's already achieved work. That is the real definition of Mr. X's Hamlet, if X really takes the puff seriously (and if he does he is much more a bad actor than hundreds of others inferior to him in every kind of stagecraft). With classic performance he obviously cannot be granted this licence, for he is imposing his personality on a work of art which already exists; his is a dead hand stifling a living work.[1]

The only point I would now add is that the word "revival", which is consistently used by actors, and which I took over without realising its significance, really makes the whole point. The play is genuinely considered dead, or at least unconscious, until the actors take it up again.

Useful confirmation for this point of view is now available in Mr. Norman Marshall's book, *The Other Theatre*.[2] He writes of the experimental work of Mr. Terence Gray at the Festival Theatre, Cambridge.

By the time he reached his last Shakespearean production at the Festival he had abandoned any pretence of respecting Shakespeare's *script*.[3] The play was *The Merchant of Venice*. It was a play that had been repeatedly asked for, as it was a favourite for examination purposes, but it bored Gray, and in his opinion would bore all the more intelligent members of his audience. *This is a point of view which at least has some justification.*[3] If Gray had produced *The Merchant of Venice* attempting to conceal his boredom

[1] *A Dialogue on Actors*, pp. 19 and 21.
[2] The book is an interesting symptom of the present situation in the theatre. Mr. Marshall is a distinguished producer at little theatres, and sees the faults of the West End theatre clearly enough. But he has no respect for drama as literature, and his conception of experimental drama is experimental acting and production of 'worthwhile' plays. One knows what that 'worthwhile' means; Mr. Marshall's lists are evidence enough.
[3] My italics.

INTRODUCTION

the production would inevitably have been dull. His method of avoiding boredom was, paradoxical though it may sound, frankly to confess his bordeom. For instance, when Portia embarked upon "The quality of mercy . . ." speech the entire court relapsed into attitudes of abject boredom and the judge whiled away the time by playing with a yo-yo, a toy which happened to be in vogue at the moment. The speech itself was deliberately delivered in a listless tone of voice as if the actress was repeating it for the thousandth time. The setting for most of the play was the banks of a canal in Venice with houses built up on either side. The middle of the stage was the canal, on which the characters moved to and fro in miniature gondolas. One scene was played with Shylock sitting on his doorstep fishing. In the final scene Shylock entered playing a barrel-organ, and the whole treatment of this character as an object of ridicule, dirty, smelly and greasy, was probably very much in the Elizabethan manner.

Whether or not the result was Shakespeare's *The Merchant of Venice* is not the point. It was what it intended to be—Terence Gray's version of *The Merchant of Venice* and it is arguable that Terence Gray's version was much more entertaining to modern audiences than Shakespeare's.[1]

This is a description of an "intelligent" production in an "intelligent" theatre in an "intelligent" book about the theatre. It can perhaps be taken as making my general point. It is an extreme case, certainly, but not at all unusual, and is certainly the logical end of all current tendencies in this kind of performance. That Mr. Gray thought that by this kind of production he was "abandoning naturalism" is the final irony.

In terms of new plays the logical result of this attitude may be seen in another of Mr. Gray's opinions, which would be very widely supported in the contemporary theatre:

The producer is an independent artist, using other artists and co-ordinating their arts into a whole which is the composite art-of-the-theatre. *The author contributes a framework, ideas, dialogue,* the designer . . . architectural form, the actors . . . sound and movement, and the whole is built up by the producer into what should be a work of *theatre*-art.[2]

Mr. Gray may be eccentric in other respects, but in this statement of faith he has described with complete accuracy the

[1] *The Other Theatre*, pp. 63-4 (Lehmann, 1947).
[2] *Op. cit.*, p. 64 (my italics).

35

normal process of presentation in the contemporary theatre. It is not surprising that dramatists like Yeats and Eliot, wishing to use drama as a serious literary form, should have asked first for change in the theatre.

> I think the theatre must be reformed in its plays, its speaking, its acting and its scenery. There is nothing good about it at present.

That was Yeats in 1903. Eliot, in 1924, wrote:

> I believe that the theatre has reached a point at which a revolution in its principles should take place.

A critical attention to the conditions of performance is, in fact, vital; not only for its own sake, but because of the effect of these conditions on the drama as a literary form. The verse play produced the theatre, but the prose play was produced by the theatre. The modern prose play began, that is to say, as a theatrical form, with the distinction from drama which that term conveys, and at a level (bearing in mind the history of the theatre) where literature, in the important sense, had virtually ceased to operate. The prose play, in the last century, has become a serious literary form; and this has been so because writers of a certain calibre have turned to it and refined it. But it bears everywhere the marks of its theatrical origin; in making a critical judgment on it, one is, inevitably, making a critical judgment of the theatre which produced and sustains it.

A good deal has happened in the drama since 1903 and 1924, but the theatre, in this essential matter of the nature of performance, is much as it was. One factor of the greatest encouragement, however, is that there are undoubtedly, in the contemporary theatre, many actors and producers who are as eager for change as the most exacting of the dramatists. Their influence is very far from dominant, and many of them, it seems to me from discussion, are still uncertain on the points of convention and performance. But the desire for intelligent and necessary change is greater than is usually realised; and there are now in progress many experiments to determine its nature. It should not be impossible, given a clear understanding of the present critical situation of the drama, to develop in practice a method of performance adequate to the full richness of the literary form. In doing this, we shall not only be making the most of the drama that we have, but also creating the conditions for a new extension and revival.

INTRODUCTION

(v)

I have considered the question of the literary nature of drama, in relation to its conventions of "character" and "action", and of language. I have also examined the relation of the verbal elements of drama to the non-verbal, visual elements which are inherent in performance. I have, finally, examined the normal assumptions of performance in the contemporary theatre, and their effect upon the drama as a literary form.

The purpose of this general discussion was the establishment of the general critical position from which the individual studies of the work of particular dramatists will proceed. I naturally wish that the general account I have given may be acceptable as a basis of study. But while the studies which follow proceed inevitably from the critical position which I have outlined, the main weight of my account and revaluation depends, not upon the general standpoint, but upon the particular judgments of individual plays. My general critical view of the modern drama was formed, not from a theoretical enquiry, but from responses to particular dramatic works. I have outlined my general view in this Introduction, not so much as a dogma which the reader must accept, but as an explanation of the method of the subsequent criticism.

I have written of these dramatists and these plays, then, with the conviction that drama is essentially a literary form, but a literary form which requires, for its communication, all the theatrical elements of performance. I have discussed the plays against a background of the theatre for which they were written, and have examined, where they were relevant, the views of the dramatists both on dramatic form and on performance. Much of my criticism is based on the analysis of particular arrangements of words for speech; this is literary analysis, but it is conceived in terms of the medium of communication. I have examined, also, questions of form and construction. It is often urged against critical analysis that it neglects these aspects of technique; but while the reminder is sometimes necessary, "construction" and "form" are, after all, no more than the conventions of literary arrangement. They demand consideration as such, but any attempt to raise them to absolute status is invalid in the same way as the similar attempts to isolate "action" and "character."

37

My selection of dramatists, both in prose and in verse, is, of course, controversial. I would defend it, if it is attacked, by saying that it seemed to me that the demonstration of a general critical position was the most important thing to be done; and that, if this general position were accepted, the actual evaluation expressed in the selection would follow. There are many histories of modern drama, but the effect of these is too often a negative, critically formless, attitude. The second part of this book concludes with an essay, *Criticism into Drama*, in which I have tried to show the vital part which criticism has played in dramatic reform and development. Criticism can only do this, it seems to me, if it goes beyond the recording of minor individual variations to the discernment of main tendencies and developments. This discernment I have attempted, not as part of that process of tidying-up which we sometimes call literary history, but as an expression of values in the drama, from which we may assess our position, and decide our future directions.

PART I

I

Henrik Ibsen

(i)

"FAME," said Rilke, "is the sum of misunderstanding which gathers about a new name." The English, indeed the European, fame of Ibsen is perhaps a case in point. It is very widely believed that his main concern was to write plays about the social problems of his day, and that his typical dramatic manner is that of the conversational play, in which every character is provided with a family, and every room with heavy furniture, a certain stuffiness in the air, and a Secret mouldering in the corner cupboard. These ideas spring from a mistake of emphasis, which, in England, began with the London performances of *A Doll's House* in 1889, and of *Ghosts* and *Hedda Gabler* in 1891. These plays—*Ghosts* in particular—were hysterically abused by a "compact majority" of the reviewers and right-thinking men of the day. "This new favourite of a foolish school," wrote Clement Scott, in a *Daily Telegraph* leading article drawing attention to his own review of *Ghosts*, ". . . this so-called master . . . who is to teach the hitherto fairly decent genius of the modern English stage a better and a darker way, seems, to our judgment, to resemble one of his own Norwegian ravens emerging from the rocks with an insatiable appetite for decayed flesh." *Ghosts* was compared to "an open drain; a loathsome sore unbandaged; a dirty act done publicly; a lazar-house with all its doors and windows open." Scott's outbursts are distinguished from others only by the lack of restraint encouraged by a fluent pen and a waiting press.

It is best, in such cases, if no attempt is made at defence. Since the attacks are irrelevant, defence will only give away the artist's case. For Ibsen, unfortunately, there were too many defenders. Ibsen*ism* and Ibsen*ites* sprang up everywhere. Mr. Shaw wrote *The Quintessence of Ibsenism*, having, it seems, decided quite firmly in advance what the plays ought to mean. What Shaw expounded in his book was hardly what Ibsen had written in his plays. But the Ibsenite emphasis on subject, as something which could be considered apart from the words of the plays, was characteristic, and it was very welcome to those many people who looked, not for a dramatist, but for a moral leader. The effect of this emphasis was to centre attention on elements in Ibsen which were in fact incidental: on the Emancipation of Women, and the Freedom of Youth; on the "whited sepulchres" of Christian fathers and gentlemen; on the slam of Nora Helmer's front door, which "brought down behind it in dust the whole Victorian family gallery." These things made the scandal, and, in the way of scandals, they made the success; they made Ibsen. When the pages were turned back to his earlier productions, it was shocks of this order which were sought, but which were not found. So it was assumed that his plays had become valuable only when he discarded verse for prose, and myth for sociology. Similarly, when later productions appeared, and were found to be neither "shocking" nor "enlightened", it was whispered that Ibsen was, after all, an old man, and that his powers might well be failing. It seemed impossible, indeed, for anyone to think about Ibsen at all, except in terms of that initial public impression. His intentions were described by Shaw:

> Shakespeare had put ourselves on the stage, but not our situations. . . . Ibsen supplies the want left by Shakespeare. He gives us not only ourselves but our situations. . . . One consequence is that his plays are much more important to us than Shakespeare's. Another is that they are capable both of hurting us cruelly, and of filling us with excited hopes of escape from idealistic tyrannies and with visions of intenser life in the future.

His methods were described by William Archer:

> . . . naturalness of exposition, suppleness of development, and . . . general untheatricality of treatment.

Worse, Archer-English, that strange compact of angularity, flatness and Victorian lyricism, was generally taken as Ibsen's own style.

These were serious errors, but they have persisted with surprising energy. The mass of Ibsen criticism, over sixty years, has done little to correct them. The best revaluation, Miss M. C. Bradbrook's *Ibsen the Norwegian*, does much to correct the excesses of Ibsenism, but, in my view, leaves the critical estimate of his work very much as it was. Miss Bradbrook has cleared the ground for a critical revaluation, but has not made it. It seems to me that the revaluation which is required is radical.

The orthodox account of Ibsen as dramatist proposes four major periods: first, the "apprenticeship", ending with *The Pretenders*; second, the major non-theatrical plays, *Brand*, *Peer Gynt*, and *Emperor and Galilean*: third, the prose plays, sometimes called the social plays, beginning with *The League of Youth* and passing through *A Doll's House* and *Ghosts* to *Hedda Gabler*; and fourth, the "visionary" plays, from *The Masterbuilder* to *When We Dead Awaken*. As a mnemonic this account has its uses; but, too often, on the naïve assumption that the development of an artist can be described in terms of the maturing and decay of an organism, it is used as a kind of graph of value. The graph, of course, is drawn on Ibsenite assumptions. Since the "social" plays were taken as the high point, the works before them must be represented as mere preparation for maturity. Similarly, since after maturity comes decline, the last works are the mere product of failing powers. What this account amounts to is a fragmentation; the Ibsenites have been the disintegrators of Ibsen. The revaluation that I propose rests on the essential unity of the work of Ibsen, a unity, incidentally, on which he always himself insisted. The fact that he was writing in a period of great experiment in the drama is important, and I hope to be able to add something to the understanding of his innovations. But it is with the unity of his work that I am mainly concerned. It is a unity too important to be given up for a pseudo-biology. What Mr. Eliot has said of Shakespeare is as true of Ibsen; "we may say confidently that the full meaning of any one of his plays is not in itself alone, but in that play in the order in which it was written, in relation to all of his other plays, earlier and later: we must know all of his work in order to know any of it."

(ii)

The part of Ibsen's work which is normally neglected, but which is essential to a critical understanding of his development, is the eleven years from 1851 to 1862, during which he worked as dramatist, producer and stage-manager in the small, struggling *Norske Theater* at Bergen, and the two succeeding years in which he was adviser to the theatre in Christiania. While Ibsen was at Bergen, one hundred and forty-five plays were produced, and seventy-five of them were French. The typical production was the play of romantic intrigue, of which Scribe was the leading exponent. The success of such a play depended on a complicated plot, moving at high speed around certain stock scenes: the confidential document dropped in public; the abducted baby identified by a secret talisman or birthmark; the poisoned goblet passing from hand to hand, and being drunk in the end by anyone but the intended victim. Characters were similarly conventional: "heavy father, innocence distressed, rough diamond, jealous husband, faithful friend."[1] The plays, that is to say, did not deal in nuances. Character and action were drawn in bold, theatrical lines: action was varied, complicated and continuous in order to provide excitement and surprise and suspense in the theatre; characters were set in a single, simple, colourful mould, in order to provoke theatrical recognition.

Now it is important to remember that for conventions of this kind one need not stay at Scribe for a model, but can go also to Shakespeare and the other Elizabethan dramatists. This fact has not been sufficiently realised: it needed Mr. Eliot to observe:

> The Elizabethans are in fact a part of the movement of progress or deterioration which has culminated in Sir Arthur Pinero and the present regiment of Europe.[2]

Mr. Eliot is here speaking in particular of "the general attitude toward life of the Elizabethans," which he describes as "one of anarchism, of dissolution, of decay." But he has previously described the aim of the Elizabethan dramatist as

> to attain complete realism without surrendering any of the advantages which as artists they observed in nonrealistic conventions . . . a desire for every sort of effect together . . .[3]

Now realism was not a primary intention of the theatre of Scribe, but, with this exception, the "desire for every sort of effect together" is a fair description of the intrigue method. The important difference between the plays of Scribe and those of Shakespeare is, however, a literary difference. The purely theatrical conventions remained very much the same; the difference was that they were used for dramatic ends of an obvious inferiority. Drama, in fact, had been reduced to a mere

---

[1] Bradbrook, *op. cit.*, p. 77.   [2] *Four Elizabethan Dramatists.*   [3] *Ibid.*

theatrical excitement. Character and action, which in the best Elizabethan drama had been primarily conventions for the expression of a larger dramatic experience, had become absolute theatrical qualities. Language, which in the best Elizabethan drama had been shaped by a deliberate convention into a medium of full dramatic range, was used by Scribe and his contemporaries for little more than sensational representation. "The advantages which as artists the Elizabethans observed in unrealistic conventions" became, with Scribe and his followers, purely theatrical. Consider the following uses of aside and soliloquy:

(a)

L: My lords, with all the humbleness I may, I greet your honours from Andronicus.
(aside) And pray the Roman gods confound you both.
D: Grammercy, lovely Lucius, what's the news?
B: (aside) That you are both deciphered, that's the news,
For villains marked with rape.

(b)

L: Ah, right, right; the papers from Peter Kanzler.
S: See, here they all are.
L: (aside) Letters for Olaf Skaktavl. (To STENSSON) The packet is open, I see. You know what it contains?

(c)

T: I know how, step by step, you've led him on, reluctant and unwilling, from crime to crime, to this last horrid act. . . .
M: (aside) Ha! Lucy has got the advantage and accused me first. Unless I can turn the accusation and fix it upon her and Blunt, I am lost.

(d)

B: You were a fair maiden, and nobly born: but your dowry would have tempted no wooer.
M: (aside) Yet was I then so rich.

(e)

M: I thank you, gentlemen.
(aside) This supernatural soliciting
Cannot be ill; cannot be good:—if ill,
Why hath it given me earnest of success,
Commencing in a truth? I am thane of Cawdor.

45

If good, why do I yield to that suggestion
Whose horrid image doth unfix my hair,
And make my seated heart knock at my ribs,
Against the use of nature? Present fears
Are less than horrible imaginings:
My thought, whose murder yet is but fantastical,
Shakes so my single state of man, that function
Is smother'd in surmise; and nothing is
But what is not.

B: Look how our partner's rapt.

M: (*aside*) If chance will have me king,
Why, chance may crown me,
Without my stir.

(f)

L: (*alone*) At last then I am at Ostraat—the ancient hall of which a
child, two years past, told me so much. Lucia. Ay, two years ago
she was still a child. And now, now, she is dead. Ostraat. It's as
though I had seen it all before, as though I were at home here.
In there is the Banquet Hall. And underneath is—the grave
vault. It must be there that Lucia lies. . . . In there—somewhere
in there is sister Elina's chamber. Elina? Ay, Elina is her name.

The first of these examples (*a*) is a structural device, rather
than a dramatic convention in the full sense. It is, like (*b*),
simply a way of keeping the audience informed of the progress
of the action. In (*c*) this device is developed somewhat further;
its function is still to explain the action, but it has a new self-
consciousness: the dramatist is using the device not only to
explain, but also to create excitement. In (*d*) we have a fairly
primitive use of the aside to provide a comment of character, a
method which is developed and transcended in (*e*) where the
soliloquy, prolonged from the aside, not only throws light on
character, but communicates a level of experience to which
both character and action are subsidiary—a part of the
essential pattern of the whole play. In (*f*) again, however, the
soliloquy is no more than a structural device, for the explanation of the action and its setting.

The first and fifth of these examples are from Elizabethan
drama; that from *Titus Andronicus* is still at the level of subter-
fuge, but the same device, in *Macbeth*, is developed to great
dramatic power. The third example is from George Lillo's
The London Merchant (1731), where the decline into theatricality
is clear: Millwood is not only conscious of himself, but of the

audience, to whom he is deliberately "playing." The remaining three examples, where aside and soliloquy are used mainly as devices to keep the action going, or for the crudest purposes of characterisation, are from a dramatist writing in the intrigue manner of Scribe: the young Henrik Ibsen.

Ibsen, writing in 1851 in the periodical *Andhrimner* (*Manden*), had severely criticised Scribe's dramatic methods, finding in the whole tendency of French drama too great a reliance on 'situation', at the expense of 'psychology.' He spoke scornfully of "the dramatic sweetmeats of Scribe & Co." But his subsequent experience in the theatre effected a modification of his views. The theatrical effectiveness of the intrigue play was unquestionable, and Ibsen set to work, quite consciously, according to its methods. *Lady Inger of Ostraat* (1855) is a typical specimen of the form:

LADY INGER: Drink, noble knights. Pledge me to the last drop. . . . But now I must tell you. One goblet held a welcome for my friend; the other death for my enemy.

NILS LYKKE: Ah, I am poisoned.

OLAF SKAKTAVL: Death and hell, have you murdered me?

LADY INGER: You see, Olaf Skaktavl, the confidence of the Danes in Inger Gyldenlove. And you Nils Lykke, can see how much my own countrymen trust me. Yet each of you would have me place myself in your power. Gently, noble sirs, gently.

This characteristic piece of business is the intrigue drama at its most normal; in the whole play Ibsen makes no significant departure from its deliberately theatrical conventions. And *Lady Inger of Ostraat* is only one example of the method of his drama at this period. In *The Feast at Solhaug* the same essential method may be everywhere observed. Here, for example, is a very favourite trick, the entry heightened by coincidence:

MARGIT: He is far from here. Gudmund cannot be coming.

BENGT: (*entering, calls loudly*) An unlooked-for guest, wife.

MARGIT: A guest? Who?

BENGT: Your kinsman, Gudmund.

This device may be seen at its most extensive in another of these early plays, *The Vikings at Helgeland*. Gunnar, believing his son Egil to have been abducted and killed by Ornulf, himself kills Thorolf, son of Ornulf. Gunnar comments:

My vengeance is poor beside Ornulf's crime. He has lost Thorolf, but he has six sons left. But I have none, none.

At this point the return of Ornulf is announced, and Gunnar calls his men to arms, crying:

Vengeance for the death of Egil.

Ornulf enters on the cry, carrying Egil in his arms. And the six sons of Ornulf have been killed in rescuing Egil from the actual abductors. Further, the killing of Thorolf was based on a *deliberate* misunderstanding: Thorolf himself allows a threat of the actual abductor to be taken as the words of his own father, even although he knows that they are not. He is, as a result, killed, but he makes no attempt at explanation. It is possible to put his death down to the Viking conception of honour; it is more to the point to ascribe it to the French conception of "situation."

Any drama must be judged in the context of its own conventions; and it is no good complaining against these plays of Ibsen on the ground of their lack of realism. The plays could have proceeded on these lines, and still have been great plays, if the dramatic experience to be communicated had been of such a kind that the conventions could have expressed it, rather than manipulated it. In plays like *Lady Inger of Ostraat*, as in so much of Scribe, the purpose of the drama is the communication of the devices. This is a fair enough definition of theatricality in any period and in any form.

A skilled theatrical craftsman might well remain satisfied with such a situation, and go on writing plays for stock. But Ibsen was always an artist, for whom the communication of significant experience must be the primary concern. Already, in these early plays, elements of the curiously consistent pattern of experience which Ibsen wished to communicate may be discerned, struggling for expression in an uncongenial form. *The Vikings at Helgeland*, for example, is built on the austere pattern of Viking law and conduct, which, with its bare unquestioned conventions of fate and retribution, is very near in spirit to Ibsen's reading of experience. Its hard, bitter consistency, and its neglect of the romantic conceptions of personality, might well have seemed to Ibsen a satisfactory convention for the expression of his own emotional pattern. It falls short of this, however, in the form in which the play is cast, because of the intrigue habit of coincidence, which reduces the tragedy from the causal to the casual.

Ibsen's next play, written after an interval of four years, which had included a profound personal crisis, is set in a different mould. He had begun it as a tragedy, to be called *Svanhild*, but it eventually appeared as his first play of modern life—*Love's Comedy*. It is a play of considerable incidental talent, but it shows more clearly than ever the false position into which Ibsen had been driven by his acceptance of contemporary theatrical techniques.

There is a certain thematic element of 'vocation', an experience to which Ibsen was to return again and again:

the essence of freedom is to fulfil our call absolutely.

There is a certain amount of reasoning about "the contrast between the actual and the ideal": another persistent Ibsen theme. Indeed, the "discussion", which Shaw acclaimed as a new element in *A Doll's House*, is similarly present here:

It's time we squared accounts. It's time we three talked out for once together from the heart.

But these elements cannot be adequately expressed in the dramatic form which Ibsen has chosen. The contrast between the actual and the ideal is seriously blurred by the fact that the central relationship—that between Falk and Svanhild—is a type situation of the romantic drama. Similarly, the beginning and end of the play are written in a kind of operetta manner: Falk sings a love-song, and a chorus of gentlemen support him. Again, there is a considerable element of caricature, which, though often incidentally successful, proceeds from an essentially different level of experience. Ibsen's intention is the expression of a theme, but the uncertainty of form is so great that the result is no more than a hybrid entertainment.

The final demonstration of the incompatibility of Ibsen's art with the theatre to which he had become apprenticed is *Kongs-emnerne* (*The Pretenders*). It is a play based on a passage of Norwegian history, and its action is the rivalry of certain pretenders to the crown. There are obvious elements of contemporary nationalist politics in it, but it cannot be read as a mere "politico-historical" play. William Archer wrote about it as if he were reviewing a history-book.

I cannot find that the Bishop played any such prominent part in the struggle between the King and the Earl as Ibsen assigned to him.

On this kind of approach, which will be familiar to readers of commentaries on the history-plays of Shakespeare, perhaps the best comment is an adaptation of Mr. Middleton Murry's well-known remark:[1] poets are not Norwegian historians; if they were they would have written Norwegian history-books. *The Pretenders* is in fact the first full embodiment of the most persistent single theme in Ibsen's whole work: the idea of *vocation*. The analysis of the relationship between the two main rivals—Hakon and Skule—is centred almost entirely on the definition of this experience. Skule is moved only by the prestige of the crown, and he knows his disadvantages against Hakon, who has the actual vocation of kingship:

> While he himself believes in his kingship, that is the heart of his fortune, the girdle of his strength.

Skule, for the purposes of faction, can assume such a vocation, and deceive even his son. But since the assumption is false, it leads only to crime, leads directly to desecration of the shrine of kingship, which his son drags from the Cathedral. Skule repents and submits to death:

> Can one man take God's calling from another? Can a Pretender clothe himself in a king's life-task as he can put on the king's robes? . . . Greet royal Hakon from me. Tell him that even in my last hour I do not know whether his birth was royal. But this I surely know—it is he whom God has chosen.

To anyone who has read *Brand*, or *Peer Gynt*, *The Masterbuilder*, or *When We Dead Awaken*, it will need no further demonstration that Ibsen is concerned here with one of his profound and lasting preoccupations: the nature of "calling" and its realisation. The rivalry for the crown is used as "a situation, a chain of events, which shall be the formula of that *particular* emotion." But *The Pretenders*, as a whole, is still cast in the form of the intrigue play. The required complication of action, so that the expected "situations" may be prepared, hampers and almost obscures the genuine expression which is achieved in the relationship of Hakon and Skule. The theatrical form, that is to say, is inadequate for the expression of the dramatic experience.

Ibsen seems to have realised this fact quite clearly. He abandoned the attempt at compromise; left Norway, left the theatre, and left off writing for the stage. The intrigue drama

---

[1] 'Poets are not tragic philosophers: if they were they would have written tragic philosophies.' *The Problem of Style.*

was his inescapable inheritance, and for the rest of his writing life he was to be profoundly affected by it. But for the moment he would turn his back on the theatre which was dedicated to its service; he would seek, without reference to the theatre, a dramatic form adequate for the expression of his significant experience.

(iii)

Ibsen had had thirteen years' practical experience of the theatre; but he only began to produce work that is now considered important when he left it. The first of these mature works was *Brand*, which was never intended for the stage, although it has once or twice been performed in its entirety, and more frequently in abridged versions. Unfortunately, Shaw's interpretation of the play as Ibsen's "exposure" of the harm caused by a fanatical idealist has so impressed itself in England that most of our versions are cut to fit that very dubious pattern. *Brand*, following *The Pretenders*, is essentially a statement on the claims of vocation; and its significant conclusion is the impossibility of fulfilling the vocation of the ideal under "the load of inherited spiritual debt." In this main theme there is no sign of satire, although one can understand why Shaw thought that there ought to have been.

The design of *Brand* is abstract, in the sense that the play is arranged, not so much to study a particular character, but to state a theme of which that character is the central element. For example, in the first act Brand defines his life in terms of vocation:

A great one gave me charge. I *must*.

And there follow, as if in a scheme of characters, objections to any absolute response: the fear of injury and death, as stated by the peasant; the devotion to happiness, as stated by Einar and Agnes; the refusal of order, in a pagan adoration of nature, as stated by the gypsy-girl Gerd. Brand reviews these three temptations to refusal, and re-affirms his faith:

War with this triple-handed foe;
I see my Call.

This formal embodiment of a theme is the general method of the play. Its next aspect is the definition of Brand's mission, which is the restoration of wholeness. The present fault in man is seen, first, as the lack of wholeness:

> Try every man in heart and soul,
> You'll find he has no virtue whole,
> But just a little grain of each . . .
> . . . . all fragments still,
> His faults, his merits, fragments all . . .
> But here's the grief, that worst or best,
> Each fragment of him wrecks the rest.

It is in opposition to this kind of fragmentary living that Brand declares his consistent "All or Nothing." He declares it, at this stage, as the means to the achievement of the ideal, the way of bridging the gulf

> Between the living world we see
> And the world as it ought to be.

Now, at first sight, this seems like Shaw's definition of the play:

> filling us with excited hopes of escape from idealistic tyrannies and with visions of intenser life in the future.

But this is to overlook the fact that it is the reforming element itself which comprises the ideal. The whole tragedy of *Brand* is that pursuit of the ideal is both necessary and futile. The call is absolute, and so are the barriers. This tension is the whole action of the play; it is summarised, in a way very characteristic of Ibsen, in the significant lines:

> Born to be tenants of the deep,
> Born to be exiles from the sun . . .
> Crying to heaven, in vain we pray
> For air, and the glad flames of day.

This is the fundamental statement in *Brand*, and perhaps in the whole work of Ibsen. The action of *Brand*, as I have said, is the demonstration of this conflict, in which Brand himself is broken. The formal implications of "demonstration", incidentally, are completely appropriate.

In the beginning, most of Brand's speeches are in specifically social terms:

> And now the *age* shall be made whole . . .
> The sick *earth* shall grow sound again . . .
> *Nations*, though poor and sparse, that live . . .

But it is part of the design of the play that this emphasis should change, that the vocation should come to be defined, not as social reform, but as the realisation of the actual self:

> One thing is yours you may not spend,
> Your very inmost self of all.
> You may not bind it, may not bend,
> Nor stem the river of your call.
> To make for ocean is its end.
>
> Self completely to fulfil,
> That's a valid right of man,
> And no more than that I will.

This realisation is not a matter of ideals. What happens is that the general aspirations come to be limited by the actual inheritance:

> To fulfil oneself, and yet
> With a heritage of debt?

By 'debt' Ibsen means hereditary guilt, a personal liability which epitomises original sin. In Brand's case, the realisation of debt comes through his meeting with his mother; he takes over both her sins and her responsibilities, and sees that the vocation must now be re-defined:

> As the morn, not so the night . . .
> Then I saw my way before me . . .
> Now my sabbath dream is dark.

Brand's mission can no longer be the reform of the world, but the actual, limited sphere of "daily duty, daily labour, hallowed to a Sabbath deed." Nevertheless, the command is still absolute, submission still necessary, even if this involves the sacrifice of life. Brand will not go to his dying mother; he will not save the life of his son. The conflict is a test of submission to the will of God, at whatever human cost. If the will to submission is strong enough, the conflict will be resolved.

> When will has conquered in that strife,
> Then comes at length the hour of Love.
> Then it descends like a white dove
> Bearing the olive-tree of life.

This, of course, is an exact prevision of the actual end of the play. It will be both love and death; when the avalanche descends ("he is white, see, as a dove") Brand cries that he has willed to his utmost strength. This, again, is the consummation which had been foreseen :

> I trust wholly in God's call . . .
> Mine is that Will and that strong trust
> That crumbles mountains into dust.

It is not, in the ordinary sense, a matter of choice. Once Brand has heard the call to wholeness, to the healing of "the fissured soul", his fate, and the fate of those connected with him, is determined. "All the generation" who have inherited sin "are doomed" :

> Blood of children must be spilt
> To atone for parents' guilt.

This is a situation with which there can be no compromise; "the Devil is compromise." Brand refuses to compromise, but, in spite of this, he is, by his inheritance, compromised. It is not that he chooses wrongly, but that he could not choose at all; he could only accept his inheritance. The voice that cries through the avalanche—"He is the God of Love"—is not some kind of retrospective criticism of Brand's actions; it is the foreseen consummation, and the assurance of mercy. Brand is one of those who come to "stand in a tight place; he cannot go forward or backward." It is, as Ibsen sees it, the essential tragedy of the human situation.

One important element of the final dramatic realisation is Ibsen's use of the figures of dove and falcon. These figures are closely interwoven throughout the play. The dove which will descend has been the ultimate love; when "will has conquered" the dove brings life. The falcon is its opposite and its counterpart. At the root of the particular sin which Brand is expiating, "a childish scene that lives in my mind like a festering scar", is his mother's robbery of the bed of his dead father, "sweeping down like a falcon on her prey." The falcon is also compromise, the mark of the devil. A great part of the effect of the climax of *Brand* depends upon these two figures. The phantom which appears to Brand in the mountains reveals itself as the falcon, and Gerd raised her gun to shoot it; "redemption", she says, "is at hand." She shoots into the mist, and the shot begins the avalanche:

> I have hit him . . .
> Plumes in thousands from his breast
> Flutter down the mountainside.

HENRIK IBSEN

See how large he looms, how white,
He is white, see, *as a dove.*

It was the falcon, and it is the dove. The transformation is the whole resolution of the play.

In this last act of *Brand,* Ibsen reaches one of the heights of his dramatic power. And he achieves this mastery by concentrating on the central dramatic element of his conception, at the expense of both 'representation' and 'situation.' *Brand* is one of the most dramatic works Ibsen ever wrote, but it is very far from what his contemporaries would call a play.

English readers are still in need of an adequate translation which would communicate something of the controlled power of the original. Herford's attempt is literal, and his lines have a surface resemblance to the metre of the original. But the difference in languages is too great, and Herford's reproductions frequently degenerate into doggerel. The other translations which I have seen and heard are, however, no better. It would seem that the verse of *Brand* is virtually untranslatable.

The achievement of *Brand* is not, of course, without fault. The social elements in the play—the figures of Dean, Sexton, Schoolmaster and Mayor—though necessary to the theme in that they define an aspect of fragmentariness—

> . . . with the best will no-one can
> Be an official and a man—

seem at times to be developed for their own sake, as caricatures. Again, it is true, as Ibsen wrote to Brandes,[1] that the theme of the play is not necessarily religious; that he "could have made Brand's syllogism" equally in art, in love, or in politics. But the formula which he has chosen is religious; and it is a weakening of its objectivity—and hence its adequacy—when elements of the *original* emotion—(Ibsen's relation to Norway and to his work, as it seems almost certain to be)—enter the art form untransmuted. Ibsen's fondness of direct speech from the stage—which made Dr. Stockmann's public meeting so congenial to him—is allowed, at a critical moment in *Brand,* to distract from the central theme with a sermon on weakness, freedom, and littleness (the speech on the mountains in Act Five). This surrender to "interestingness"—a surrender similar to the elaboration of the social caricatures—is a failure of

[1] Letter of 26 June 1869 (*Breve,* 1, p. 68).

55

discipline. And it is not merely an incidental failure. The desire for directness is part of the same failure as the tendency to dissociation. "As a character, Brand convinces,"[1] writes Miss Bradbrook. Even if this were relevant, I do not think it would be true. One is not making the naïve complaint that Brand is not "a human being." "The persons ultimately are not human at all, but purely symbols of a poetic vision." But there is a pervasive limitation of substance in the experience of which Brand is an expressive convention. The complaint is not that Brand is an "attitude", as William Archer commented; but that the level of the attitude seems to be only diagramatically related to detailed human experience. In the final act, we do not feel this. But the Brand of the earlier acts has the crude lines of a theoretical creature; he has, it would seem, no roots; not because the experience which contains him is inorganic or insubstantial; but because it is *now*, as manifested, rootless; it has been dug up and exhibited at the level of conscious debate.

The point is really one of convention. *Brand* is, essentially, a morality play, with its characteristic isolation of a central figure against whom certain forces and attitudes embodied in characters are pitted. But Ibsen could not fully command the integrity of form which such a play demands. There is always a tendency to blur the central pattern by touches of a different kind of "personality"; so that we come to look, not at the pattern, but at the man, and question the adequacy of his substantiation. Yet the play, if we understand its essential type, is a very considerable achievement. It is better read, however, than performed. And this is because the conditions of modern performance, with their insistent emphasis on "personality" and on substantiated characters, are quite unsuited to the communication of an essentially impersonal dramatic form. This is the real measure of Ibsen's departure from the theatre of his day.

Such attention to Ibsen's work as has been primarily concerned with abstracting his philosophy is responsible for the normal bracketing of *Brand* and *Peer Gynt*, Ibsen's next play. *Brand*, it is said, is the examination of unswerving will; *Peer Gynt* the examination of constantly swerving lack of will. In one sense this is true, but preoccupation with the point has prevented most critics from remarking the great difference between the plays, which are similar only in that both are

[1] *Op. cit.*, p. 51.

non-theatrical. *Peer Gynt* is a very different work from *Brand*, and requires quite different consideration.

Peer Gynt is a romantic fantasy, or, as Ibsen called it, a "caprice." It is cast in the traditional form of the quest, but it is a quest, unlike that of Brand, which is devoid of self-consciousness of the more usual kind. It is casual as all fantasy is casual, and at the same time as systematic. The quest of Peer is, in a real sense, itself a fantasy; in the illusion of self-sufficiency he is moving steadily away from that which he wishes to find; in seeking he is hiding; his straight road is the "round about" of the Bojg: his eye is "scratched" by the trolls, his vision is blindness.[1] To the demonstration of fantasy of this order the tone of the poem is particularly well suited; at the taken level, which is very uniform throughout, there is surprising richness. If not his most important, *Peer Gynt* is Ibsen's most consistently successful work.

Peer's inheritance is fantasy. As his mother, Ase, explains:

> And of course one is glad to be quit of one's cares
> And try all one can to hold thinking aloof.
> Some take to brandy, and others to lies.
> And we? Why we took to fairy tales
> Of princes and trolls and of all sorts of beasts;
> And of bride-rapes as well. Ah, but who could have dreamed
> That those devils' yarns would have stuck in his head.

But in fact it is this inheritance which Peer will act out. It is the expression of fantasy which he understands as the expression of self. He is led by it, inevitably, to the trolls. In mating with the Green Woman, he is confirming this negative existence:

GREEN WOMAN: Black it seems white, and ugly seems fair.
PEER GYNT: Big it seems little, and dirty seems clean.
GREEN WOMAN: Ay, Peter, now I see that we fit, you and I.

The fantasy of the troll-world is sufficient to itself:

DOVRE-KING: Among men the saying goes: Man be thyself.
At home here with us, in the tribe of the trolls
The saying goes: Troll, to thyself be—*enough.*

---

[1] For an exceptionally brilliant treatment of this theme I would refer to the novel *Die Blendung*, by Elias Canetti (1935). This work has been well translated by C. V. Wedgwood (Cape, 1946), but the English title *Auto-da-Fe* fixes the reader's attention on aspects of the novel which are less important than the brilliant exposition of fantasy to which the German title refers.

For such self-sufficiency, however, as Peer quickly discovers, it is necessary to blind oneself, to mutilate one's senses:

> DOVRE-KING: In your left eye first.
> I'll scratch you a bit, till you see awry.
> But all that you see will seem fine and brave.

Peer refuses to be mutilated, and when the trolls attack him, he saves himself by calling on his mother; by calling, that is to say, on an actual relationship. The theme of self-mutilation is taken up again in the scene where Peer, in the forest, sees a youth cut off his thumb to avoid serving in the army. It is a determination which contrasts with his own impotence:

> Aye, think of it, wish it done, even will it,
> But do it! No, that's past my understanding.

The Bojg, that "familiar compound ghost", the amorphous creature which conquers but does not fight, is a similar temptation to fantasy. It is a kind of reality which Peer cannot enter, and in his failure he accepts its advice to "go round about."

Peer's protection, his only relation with reality after the death of his mother, is expressed in Solveig:

> If you dare dwell with the hunter here,
> I know the hut will be blessed from evil.

But he cannot stay with her, because of the debt which he has contracted: the child of the Green Woman. He can see the Green Woman as she is—a hag. But, as she reminds him:

> If you would see me fair as before
> You have only to turn yonder girl out of doors.

Solveig, in fact, is the guarantee of his actual sight, and hence of his actual existence. Yet he cannot stay with her; he cannot understand repentance. His only way is the "round about" of the Bojg.

The Fourth Act, which is looser and less integrated dramatically than those preceding, deals with his travels "round about." It is a history of fantasy and deception, the expression of his fantasy of self to the point where he is crowned by the madmen as the "Emperor of Selfhood." That is the consummation of the fantasy, and it is succeeded, in the Fifth Act, by the long way back to reality. As the Strange Passenger promises him:

> I'll have you laid open and brought to the light.
> What I specially seek is the centre of dreams.

When he is back in his own country, Peer sees the funeral of the man who had mutilated himself: "he followed his calling." It is a definition of his own life. There follows the auction of his own childhood possessions, and through these layers Peer seeks the centre of his own reality. But, as he strips the onion:

> To the innermost centre
> It's nothing but swathings, each smaller and smaller.

Peer has, in fact, no self. As the Button Moulder tells him:

> Now you were designed for a shining button
> On the coat of the world; but your loop gave way;
> So into the waste-box you must go,
> And then, as they say, be merged in the mass.

His failure (when his attachment to reality had "given way") is a failure to realise the nature of self. He has followed the troll maxim—"to thyself be *enough*." In other words, he has refused his vocation, "has set at defiance his life's design." "To be oneself", says the Button Moulder, "is to slay oneself." To respond to vocation is imperative, at whatever apparent cost. The actual self, rather than the fantasy of self, demands fulfilment, through response to "the design":

> To stand forth everywhere
> With the Master's intention clearly displayed.

Peer has chosen the negative way, is now simply a "negative print", in which "the light and shade are reversed." And now that he has been brought to see this, he can at last reverse the reversal:

> Round about, said the Bojg. No. This time at least
> Straight ahead, however narrow the path.

He returns to Solveig, in whom he has remained

> as myself, as the whole man, the true man.

Solveig is both wife and mother; is the guarantee of his existence.

> PEER: My mother; my wife; thou innocent woman.

And the return is not only to Solveig, but to God:

> SOLVEIG: Who is thy father?
> Surely He that forgives at the mother's prayer.

So, for the moment, Peer finds himself and his rest, while the Button Moulder waits for him at the last cross-roads.

Peer Gynt, clearly, springs from the same source in experience as most of Ibsen's major work. Indeed, by the time *Brand* and *Peer Gynt* were written, every major theme of his later work had been not only conceived but put into words. *Peer Gynt's* success, and its difference from *Brand*, is that the mythological and legendary material which Ibsen uses provides a more completely objective formula for the central experience than any he found before or after. The Fifth Act, in particular, is magnificently *present* as drama. The images of the burned forest, of the auction, of the stripped wood-onion are part of a controlled pattern of realised experience, in which the images which function as characters—the Strange Passenger and the Button Moulder—are perfectly in place. The material is deliberately unrealistic—for the Act is an exposition of Peer's death and redemption; it is concerned, not with persons, but with a body of dramatic imagery "such that, when the external facts, which must terminate in sensory experience, are given, the emotion is immediately invoked." The consistent legendary atmosphere of the play makes contemporary performance perfectly possible, although there is usually a disappointing lack of emphasis on the essential *verbal* pattern. This is an aspect of the real contemporary difficulty of understanding *Peer Gynt*; for it is in the distance of the play from what is now understood as "personality" that the difference between the dramatic method of *Peer Gynt* and the methods, both of the intrigue drama which he had rejected, and of the naturalist drama which he was to create, is most clearly evident. In *Peer Gynt* words, once again, are the sovereign element in drama.

(iv)

Brand and *Peer Gynt* had been written in Italy. In 1868, the year after *Peer Gynt* appeared, Ibsen went to Germany. He was then forty. In the next ten years he produced only three plays: the long *Emperor and Galilean*; *The League of Youth*; and *Pillars of Society*. He then returned to Rome. The whole of this period in Germany (the evidence is everywhere in the letters) was clearly a period of great crisis, in at least three important aspects of his life: his religion, his political philosophy, and his dramatic technique. It is beyond my scope in this study to consider either of the first two aspects, which can in any case only be approached obliquely. But the dramatic issue of this period was the modern prose play as we know it, so that the period is clearly a vital one. If either of the former studies—of the change in Ibsen's spiritual and political attitudes—could be competently undertaken they would be of the very greatest value. For it is impossible to believe that the change in the emphasis of his work was simply a literary question; just as it is impossible to believe that the methods of naturalist literature are a matter of casual technical choice, unrelated to major changes in human outlooks.

About the technical change Ibsen is explicit. Writing to his publisher about *The League of Youth*, he declares:

It will be in prose, and in every way adapted for the stage.

He has decided to abandon verse, and cultivate

the very much more difficult art of writing the genuine, plain language spoken in real life.[1]

Of *Emperor and Galilean* he writes:

The illusion I wished to produce was that of reality. I wished to leave on the reader's mind the impression that what he had read had actually happened. By employing verse I should have counteracted my own intention. The many, everyday insignificant characters, whom I have intentionally introduced, would have become indistinct and mixed up with each other had I made them all speak in rhythmic measure. We no longer live in the days of Shakespeare. . . . The style ought to conform to the degree of ideality imparted to the whole presentment. My play is no tragedy in the ancient acceptation. My desire was to depict human beings and therefore I would not make them speak the language of the gods.[2]

[1] *Correspondence*, letter 171.
[2] Letter to Edmund Gosse, quoted in Archer's Introduction (*Collected Works*, Heinemann). It is worth noting at this point that it is not correct to say, as does Miss Bradbrook in *Ibsen the Norwegian*, that Ibsen 'thought that poetry was *harmful* to the drama.' In 1883 he certainly said that 'verse has done *acting* considerable harm', and that 'verse forms will scarcely be of any significance in the drama of the future.' But in June 1884, he wrote: 'I certainly remember that I once expressed myself disrespectfully with regard to verse; but that was a result of my own momentary attitude to that art form.' 'Dramatic categories', he added, 'must accommodate themselves to literary fact.' It is significant also, in his comment on the harm verse has done to acting, that he instances the iambic pentameter, and describes his own work as '*writing poetry* in straightforward, realistic everyday language.'

The statements, and their root attitude, are self-explanatory; but certain of their implications deserve comment. Perhaps the key phrase is "in every way adapted for the stage." After the independence of *Brand* and *Peer Gynt*, Ibsen is returning to the contemporary theatre. It is indeed a return, rather than a new departure. The practices of the intrigue drama, which he seemed to have abandoned in despair, are to be accepted again. Ibsen will introduce new elements—prose dialogue and modern settings—but the fundamental dramatic practices of the old stage will remain his framework.

Of the three plays which he wrote in Germany, *Emperor and Galilean* is clearly the most ambitious: when he had finished it Ibsen regarded it as his *hauptwerk*, and at the end of his writing life he retained this opinion. *Emperor and Galilean* is a poetic drama, cast in the form of a realistic historical play. That is its basic contradiction, and its importance as a transition in Ibsen's development. The contradiction is evident in Ibsen's own account of the work:

> I am putting into this book (*sic*) a part of my own spiritual life; what I depict I have, under other forms, myself gone through, and the historic theme I have chosen has also a much closer relation to the movements of our own time than one might at first suppose . . . I have kept strictly to history. . . . And yet I have put much self-anatomy into the work.[1]

The history, that is to say, was chosen as a means of expression for a particular pattern of experience. But Ibsen adds to this other interests; he wishes to "depict human beings" to offer a philosophy,[2] and to draw a moral for the times. The contradiction of the work is between these public aims and the essential experience.

Of the central theme the most important elements are the relationship between Julian and Maximus, between Julian and Agathon, and between Julian and Makrina. Julian is the slave of vocation; he is born to be Achilles:

JULIAN: Why was I born?
VOICE: To serve the spirit. . . .
JULIAN: What is my mission?
VOICE: To establish the empire.

[1] Letter to Edmund Gosse.
[2] 'That positive view of life which my critics have long asked of me, I shall provide.'

JULIAN: What Empire?
VOICE: The empire. . . .
JULIAN: By what power?
VOICE: By *willing*.
JULIAN: What shall I will?
VOICE : What thou must.

This vocation is reinforced by other auguries. The conflict
to which he is called is at one level that between Caesar and
Galilean, in historical as well as in absolute terms; at another
that between flesh and spirit; at another that between the old
beauty and the new truth:

> JULIAN: All that is human has become unlawful since the day
> when the seer of Galilee became ruler of the world. Through
> him, life has become death. Love and hatred, both are sins.
> Has he, then, transformed man's flesh and blood? Has not
> earth-bound man remained what he ever was? Our inmost
> healthy spirit rebels against it all;—and yet we are to will in
> the teeth of our own will. Thou shalt, thou shalt, thou shalt.[1]

It is so with

all who are under the terror of the revelation.

But:

> JULIAN: There must come a new revelation. Or a revelation of
> something new. It *must* come, I say, because the time is ripe. . . .
> The old beauty is no longer beautiful, and the new truth is no
> longer true.

To his doubts:

> Was I the chosen one? The "heir to the empire," it said. And
> what empire—? That matter is beset with a thousand un-
> certainties.

Maximus opposes his confident prophecy:

> JULIAN: Then tell me. Who shall conquer? Emperor or Galilean?
> MAXIMUS: Both the Emperor and the Galilean shall succumb. . . .
> Does not the child succumb in the youth, and the youth in the
> man? Yet neither child nor youth perishes. . . . You have
> striven to make the youth a child again. The empire of the flesh
> is swallowed up in the empire of the spirit. But the empire of the

---

[1] An interesting comparison might be made with D. H. Lawrence's *The
Man Who Died.*

spirit is not final. . . . Oh fool, who have drawn your sword against that which is to be—against the third empire in which the twin-natured shall reign.

JULIAN: Neither Emperor nor Redeemer?
MAXIMUS: Both in one, and one in both.
JULIAN: Emperor-God. God-Emperor. Emperor in the kingdom of the spirit, and God in the kingdom of the flesh.
MAXIMUS: That is the third empire, Julian.

This empire Julian will seek, as Agnes said of her life with Brand,

Through darkness to light.

Julian becomes ambitious of world-conquest, and a violent persecutor of the Christians. At the climax he burns his fleet, and this is followed by silence. At the moment of believing himself the Messiah to whom both Emperor and Galilean shall succumb, Julian is conquered by the Galilean.

JULIAN: What if that at Golgotha was but a wayside matter, a thing done, as it were, in passing, in a leisure hour? What if he goes on and on, and suffers and dies and conquers, again and again, from world to world?

Even while he seeks the "beautiful earth" (which Peer Gynt had betrayed), and the city of the sun, his mission is not forgotten.

MAKRINA: In him dwells a greater than he . . . In him will the Lord God smite us even to death.

As Brand was taken by Gerd for the Redeemer, so the death of Julian reminds us of the death on the cross:

AGATHON: With Christ for Christ!
(He throws his spear; it grazes the Emperor's arm and plunges into his side) . . .
AGATHON: The Roman's spear from Golgotha.

As he had come from the sacrifice in the catacombs with the cry

It is finished.

so now, as he dies, he speaks these deliberately reminiscent words:

Beautiful earth, Beautiful life . . . Oh, Helios,
Helios, why hast thou betrayed me?

Over his body, Maximus declares:

Led astray like Cain. Led astray like Judas. Your God is a spend-thrift God, Galileans. He wears out many souls. Were you not then, this time either, the chosen one; you, a victim on the altar of necessity . . . But the third empire shall come. The spirit of man shall re-enter on its heritage.

And the Christian Makrina makes the last judgment.

MAKRINA: Here lies a noble, shattered instrument of God.

BASIL: . . . Christ, Christ, how came it that thy people saw not thy manifest design? The Emperor Julian was a rod of chastise-ment, not unto death but unto resurrection.

MAKRINA: *Terrible is the mystery of election* . . . Erring soul of man—if thou wast indeed forced to err, it shall surely be accounted to thee for good on that great day when the Mighty One shall descend in the clouds to judge the living dead and the dead who are yet alive.

At its close, the play takes us back to the world of Brand, and forward to the world of *When We Dead Awaken*. Judged on these elements alone, Ibsen's opinion of the worth of the play might be substantiated. But this essential theme is embedded in a great mass of historicism, social satire, and philosophical debate. The historical episodes, particularly in the second part, are tedious, and the whole crude mechanism of the prose exposition destroys the intermittent vitality. *Emperor and Galilean* could hardly be staged; but in writing it Ibsen was fashioning a theatrical method which limited his essential interests.[1]

In the two other plays of this period, Ibsen presents us with intrigue drama in modern Norwegian dress. It is not necessary

[1] A point which perhaps deserves mention is the amount of apparent reminiscence of *Macbeth* in the work. As Miss Bradbrook has pointed out (*op. cit.*, p. 65), the prophecy of Julian's invulnerability is a deceptive strata-gem similar to that of the Witches' declaration to Macbeth. Julian's auguries generally resemble the Witches. Helena's urging of Julian to kill Constantine seems reminiscent of Lady Macbeth's words to her husband before the death of Duncan. A much more certain example, in the generally reminiscent scene of the death of Helena, is when the murder of Helena is covered by the hasty killing of her two guardians:

DECENTIUS: Call me hasty if you will, noble Caesar. But my love to the Emperor . . . would in truth be less than it is if, in such an hour, I were capable of calm reflection.

There is, of course, a possible further reminiscence of Shakespeare's play in *Lady Inger of Ostraat* (in particular the sleep-walking scene).

to examine them in detail, but simply to record their methods as a step in the evolution of the romantic melodrama into the naturalist. *The League of Youth* is an entertaining account of parish-pump politics, with Peer Gynt degenerated to the social caricature of Stensgard. There are the expected "portraits of human beings"—local printer, doctor, student, industrialist, landowner, and widow. The mechanism of the plot rests on characteristic devices: deliberate misunderstandings, substituted letters, complicated intrigue, "the classic quid pro quo of the proposal by proxy mistaken for the proposal direct";[1] forged bankbills, and a "set to partners" happy ending. It is the "well-made play" with a certain flatness, which "comes of the local situation." *Pillars of Society* is very similar. Its plot is extraordinarily complicated; it is, in both senses, intrigue, and the result is an overall satire (on a very slight scale, as I take it) of the kind represented by the ironic title. It is possible to admire the ingenuity of the plot, which has been compared to that of a detective story. But in spite of its skilful carpentry, *Pillars of Society* is crude. Everything in it is a simplification of the order of Lona's last cry:

The spirits of truth and freedom—*these* are the pillars of society.

The skill is the *result* of simplification; the flawless plot is designed to exclude any real complexity. For a man who had done such work as Ibsen, the play is extremely immature. But *Pillars of Society* is not prentice-work. By the Ibsenites, indeed, it is represented as his entrance on maturity. For all the while he had in his pocket the plans for *A Doll's House*.

To each succeeding generation, and equally to our own, Ibsen is above all the writer of *A Doll's House* and of *Ghosts*.[2] The plays have been interpreted, paraphrased, acted and rewritten into a numb and stale prestige. *A Doll's House* is now, as it has always been, a social rather than a literary phenomenon. Its excitement lay in its relation to feminism, and, although Ibsen rejects the ascription of support for feminism,[3] in practical terms this hardly seems to matter.

---

[1] Archer's Introduction to the play, Heinemann *Collected Works*, Vol. VI (p. xii).

[2] It is also understood, by some, that he wrote a libretto for Grieg.

[3] 'I thank you for drinking my health, but I must reject the honour of having consciously worked for the woman's cause. I am not even clear what the woman's cause really is. For me it has been an affair of humanity.'—Speech to the Norwegian Society for the Woman's Cause, May 26, 1898.

What was it that made *A Doll's House*, as drama, appear so strikingly original? That it dealt with "real people in real situations"? This is surely very questionable. The characters of the play differ very little from the usual types of romantic drama: the innocent, childlike woman, involved in a desperate deception; the heavy, insensitive husband; the faithful friend. Similarly, the main situations of the play are typical of the intrigue drama: the guilty secret, the sealed lips, the complication of situation around Krogstad's fatal letter. The appearance of Krogstad at the children's party is a typical 'situation': the villain against a background of idyllic happiness (all the best murders are committed in rose-gardens). None of this is at all new, and it is the major part of the play.

But the novelty, it is said again, is that these deliberate romantic puppets are suddenly jerked into life. This, I think, is true, in one definite sense. But one must be careful in defining the mechanism of change. According to Shaw, this mechanism is the "discussion"—the movement into a new kind of reality with Nora's famous words:

> We must come to a final settlement, Torvald. During eight whole years ... we have never exchanged one serious word about serious things.

Now this is certainly an important change of mood, but one doubts whether "discussion" is the right word for it. What, in any case, is *discussed* in *A Doll's House*? The final scene between Nora and Torvald is not so much a discussion as a *declaration*. It is this in two ways: first, in Nora's declaration that she will leave Torvald; and second, in that it is a stated moral of the play. Now Torvald attempts to dissuade Nora, but his objections do not seem to be made in any substantial personal way. They are more like cues for her declaration; stock social objections which the play as a whole (and not necessarily Nora) must answer:

TORVALD: Are you not clear about your place in your own home? Have you not an infallible guide in questions like these? Have you not religion?
NORA: Oh, Torvald, I don't really know what religion is.
TORVALD: What do you mean?
NORA: I know nothing but what Pastor Hansen told me when I was confirmed. He explained that religion was this and that. When I get away from all this and stand alone, I will look into

that matter too. I will see whether what he taught me is right, or, at any rate, whether it is right for me.

My own judgment of passages like these is that they do not represent a "living confrontation between actual people", but are rather straight, single declaration. Torvald's questions, that is to say, are devices of the argument. They are, in fact, rhetorical questions, and could, essentially, be all spoken by Nora herself:

"You may say, have I not an infallible guide in questions like these? Have I not religion? I can only answer that I know nothing but what Pastor Hansen told me . . . etc."

The point is important, because it indicates the level at which the play operates. It is not that we get a dramatic presentation of more substantial experience than is common in the late romantic drama. The experience is of the same limited kind, and is presented according to the same conventions. Then, in the statement of the moral, we get an unusual conclusion. The play does not go deeper than the usual mechanism of intrigue; it does not undercut the assumptions of romantic drama, with its mechanical versions of experience; it merely provides a reversal within the romantic framework. It is not a new positive dramatic standard; it is simply *anti*-romantic, a negative within the same framework of experience. That the negative is justified, on moral grounds, is probably true; and the play is valuable as a rejection of the romantic morality. But it is only a rejection of conclusions; it is not a rejection of the limited romantic conventions of experience. That is why the term "problem play" or "thesis play" is justified. The term suggests abstraction, and abstraction is what we have. There had always been problems in drama, but in the greatest drama these were set within a body of specific experience which was not limited by the conventions of "situation" and "type character." In the Elizabethan drama, the "situations" and "type characters" were often present; but the range of the play's language provided, in the best work, the essential body of immediate and compelling specific experience. When the range of dramatic language was limited, the situations and type characters became merely mechanical: devices of communication for which no substantial communication had been devised. Ibsen's rejection of the conventional moral ending was only a limited cure for this deficiency—a partial negative within an essential acceptance. Any full cure would have involved the restoration of total dramatic substance.

A Doll's House, then, is an anti-romantic play, in the sense of the limited negative which I have defined. Naturalism, as it has been widely practised, is anti-romantic in this same limited sense. Strindberg, as we shall see, proposed that naturalism should attempt to restore the whole substance. But the naturalism which came to dominate the theatre was of the more limited kind. It is in this respect that one must emphasise that naturalism is a legitimate child of the romantic drama; a child which makes a limited rejection of its parent, but which remains essentially formed by its general inheritance. The anti-romantic drama, down to the *teatro grottesco* and the work of Pirandello, is to be essentially understood in this way. For Ibsen, who in *Brand* and *Peer Gynt* had attempted, with considerable success, to restore substance, the development which *A Doll's House* typifies is to be seen as essentially regressive. The fact that Nora and Torvald and Krogstad and Rank can function *simultaneously* as the stock figures of romantic melodrama and of the problem play is only one local indication of this general and vital fact.

Ghosts is a play of the same essential kind as *A Doll's House*, but it is of a very different temper. Its issues are more serious, and Ibsen is more concentrated on their resolution. The condensed power of the play, however we may finally judge it, is undeniable. The situation which Ibsen examines is more nearly isolated from the irrelevant concessions to theatrical intrigue than all but a few others of his plays in this *genre*. The mechanical logic of its resolution is clear and exact. From the moment that the intriguing Engstrand appears in the first few words of the play—

ENGSTRAND: It's the Lord's own rain, my girl.
REGINA: It's the devil's rain, *I* say.

—the movement to inevitable disaster is played out at top speed. The only modern plays comparable with it in theatrical terms are Strindberg's *Lady Julie* and Ibsen's own *Hedda Gabler*.

The theme of *Ghosts* is not a new one in Ibsen. The reduction of Osvald to a state of death in life, calling for the sun, is closely related to the last cry of Brand—

Blood of children must be spilt
To atone for parents' guilt

DRAMA FROM IBSEN TO ELIOT

—and the last cry of Julian:

Oh, Helios, Helios, why hast thou betrayed me?

That the inherited debt is a matter of physical disease is only incidental. It was not only the pity and suffering associated with hereditary disease which mattered to Ibsen; although for obvious reasons it was what mattered to his admiring or repelled audience. The essential experience of *Ghosts* is not disease, but inheritance.

There is a curious ambiguity in the play, one's sense of which is reinforced when it is considered in the context of Ibsen's work as a whole. The specific text for consideration of this is Mrs. Alving's famous speech:

Ghosts! . . . I almost believe we are all ghosts, Pastor Manders. It is not only what we have inherited from our fathers and mothers that walks in us. It is every kind of dead idea, lifeless old beliefs and so on. They are not alive, but they cling to us for all that, and we can never rid ourselves of them. Whenever I read a newspaper I seem to see ghosts stealing between the lines. There must be ghosts the whole country over, as thick as the sands of the sea. And then we are all of us so wretchedly afraid of the light.

Here is the element of protest against subscription to dead beliefs, and the cry for light. But it is not simply a banner of the enlightenment, in the manner of the declaration of Lona in the First Act of *Pillars of Society*:

I'm going to let in some fresh air.

For it is recognised that

We can never rid ourselves of them.

We are the creatures of our past. From the moment of our birth we are inevitably haunted, by every inherited debt. In *Brand*, Ibsen had written

Born to be tenants of the deep,
Born to be exiles from the sun . . .
Crying to heaven, *in vain* we pray
For air and the glad flames of day.

And in *Brand* and *Emperor and Galilean* the progress had been, inevitably, "through darkness to light." Osvald, in *Ghosts*, was

70

born to be an exile from the sun: in the final resolution of his life he prays in vain for the "glad flames of day":

Mother, give me the sun.

The parallel with Julian is very close. Osvald, like Julian, had sought Helios:

Have you noticed that everything I have painted has turned upon the joy of life?—always, always upon the joy of life?—light and sunshine and glorious air.

Osvald is as clearly as Julian a "sacrifice to necessity." But there are two important differences, in Ibsen's treatment of this recurrent theme, in *Ghosts* from his earlier, and from his later, treatments of it. The assurance of mercy is lacking; the absolution which was pronounced over Brand and Julian, and which was to be pronounced again over Rubek, is not given to Osvald. He goes out in his madness, amid a fumble for the physical alleviation of his pain. This significant omission is related to the other new element in the play, the suggestion that the way "through darkness to light" is a false way:

OSVALD: In the great world people won't hear of such things. There, nobody really believes such doctrines any longer.

It is the tone of the enlightenment, on which the Ibsenites seized.

There are hints, it is true, that Ibsen had not really changed his position. The idea of absolution had in many of his plays been bound up with the idea of woman: it is Solveig who absolves Peer Gynt, Makrina who absolves Julian; each is described as "the pure woman." In *Ghosts* Osvald expects the act of mercy (although a different kind of mercy) from Regina. It is her refusal to act for him that denies him his peace. Again, the pursuit of "lijvsglaeden", which seems to be otherwise represented as a positive, is hinted at as responsible for the sins of Captain Alving which begin the cycle of destruction. And the *uninsured* orphanage, to which Osvald is explicitly related, may suggest the very lack of the assurance of mercy which is caused by Mrs. Alving's absence of faith.

From these elements, in conjunction with those parts of the play which are directly comparable to earlier themes in Ibsen, it would be possible to construct a reading which would set *Ghosts* at the level of Ibsen's more significant work—a reading which would be directly opposed to the normal reading of the Ibsenites. I feel, however, that this would be wrong, although such modifications of the normal view of the play as I have suggested ought to be enforced. But *Ghosts* is profoundly inconsistent, unless it is taken at the very simplest level, and most of its implications ignored. *Emperor and Galilean* has been represented by many critics as the product of a period of chaos. The remark is altogether more applicable to *Ghosts*. Ibsen has half-accepted naturalist attitudes to suffering, and expounds them with his usual force. But at root a very different attitude remains, and the tension between these incompatible values is not resolved. Deprived of this essential consistency, *Ghosts* tends always to disintegrate into melodrama. The method of the play is very like that of melodrama, but it might have achieved the status of tragedy if the fundamental attitude to suffering had been certain and controlling. One feels at the end of the play the recoil from a horror which the dramatist has not been able fully to understand. The disturbing power of the play is sufficient evidence of the reality of the horror, but the succeeding emotion is incomplete, because of the essential failure of resolution.

(v)

In *Pillars of Society*, the leaky ship *The Indian Girl* becomes, in a sense, the play. The fortunes of all the persons are involved with it, and it would be possible to take it as an overall judgment on the dramatic situation. In *A Doll's House* the *tarantelle* which Nora dances sums up the total situation of the play in a form which does not depend on words. In *Ghosts* the orphanage built in memory of Captain Alving, which is uninsured and which is burned down (it is a "whited sepulchre") is a similar statement of the total situation of the drama. In *An Enemy of the People* moral turpitude seems to find its material equivalent in the infected baths. In *The Wild Duck* the title-phrase, and the strange attic, summarise the total situation. In *Rosmersholm* the white horses seem to embody the past which gives meaning to the play. *Hedda Gabler* has a clear relation to the famous pistols.

All these elements, and some others in the last plays, comprise what is called Ibsen's "symbolism." The following abstract of certain statements about this method may form a basis for discussion. Consider:

Ibsen has no symbolism.—GEORG BRANDES.[1]

---

[1] *Ibsen and Bjornson, Dramatic Opinions*, p. 31.

In Ibsen's case realism and symbolism have thriven very well together for more than a score of years. The contrasts in his nature incline him at once to fidelity to fact, and to mysticism.

GEORG BRANDES.[1]

Ibsen makes use of symbolism . . . I should like to know the meaning of the house of a hundred stories built by Solness, from which he falls and breaks his neck.—EMILE FAGUET.[2]

The play (*A Doll's House*) is life itself. It has its symbol and it lays hold on the sympathy of the reader. But again it fails of artistic completeness. The symbol does not fit at all points.

JEANNETTE LEE.[3]

In (*The Wild Duck*) and in *Rosmersholm* Ibsen perfected his own special power: the power to infuse the particular, drab, limited fact with a halo and a glory . . . Ibsen had suppressed the poet in himself but this suppressed power lights up all his writing, giving it not only the rich concentration of *A Doll's House*, but the unifying cohesion of the symbolic.—M. C. BRADBROOK.[4]

The rationalist students of Ibsen tried to pin a single meaning on to his symbols: was the wild duck symbolic of Hedvig or of Hjalmer or of Gregers? Was Gregers a portrait of Ibsen or was he not? No-one is likely to react in that way now.—M. C. BRADBROOK.[5]

That the play is full of symbolism would be futile to deny; and the symbolism is mainly autobiographic. The churches which Solness sets out by building doubtless represent Ibsen's early romantic plays; the homes for human beings his social dramas; while the houses with high towers merging into castles in the air, stand for those spiritual dramas on which he was henceforth to be engaged.

WILLIAM ARCHER.[6]

Take for instance the history of Rubek's statue and its development into a group. In actual sculpture this development is a grotesque impossibility. In conceiving it we are deserting the domain of reality and plunging into some fourth dimension where the properties of matter are other than those we know. This is an abandonment of the fundamental principle which Ibsen over and

---

[1] *Op. cit.*, p. 115.
[2] Quoted in *The Ibsen Secret*—Jeannette Lee (pp. 4 and 116).
[3] *Op. cit.*
[4] *Op. cit.*, p. 98.
[5] *Op. cit.*, p. 99.
[6] Introduction to *Masterbuilder Solness*—Collected Works.

over again emphatically expressed—namely, that any symbolism his work might be found to contain was entirely incidental, and subordinate to the truth and consistency of his picture of life.

WILLIAM ARCHER.[1]

Hedda Gabler *is* the pistol.—JEANNETTE LEE.[2]

The term "symbolism", one might comment, has been a little over-used. Indeed, one cannot help feeling that it had better not have been used at all. But how exactly may one define in dramatic terms the element to which it refers? To begin with, certain distinctions in Ibsen's practice must be noted.

In *Pillars of Society* the unseaworthy ship is not a dramatic device; it is nowhere shown. It is an external element and its main purpose is that of a precipitant in the action. Beyond this purpose, applied to the total situation of the play, it is merely a suggestive analogy. In *A Doll's House* the *tarantelle* is a distinctly theatrical device; it adds nothing to the essence of the play, but serves, in presentation, to heighten a situation of which the audience has already, in direct terms, been made aware. To call it symbolism is somewhat misleading. It is the kind of device which Strindberg developed in the mimes of *Lady Julie*, a reintroduction of the elements of dance. It may be considered as theatrically effective and valid; it may, on the other hand, be seen as the starting-point of a mechanism familiar to us from contemporary plays—the heightening of a situation by "music off" (which has become the bludgeoning musical accompaniment of the films).[3] In *Ghosts* the device is similar to that of *The Indian Girl*. The situation is described in direct terms, but it is reinforced theatrically by the fire. Inevitably we begin to consider this with a prejudice. The very success of *Ghosts*, which inspired wearisome imitation, has made many of us a little antipathetic to fires, fogs, and sunlight as elements of representational atmosphere in the theatre. The device, that is to say, comes very near to the provision of "stage atmosphere", referring back to the snowstorms in which the

[1] Introduction to *When We Dead Awaken*.
[2] *Op. cit.*
[3] Mr. Noel Coward is probably responsible for the 'End of Act Two' mechanism which is now stereotyped. It is the period of the big emotional crisis, worked out between tight lips with one of its principals playing the piano. The scene usually ends with one or the other or both slamming out through the french windows.

heroines of melodrama went out into the cruel world, and forward to the wind-machines of the contemporary playhouse. The orphanage in *Ghosts* is rather more particular than that; (and particularity is an important test of this device; when it is not particular it is simply "atmosphere"). It is difficult, however, to consider it as anything but an illustrative analogy, heightening the emotional effect of a situation which might otherwise fail to satisfy. And this point should serve to remind us that any device of this kind cannot be considered as a separate entity. Its quality rests almost solely on the quality of the experience to which it is related. If this experience, which will normally be communicated by language, is crude, flat, or incomplete, the "symbol" can be clearly seen as a substitute effect. And it is exactly as a substitute for satisfactory communication through language that devices of this kind have been elaborated.

In *An Enemy of the People* the infected baths are a non-visual element of the plot, giving Ibsen the opportunity to launch the crusading Stockmann. It is true, as with *The Indian Girl*, that the infected baths may serve as an analogy for a corrupt society. But we do not need to ask ourselves anxiously whether they are symbolic. The analogy is expressly made, by Stockmann, in his speech at the public meeting. The play is not offered as anything more than a polemic (in reply to the vituperation which had greeted *Ghosts*) and as such it is still alive. The rhetoric against the compact, complacent liberal majority; the attack on sentimental devotion to the masses— "the masses are only the raw material from which a *people* is made"; the emphasis on the aristocratic principle (as opposed to the mediocrities who win popular applause); the declaration of the function of the conscious minority: all these still make good listening. Ibsen's desire to let loose some direct speech-making found its promised land in the famous scene at the public-meeting. The play has been used as a banner by almost everyone, from anarchists to conservatives. In general terms, of course, they are all quite right. And this is the point about the analogy of the baths: in all political speeches analogy is a safe substitute for particularity. *The Indian Girl* is owned by the same company as the ubiquitous Ship of State. Dr. Stockmann's polluted baths have become the "swamp of mysticism and pornography" of M. Zdhanov.

But perhaps for those who make a case for Ibsen's use of symbolism in his prose plays, none of the works mentioned would be a main text. Such a text would almost certainly be *The Wild Duck*. This play, written in 1884, when Ibsen was 56, is frequently singled out by his critics as his greatest work.

Ibsen wrote of it to his publisher:

> The characters, in this play, despite their many frailties, have, in the course of our long daily association, endeared themselves to me. However, I hope they will also find good and kind friends among the great reading-public, and not least among the player-folk, to whom they all, without exception, offer problems worth the solving.[1]

The play does as much as the fully naturalist play could ever do. It presents a richly assorted selection of characters, an interesting plot, and a high strain of emotion. The play is very skilful, and shows the elaboration of Ibsen's methods at this period at its most successful.

Clearly the central point for analysis is the wild duck, and its function. Now I think it is very satisfying to rebuke the rationalists for trying to "pin the symbol" on to one or other of the characters; but the quarrel one makes in this respect is not really with William Archer and his men, but with Ibsen. What is the point which Ibsen makes about the bird?

> HIALMAR: She has lived in there so long now that she has forgotten her natural wild life; and it all depends on that.

The wild duck is an explicit figure for broken and frustrated lives. It is related to Hedvig:

> My wild duck; it belongs to me;

the child who, when urged to sacrifice the wild duck to prove that she loves her father, shoots herself. Gregers tells the father, Hialmar:

> You have much of the wild duck in you.

Hialmar thinks of the duck as his wife, Gina, the damaged present (the seduced maid) of the elder Wehrle:

> Mr. Wehrle's wing-broken victim.

The damaged bird is also related to the elder Ekdal, who had been ruined by Wehrle:

> HIALMAR: Are you alluding to the well-nigh fatal shot that has broken my father's wing?

[1] Quoted by Archer in his Introduction (p. xviii).

It is to Wehrle that all the damage goes back:

EKDAL: He was shooting from a boat, you see, and he brought her down . . .

HEDVIG: She was hit under the wing so that she couldn't fly.

GREGERS: And I suppose she dived to the bottom.

EKDAL: Of course. Always do that, wild ducks do. They shoot to the bottom as deep as they can get, sir, and bury themselves fast in the tangle and seaweed, and all the devil's own mess that grows down there. And they never come up again.

GREGERS: But your wild duck came up again, Lieutenant Ekdal.

EKDAL: He had such an amazingly clever dog, your father had. And that dog—he dived in after the duck and fetched her up again.

GREGERS: (*turning to* HIALMAR) And then she was sent to you here.

Gregers, Wehrle's son, becomes conscious of the debt, and sets out to pay it, in service to "the claim of the ideal." All he does is to finish off the work which his father had begun.

Ibsen speaks of *The Wild Duck* as occupying

a place apart among my dramatic productions; its method of progress is in many respects divergent from that of its predecessors.

This has never been satisfactorily explained; but it would seem that the change is that the device, the "symbol", is used at every point in the presentation. It sets the total atmosphere of the broken, frustrated people who have forgotten "their natural life", and is the embodiment of the debt which Gregers so fatally pays. It thus covers the whole of the situation and action. In this respect it resembles the orphanage of Captain Alving or the infected baths or the unseaworthy ship. But it also does more: it is a means of definition of the main characters, who are all explicitly "revealed" in its terms. And it is this preoccupation with "character-revelation" that is the really new element of the play.

Like all such plays, the humanity it depicts is of a rather special kind. The key word, used by all its critics, is "charm." This useful word (it can be alternated with "delicacy") covers the two extremes of character: the pathetic, lyrical Hedvig, a charming child; and the old caricature Ekdal, with his uniform cap and his secret drinking. There is something very conscious about this charm, an unmistakable quality of theatrical artifice. The characters laugh at each other, and we see our cue and join them. Then the laughter fades on our lips, which tremble; a cry of pathos, a glance at the attic, and we have passed to the identity of full, lovable human beings, poised between laughter and tears. The very thing, in fact, for an evening at the theatre.

This is a difficult judgment, but I think it is true that, in spite of the substantial human emotions *behind* the play, the actual effect is sentimental. "We are evidently intended to accept the character's sentimental interpretation of himself," Mr. Eliot wrote, of the earlier sentimental drama. In *The Wild Duck* this process is taken further: we are evidently intended to accept the sentimental self-interpretation of *all* the characters in the play, the whole group. And the focus of this intention is the figure of the wild duck.

The method almost succeeds; indeed it succeeds entirely for all those who are satisfied by this essentially naturalist mode of consciousness. The difficulty is that one can see how nearly Ibsen succeeded in establishing, through the figure of the wild duck, a total form, which would achieve dramatic concentration and unity. The reason for his failure, it seems to me, is that the characters, who have, "in the course of our long daily association, endeared themselves to me," take charge. The relaxation of judgment implied in Ibsen's phrase made of the figure of the wild duck, not a *form*, within which all the emotions of the play might be controlled and valued, but simply a pressure-point for all kinds of feeling: mature and immature, genuine and calculated, precise and vague. By its very function of uniting such varieties of feeling, it prevents that process of distinction and evaluation which a play of strong, overt emotion particularly needs. The figure, that is to say, while intended to integrate the minutely observed details of the drama, integrates only at the level of theatrical effect; its very sufficiency prevents the achievement of a more conclusive dramatic form.

Rosmersholm, the next play, is a more substantial work than anything Ibsen had written since *Peer Gynt*. It realises the tension which had lain behind *Brand*—the inevitable conflict between response to vocation and inherited debt. Ibsen examines this experience in a double aspect, through Rosmer and Rebekke, but it is a single experience, just as, in the play, Rosmer and Rebekke come to realise:

We are one.

Rosmer is a creature of his past, the "death in life" of Rosmersholm. To fight his way out to life, to bring light

> where the Rosmer family has from generation to generation been a centre of darkness

his own strength is insufficient. While he has faith in Rebekke he can act; but the dead voice of Beata, revealed in her letter to Mortensgaard, ends his illusions. He has no choice. Against a past which was dark, Rebekke opposes ideas of emancipation. But the ideas "have not passed into her blood." She becomes simply predatory, and the ideal of a "pure" partnership with Rosmer in his crusade for nobility—a crusade to which she persuades him—becomes an "uncontrollable" physical passion which drives her to destroy his wife. From this guilt there is no living absolution. From this guilt Rosmer himself is not free; the very fantasy of his purposed nobility, his inherited inability to live, is her silent abettor. The freedom which might have been expected when Beata is gone is simply illusory. Guilt, the inheritance of Rosmersholm, has "infected her will."

> I have lost the power of action, Rosmer.

With both, in the words of *When We Dead Awaken*, it is

> a place where you stick fast, you cannot go forward or backward.

The crusade for nobility, like the "brief mountain-vision" of Brand, is nothing more than an "immature idea":

> We cannot be ennobled from without.

By whatever system their position is judged, the reality is the same:

> REBEKKE: I am under the dominion of the Rosmersholm way of life, now. What I have sinned—it is fit that I should expiate.
> ROSMER: Is *that* your point of view?
> REBEKKE: Yes.
> ROSMER: Well then, *I* stand firm in our emancipated view of life, Rebekke. There is no judge over us; and therefore we must do justice upon ourselves . . . If you go, I go with you.

They die in the millrace, the stream of the old Rosmersholm:

> The dead woman has taken them.

79

Rosmersholm is an impressive play, with its finely worked texture, and its authentic particularity. If one hesitates to judge it a complete success, it is because one is uncertain about the nature of the characters. With Rosmer, and especially with Rebekke, there is an element of the familiar suggestiveness of naturalism—the hint at the unrevealed, the private motives which underlie their conduct and professions. Both are studied in much greater detail than the Hedvigs, Noras, Selmas, Ekdals, Osvalds and the like of his immediately preceding plays; *Rosmersholm* is almost free of the conscious charm of parts of *The Wild Duck*. But the very scale of their creation imposes difficulties. It involves a degree of detail which cannot fully be realised in the explicit, spoken framework of the play. The refinement of the characters, one might say, is a fictional refinement; the degree of attention to motive and behaviour is that of the psychological novel. But, as characters in the play, Rosmer and Rebekke must function as conventional, explicit figures; they must go towards a dénouement which is at quite a different level of reality. All that part of their creation which cannot be directly realised in the play is conveyed by hint and by implication. Thus one is being continually led away from what is explicitly presented. The characters are at the same time explicit figures of the drama and as it were summaries of the slowly realised figures of the novel.

The use of the figure of the white horses (the play was originally to be called *The White Horses*) does not resolve this difficulty. The white horses embody the past of Rosmersholm, the past which determines the lives of Rosmer and Rebekke. To this extent, the figure is successful, but the success establishes the play all the more firmly at a level of convention with which aspects of the characterisation are not compatible. The great power of the play cannot hide the incongruities: the tendency, on the one hand, to the detailed realism of the novel, and, both in speech and in action, to the naturalism of the stage (cf., for example, the death of Brand, which is within the drama, and the death of Rosmer and Rebekke, which is represented only by the bathos of the commentary of the housekeeper); and, on the other hand, the explicit, formal pattern of the romantic drama, with its white horses, its double suicide and its inexorable Fate.

There is one aspect of the play to which attention must be drawn, as part of the exposition of Ibsen's essential attitude to experience. *Rosmersholm* has been spoken of as a play of the

Enlightenment; but it is in fact quite the opposite. When Rosmer speaks of atonement, Rebekke asks:

> If you were deceiving yourself? If it were only a delusion? One of those white horses of Rosmersholm.

But Rosmer answers equivocally:

> It may be so. We can never escape them, we of this house.

It is the cry of Mrs. Alving; faced by the ghosts:

> We can never rid ourselves of them.

The command to attempt emancipation from the past is insistent; it is one aspect of "vocation." But the attempt, in Ibsen, is almost certain to fail. This is the persistent pattern. In *The Wild Duck*, we should not have heard so much of Ibsen's supposed repudiation of his former attitudes, if his actual work, and not merely Shaw's exposition of it, had been sufficiently known. For Ibsen recognised, in experience, both the command to emancipation, and its consequences. Hedvig Ekdal is not the first casualty of a pursuit of truth; there were also Brand and the Emperor Julian.

Rosmersholm is the essential introduction to the last plays, but, before proceeding to them, Ibsen wrote two very individual works—*Lady from the Sea*, and *Hedda Gabler*. More justly than any other work of Ibsen, *Lady from the Sea* could be called a problem play. Ellida had been, in the words of Brand, "born to be a creature of the deep." This sense of origin, which is so crucial in Ibsen, seems here to be considered a mere obsession, susceptible to direct cure.

> WANGEL: I begin to understand you, by degrees. You think and conceive in images, in visible pictures. Your longing and yearning for the sea, the fascination that he, the stranger, possessed for you, must have been the expression of an awakening and growing need for freedom within you—nothing else . . . But now you will come to me again, will you not, Ellida?
>
> ELLIDA: Yes, my dear, now I will come to you again. I can now, for now I come to you in freedom, of my own will, and of my own responsibility . . . And we shall have all our memories in common.

And again:

BALLESTED: Human beings can acclimatise themselves.
ELLIDA: Yes, in freedom they can.
WANGEL: And under full responsibility.
ELLIDA: *That* is the secret.

This is the only positive example, in Ibsen's work, of the idea of acclimatisation, of the past being overcome and absorbed into a living present. The Ellida theme in the play is powerful, and the tone of statement in its resolution is only unsatisfactory because the play as a whole is a hybrid of so many methods and achieves no compelling total form. The early acts are remarkable mainly for their observation of the *lokale forholde*; in the development of the group of characters there is a looseness of technique which is surprising when one remembers the play's date. As a result, the Ellida theme is blurred, and does not achieve major emotional effect. It seems a half-felt *example*, and its resolution comes to appear didactic for this reason.

Hedda Gabler may also be taken as a psychological study, but it is a very much more powerful play. Ibsen wrote to Count Prozor:

> The title of the play is *Hedda Gabler*. My intention in giving it this name was to indicate that Hedda, as a personality, is to be regarded rather as her father's daughter than as her husband's wife.

For Hedda is still, fundamentally, a child, and a child of her particular past. She is the daughter of a General, with the narrow traditions of a military caste behind her; she has inherited the ethical nullity of her class. She cannot, like Ellida, find herself through freedom and responsibility. Freedom is inhibited by what she and Lovborg call cowardice, a dread of scandal. The dread is of adult responsibility, as here with the possibility of a child:

BRACK: A new responsibility, Fru Hedda?
HEDDA: Be quiet! Nothing of that sort will ever happen. . . . I have no turn for anything of the sort. . . . No responsibilities for me! . . . I often think there is only one thing in the world I have any turn for. . . . Boring myself to death.

Like Peer Gynt, and perhaps like Julian, her only outlet is the fantasy of self. (Her desire to see Lovborg with "vine-leaves in his hair" recalls Peer's wish for the same adornment when he is with Anitra; or Julian's assumption of a wreath of vine-leaves when, at the moment of his apostasy, he impersonates Dionysus.) But just as even Peer Gynt's myth of self-sufficiency could be sustained only by his inherited talent for romancing, so Hedda's is only thinkable while she retains "General Gabler's pistols." At every crisis, at every contact with a real situation, she has no equipment but her negative, and ultimately destructive, tradition; at every crisis she acts with the pistols. One might say that the only thing which explains and holds together the "overwhelming and incomprehensible" Hedda is the embodiment in General Gabler's pistols of her pre-adult amorality.[1]

But this use of the pistols is not Ibsen's only resource. The situation is expounded in its own terms, explicitly. We see this in the passage quoted above, and in this characteristic question:

BRACK: Why should you not, also, find some vocation in life, Fru Hedda?

HEDDA: A vocation, that should attract me?

BRACK: If possible, of course.

HEDDA: Heaven knows what sort of vocation that could be.

The mechanical logic of Hedda's destruction is completely convincing, as well as being very exciting in the theatre. I find myself agreeing with Mr. Wolf Mankowitz when he writes:

In a sense *Hedda Gabler* is a farce.[2]

It is, indeed, the kind of savage farce which it is traditionally difficult to distinguish from melodrama: Mr. Eliot's example in this *genre* was Marlowe's *Jew of Malta*; from contemporary work one might add Canetti's *Auto-da-Fe*. Strindberg's *Lady Julie* is closely related, and Ibsen certainly seems to have been very conscious of Strindberg's work at this time. The plays form an interesting ground for comparison, and, although Strind-

[1] Mrs. J. Lee (*op. cit.*) tells us (enthusiastically, and many times) that Hedda *is* the pistol; that 'the chief character is not a woman, but a slim, straight, deadly weapon.' That the pistols have other significance, in conjunction with the vine-leaves, as a Dionysian phallic symbol, has also been broached. It is interesting that in his first draft Ibsen put less emphasis on the pistols, and more on the blue-and-white-leaved manuscript. This, in conjunction with the afterthought of the tarantelle in *A Doll's House*, suggests that Ibsen used these devices to illustrate a theme which he had already formulated explicitly.

[2] *The Critic*, Autumn 1947, p. 82. With Mr. Mankowitz's analysis I substantially agree, although—a minor point—he has surely transposed the names of Thea and Berta.

berg's play was written three years earlier, the question of
influence would not be a simple one to determine. For although
there are many features in Ibsen's play which seem simply
reminiscent, Ibsen was in fact, in *Hedda Gabler*, consolidating
the features of much of his early work—work of which the
younger Strindberg was well aware. *Hedda Gabler*, too, is
thematically centred in Ibsen's major work, for, like so many
others, Hedda is destroyed by her inherited debt. But there is
no mercy; "merciless" indeed might well indicate the predominant mood of Ibsen's treatment. There is no absolution.

Hedda Gabler is a theatrical *tour-de-force*, but it is not a
completely satisfying play. It tends continually outwards to a
body of experience which the play itself cannot realise. One
might say that it is like a powerful dramatisation of a novel;
the tone of its thorough analysis is, at many points, one of
implication only. This has allowed it to be widely misunderstood.
The end of the play is deliberate bathos; the comment on
Hedda's suicide—

People don't do such things

—is the exact mood of savage farce. But it is normally played
with a certain sympathy. Hedda is as mercilessly confounded
as, say, Volpone; but the lack of final control in the total words
of the play allows the tone to be frequently missed, and Hedda
degenerates to an exciting *femme fatale*. It is the familiar lack
of adequacy of a complete dramatic form. In his continuing
search for such a form, Ibsen was now to go back on his
development, and increasingly to neglect his reference to the
contemporary theatre.

(vi)

"Look!
When I left the country I sailed by here ...
In there, where the screes and the clefts lie blue,
Where the valleys, like trenches, gloom narrow and dark,
And lower, skirting the open fiords:
It's in places like *these* human beings abide.
They build far apart in this country ..."

The speaker of these words is an old white-haired man, of
a "somewhat hard expression", who leans on the rail of a ship
from the South, approaching the coast of Norway at sunset.

84

He is returning to the land of his birth, from which as a young man he had gone into exile. To his side, a minute later, comes a Strange Passenger, offering to buy and take possession of his dead body. What the passenger seeks, he explains, is the "centre of dreams."

The name of the old man is not Henrik Ibsen, but Peer Gynt. Ibsen had written *Peer Gynt* in the early years of his own exile, in 1867. In 1891, after twenty-seven years of exile, Ibsen made his own return to Norway. He was then sixty-three, and an acknowledged master of European drama. In the next eight years he wrote his four final plays.

"You are essentially right," Ibsen wrote to Count Prozor, "in assuming that the series which ends with the Epilogue (*When We Dead Awaken*) began with *The Masterbuilder*." The last plays have indeed long been recognised as a group; but it is less often realised that they are a group very much within Ibsen's work as a whole. The immediately preceding plays had foreshadowed something of their mood; and the return from exile is not only to Norway, but to the world of *The Pretenders, Brand,* and *Peer Gynt.*

The Masterbuilder resembles *Brand* and *When We Dead Awaken* in the final climb to annihilation, but the fact that Solness falls by his own act, whereas Brand and Rubek are overwhelmed by an external force, the avalanche, marks an essential difference of resolution. The use of fire as a crisis in development relates *The Masterbuilder*, in a minor degree, to *Little Eyolf*, where the love of Allmers and Rita is described as a "consuming fire", but it relates even more to the burned forest of *Peer Gynt*, to the fire at the old house in *On the Vidda*, to the burning of Julian's fleet in *Emperor and Galilean*, to Hedda Gabler's crucial burning of Lovborg's manuscript, and to the fire in *Ghosts* which destroyed the memorial to Captain Alving. The theme of the unborn children in *The Masterbuilder* relates back to *Hedda Gabler* as well as forward to *When We Dead Awaken*. Similarly, in *Little Eyolf*, the figure of the Rat-Wife relates, not to any of the last plays, but to the Strange Passenger in *Peer Gynt* ("there went Death and I, like two good fellow-travellers"), and to the Stranger in *Lady from the Sea*. The drowning of Eyolf may similarly be related to the incident in *The Wild Duck*, in which old Wehrle shoots the wild duck, which falls "to the bottom of the sea, as deep as it can get."

Further, the important experiences of *vocation* and of *debt*, which appear directly in all the last plays, appear also, as we have seen, in *The Pretenders, Brand, Peer Gynt, Emperor and Galilean, Ghosts, Rosmersholm,* and *Hedda Gabler. Little Eyolf* ends in a resolution within life, as had *Lady from the Sea,* and, equivocally, *Peer Gynt. The Masterbuilder, John Gabriel Borkman,* and *When We Dead Awaken,* like *Brand, Emperor and Galilean, Ghosts, Rosmersholm* and *Hedda Gabler,* have their only solution in death.

And, if the last plays cannot be set apart in theme, neither can they in technique. *Little Eyolf* resembles *Rosmersholm* and, more particularly, *Lady from the Sea* more than it resembles *John Gabriel Borkman.* The method of *The Masterbuilder* is more that of *Rosmersholm* or of *Ghosts* than of *When We Dead Awaken. John Gabriel Borkman* and *When We Dead Awaken* have important resemblances of theme, but, as plays, they are as different as, say, *Rosmersholm* and *Brand.*

What I am arguing is that we should not let biography usurp the functions of criticism. The Ibsenites, having placed Ibsen's maturity somewhere between *Ghosts* and *Rosmersholm,* prolonged their biological simile and dismissed the last plays as a decline. "Down among the Dead Men," said Shaw, and Down, Down, Down was the estimate of the last plays as they appeared. Mysticism, hypnotism, symbolism, supernaturalist dotage; these are the terms which abound in the usual accounts. And it is true that these elements, or elements resembling them, appear in the last plays. But they appear also almost everywhere in Ibsen's work. It is only in the sterilised Ibsen figure presented by his dogmatic admirers that they are not seen as a consistent and essential element of his art. The last plays, then, cannot be explained, or explained away, as a period. Our judgment of them is an integral part of our general judgment of Ibsen. The immediate directive for criticism is that the four plays demand consideration each as an individual work of art; and not within any artificially localised context, but in the context of Ibsen's work as a whole.

The Masterbuilder is in some ways the most interesting of these final plays. It is a powerful realisation of the experience of guilt and retribution; conscience is altogether the wrong word.

All that I have succeeded in doing, building, creating . . . all this I have to make up for, to pay for. And not with my own happiness only, but with other people's too. That is the price which my position as an artist has cost me, and others. And every single day I have to look on while the price is paid for me anew. Over again, and over again, and over again for ever.

HENRIK IBSEN

The foundation of Solness's career was the burning of the old house which he and his wife had inherited. The fire may not have been his fault; in practical terms, it clearly was not. Yet:

... Suppose the fault was mine, in a certain sense. All of it, the whole thing. And yet perhaps—I may not have had anything to do with it.

When Hilde asks:

But may it not come right, even yet?

Solness answers:

Never in this world, never. That is another consequence of the fire.

Solness is the agent of his own fate; he climbs himself to the tower from which he falls. But

... it is not one's self alone that can do such great things. Oh no, the helpers and servers, they must do their part too. But they never come of themselves. One has to call upon them very persistently; inwardly, you understand.

To this last scene of his life, Hilde, the "bird of prey", has been called, *by himself*. She is the "helper and server" of his final payment.

"What is the meaning," asked M. Emile Faguet, "of the house of a hundred stories, built by Solness, from which he falls and breaks his neck?" It was not as high as all that, but the question, in one form or another, is a very frequent one. It is, of course, a question that cannot be answered, except within the terms of the play. The tower is not something else. It is a part of the play's landscape which one has to accept, as were the mountains in *Brand*, the shipwreck in *Peer Gynt*, or the ocean in *Lady from the Sea*. None of these elements is a symbol, in dramatic terms, except in the sense that everything in a work of literature—event, character, landscape—is symbolic. All such elements are organised by the writer so that in the work as a whole they may elicit a particular response of feeling. It is of course true that certain elements in *The Masterbuilder*—the tower itself, the crack in the chimney, the nine dolls which Aline carried under her heart, the dreams of Solness and Hilde that they are falling, with their "legs drawn up under" them—are capable of an explanation in Freudian

87

terms, in the same way as are the pistols in *Hedda Gabler*, or the gallery of John Gabriel Borkman. But one cannot abstract certain elements of a work, and try to explain them outside its terms. The substance of a play—the total organisation of words, and those visual elements which the author prescribes —either conveys the experience he wishes to communicate, or it does not. If it does not, the failure is one of dramatic creation: the substance is inadequate to the feeling. Perhaps the argument about symbols in *The Masterbuilder* arises from an impression that there is in the play some such failure of substance.

This failure, perhaps, is of the kind Mr. Eliot suggested with relation to *Hamlet*: that there is in the play something which the author "could not drag to light, contemplate, or mani-pulate into art." But perhaps one's uneasiness is better stated in another way. Perhaps it is the dramatic *method* that one questions: the method, that is to say, of communicating experience, not so much through characters, and not, in any final way, through speech, but rather by means of objects: things on or off the stage which are made to bear significance. This is not a method that one can best discuss in the abstract; it is a matter of responses to particular plays. In *The Master-builder* I think one is probably right in ascribing the final weakness of the play to the dramatic vagueness of the whole formula of the "building." The formula is, at moments (in the climb to the tower, for example), powerful; but as a whole it is both equivocal and over-exact; it lacks any complete force of realisation.

The particular achievement of *Little Eyolf*, the play which, after the customary two-year interval, next appeared, is that it virtually dispenses with "characters", in the sense in which Ibsen, and the naturalist theatre after him, understood the term. The main persons of the play are not so much independ-ent portraits, as aspects of a central dramatic concept. This concept is that of Eyolf, the embodiment of remorse. Eyolf is not only the crippled child whose "calling" is to be a soldier. Eyolf is Asta, the woman with whom Allmers had lived in happiness, and also Allmers himself. Rita, with her "gold, and green forests", comes to be governed by Eyolf, first in her desire to be rid of the child's "evil eye", and later by the wide-open eyes of the drowned child staring up at her from the depths. The Rat-Wife is a "helper and server." Only Borgheim, the faithful roadbuilder, is part of the usual mechanism of character. The rest exist only as aspects of the specific consciousness of Eyolf.

The play is written in an even, restrained language, which bears the tone of analysis rather than declamation. It is the language to which Ibsen was to return in *When We Dead Awaken*. After parts of *The Wild Duck* and *Masterbuilder Solness* this cool, tempered style is particularly satisfying, difficult as it is to render into English of similar quality.

The child Eyolf is crippled as a direct result of Allmers' betrayal of himself for the "gold, and green forests", in the person of the beautiful Rita:

ALLMERS: You called, you, you, you—and drew me after you.
RITA: Admit it. You forgot the child and everything else.
ALLMERS: That is true. I forgot the child, in your arms.
RITA: This is intolerable of you.
ALLMERS: In that hour you condemned little Eyolf to death.
RITA: You also. You also, if it is as you say.
ALLMERS: Yes, call me also to account, if you wish. We both have sinned. There was, after all, retribution in Eyolf's death.
RITA: Retribution?
ALLMERS: Judgment. Upon you and me. Now, as we stand here, we have our deserts. While he lived, we let ourselves shrink from his sight, in secret, abject remorse. We could not bear to see it, the thing he must drag with him.
RITA: The crutch.

With Rita the impulse was passion, the desire for absolute possession of the man she had bought. With Allmers, the crippling of Eyolf is the result of an older debt. His love for Asta began as payment of a debt inherited from his father:

I had so much injustice to compensate.

And, further back, the sin of Asta's mother cripples their life. For Asta was not the child of Allmers' father, but of another, and her mother had lied. The love of Allmers and Asta could never be consummated because of an assumed blood-relationship, which was, in fact, only the covering of this lie. So Allmers married Rita, and the cycle of retribution widened. For their "love" was only

a consuming fire.

It was Asta, "Little Eyolf" as Allmers had habitually called her, who forced them on each other under the crippling weight of her mother's lie.

And then the crippled child is drawn away by the Rat-Wife, the "sweetener of the earth", drawn away and drowned in the depths of the fiord:

> ALLMERS: How merciless the fiord looks today, lying so heavy and drowsy, leaden-grey, with splashes of yellow, reflecting the rain-clouds.
> ASTA: You must not sit staring over the fiord.
> ALLMERS: Yes, over the surface. But in the depths—there sweeps the rushing undertow.
> ASTA: For God's sake, do not think of the depths.

But from the depths the "little stranger-boy" stares up with wide-open eyes. And the crutch—floats. These are the substance of remorse.

After Eyolf's death, Allmers dreams that he sees him whole and alive again, and thanks and blesses—whom? He will not name God; his faith has long been lost. In his trip to the mountains, however, in contact with "the loneliness and the great waste places", he had become conscious of death:

> There went death and I, like two good fellow-travellers.

In the light of this consciousness, his life-effort had seemed insubstantial. And when his fellow-traveller took Eyolf, to whom he had turned for solace but whom he had never really possessed,

> Then I felt the horror of it; of it all; of all that, in spite of everything, we dare not tear ourselves away from. So earthbound are we, both of us. . . . And yet, an empty void on all sides.

Allmers had reached, in Conrad's phrase, the "heart of darkness"; his cry is that of the dying Kurtz—"The horror, the horror." But Allmers attempts to fill the void, in caring for the children of the quayside, which Rita has undertaken

> to make my peace with the great open eyes.

It is the resolve of Brand:

> Daily duty, daily labour,
> Hallowed to a Sabbath deed.

> ALLMERS: We have a heavy day of work before us, Rita.
> RITA: You will see—that now and then a Sabbath peace will descend on us.

ALLMERS: Then perhaps we shall know that the spirits are with us—those whom we have lost. . . .
RITA: Where shall we look for them?
ALLMERS: Upwards. Toward the peaks. Toward the stars. Toward the great silence.

This ending of the play should make it clear that what Ibsen has in mind is not an "acclimatisation", although a summary of the action, showing Allmers and Rita filling their personal loss with an ennobling social effort might indicate some such idea. The word is *acceptance*, in its religious sense; the final acceptance of the concept of "Eyolf."

John Gabriel Borkman, like *Little Eyolf*, expresses a situation in which very little is possible. Its persons are essentially shadows; creatures of an inevitable Death, which they must learn to accept;

Never dream of life again. Lie quiet where you are.

Borkman, Gunhild, and Ella can no more break out of their deadlock than could Allmers and Asta and Rita. They can move, but only into the death of Borkman.

Yet the method of the play is very different from that of *Little Eyolf*. It is not only John Gabriel Borkman who paces the long gallery, to the arranged playing of the *danse macabre*; it is the ghost of the romantic theatre. The end of the play is the conventional finale of the romantic tragedy, the joining of hands over the dead:

We twin sisters, over him we have both loved.
We two shadows, over the dead man.

The play as a whole is the last act of a romantic tragedy. The other acts are included, are assumed, by what is known as Ibsen's "retrospective technique." But one must not think of this technique in terms of a textbook "device" to provide economy. The manner is retrospective because the whole experience of the play is retrospect. Those critics of the play who "tell the story" of the ruined banker, starting at the beginning and leading up to the end, miss the essential point. It is not Borkman's past, his "story", which matters, but his attitude to the past. The tension of the play is between Borkman's retrospect, which is his life, and his actual condition, which is death.

91

DRAMA FROM IBSEN TO ELIOT

In *When We Dead Awaken*, Ibsen made his last attempt:
the dramatic epilogue to his whole response to "calling."
When We Dead Awaken is an epilogue, but it is also a drama.
To argue that it is "not really a play at all" is simply to argue
that it is not a naturalist play. The work has always been
curiously misunderstood.

The most notable single factor about the technique of *When
We Dead Awaken*, for which there is a certain precedent in
Little Eyolf, and a clear precedent in *Brand* and *Peer Gynt*, is
Ibsen's rejection of the "individual personality" as the basis
of the character-convention in drama. Rubek, Irene, Maia,
Ulfheim, are "ultimately . . . not human at all, but purely
symbols of a poetic vision." The "drama is enacted by symbolic creatures formed out of human consciousness; puppets if
you like; but not human *individuals*."

Rubek and Irene conceived and formed, in their youth, a
child, the lovely image of

the Resurrection, a pure woman awakening to light and glory.

But Rubek, for his life-work, rejected the real Irene, under the
command that had lain on Julian:

"Kill the body that the soul may live."

He rejected his human destiny, his own and that of Irene. He
was concerned only with his "vocation", with the statue that
would bring him glory, that would be placed in museums—
"grave-vaults" as Irene calls them. He says, much later:

RUBEK: All this talk about the artist's vocation and the artist's
mission and so forth began to strike me as being very empty,
and hollow, and ultimately meaningless.
MAIA: What would you put in its place, then?
RUBEK: Life. . . . Is not life in sunshine and beauty a hundred
times better worth while than to hang about to the end of your
days in a raw damp hole, wearing yourself out in a perpetual
struggle with lumps of clay and blocks of stone?

Irene, too, has betrayed her destiny:

It was self-murder, a deadly sin against myself. And that sin I can
never expiate . . . I should have borne children into the world,
many children, real children, not such children as are hidden
away in grave-vaults.

With Rubek, the rejection of life affects his art also:

I learned worldly wisdom in the years that followed, Irene. "The Resurrection Day" became in my mind's eye something more and something—more complex. The little round plinth, on which your figure stood, erect and solitary, no longer afforded room for all the imagery I now wanted to add . . . I imaged that which I saw with my eyes around me in the world . . . I expanded the plinth, made it wide and spacious. And on it I placed a segment of the curving, bursting earth. And up from the fissures of the soil there now swarm men and women with dimly-suggested animal faces. Women and men, as I knew them in real life . . . I had, unfortunately, to move your figure a little back. For the sake of the general effect.

This was "the masterpiece that went round the world", which made Rubek famous.

MAIA: All the world knows it is a masterpiece.
RUBEK: "All the world" knows nothing. Understands nothing . . . What is the good of working oneself to death for the mob and the masses, for "all the world"?
MAIA: Do you think it is better, that it is worthy of *you*, to do nothing at all but a portrait bust now and then?
RUBEK: These are no mere portrait busts I can tell you. There is something equivocal, something cryptic, lurking in and behind those busts—a secret something that the people themselves cannot see . . . I alone can see it. And it amuses me unspeakably. On the surface I give them the "striking likeness", as they call it, that they all stand and gape at in astonishment. But at bottom they are . . . simply the dear domestic animals, Maia. All the animals which men have bedevilled in their own image, and which have bedevilled men in return . . . It is these equivocal works of art that our excellent plutocrats come and order from me. And pay for in all good faith. . . .

The situation of Rubek and Irene can be summarised in the words of Julian:

The old beauty is no longer beautiful, and the new truth is no longer true.

Irene, the lovely, innocent woman, has become the naked poseur at variety shows. The new truth, "the striking likeness", is a simply zoological naturalism.

Irene has played out lust into madness.

> They lowered me into a grave-vault, with iron bars before the loophole, and with padded walls, so that no one of the earth above could hear the grave-shrieks.

The vision of innocence is dead and crippled. And Rubek, the "strong man who stands alone", has simply, like the scorpion, emptied his poison into the soft flesh, and is incapable of a living relationship. His marriage to Maia is simply

> a tedious coasting-voyage to the north.

He is capable, indeed, of remorse:

> Let me tell you how I have placed myself in the group. In front, beside a fountain . . . sits a man weighed down with guilt, who cannot quite free himself from the earth-crust. I call him remorse for a forfeited life. He sits there and dips his fingers in the stream— to wash them clean—and he is tortured by the thought that never, never will he succeed.

But Irene tells him:

> You are nerveless and sluggish and full of forgiveness for all the sins of your life, in thought and in act. You have killed my soul, so you model yourself in remorse, and self-accusation, and penance— and with that you think your account is cleared.

All that is certain is:

> IRENE: We see the irretrievable only when . . .
> RUBEK: When? . . .
> IRENE: When we dead awaken.
> RUBEK: What do we really see then?
> IRENE: We see that we have never lived.

But the "two clay-cold bodies, playing together by the Lake of Taunitz", make one last attempt: to spend

> a summer night on the uplands . . . for once live life to its uttermost, before we go down to our graves again.

Maia is happy with the hunter Ulfheim; Rubek and Irene believe they are free. But as they climb, they come, in Ulfheim's words,

> to a tight place where you stick fast. There is no going forward or backward.

While Maia sings triumphantly, from the depths below, of her freedom, Rubek and Irene, high up on the snowfield, are engulfed by the avalanche, and perish. Over them, the Sister of Mercy makes the sign of the cross before her in the air, and pronounces the blessing:

Peace be with you.

It is the last absolution.

There is hardly any action in the play, and certainly no individual characters. The work is not a return to poetic drama, but it holds related intentions. In the technical sense, the interesting development is one that has become historical. Perhaps under the influence of Strindberg, and certainly under the weight of his ruthless self-analysis, Ibsen has here written what came to be called an expressionist play. The "speaking likeness" of naturalism is realised for what it is, and rejected. The statue which is central in the play is clearly a development of Ibsen's earlier attempts at "symbolism": an external framework for examination of a pattern of experience. But it is the characters which are new. The expressionist play has been described as a "manifestation of an inner, autobiographical drama, projected into characters which are posed in contrasted poles." This would be a just description of *When We Dead Awaken*.

"The tight place, where you stick fast; there is no going forward or backward." When he had finished *When We Dead Awaken* Ibsen talked of "perhaps another attempt—in verse." But he had reached the end of his strength; he collapsed into physical and mental impotence, and passed his last years in a form of living death.

(vii)

The revaluation of Ibsen which I propose may be summarised under its two main headings: the nature of his experience as an artist; and his development of dramatic form. As to the first, it seems to be unquestionable that Ibsen's interest was not in the abstract problems which Shaw assigned to him. He was always concerned with a more traditional function of the dramatist: the communication of a seen pattern of particular experience. He was not, as a dramatist, interested in Heredity, but in the experience of inheritance; he was not interested in Idealism, but in the experience of vocation. The fact that his pattern was a strangely consistent one confirms this view. The essence of his drama underlies and persists through all the varied periods of his development. The question of the moral or metaphysical adequacy of this pattern is a quite separate issue, which one cannot treat within the boundaries of criticism. But one point may be made. The pattern was a deeply personal one, as may be seen in its very persistence. And this "personal" element is perhaps one of the limitations of the achieved work. "The more mature the artist, the more separate in him is the man who suffers and the mind which creates." Mr. Eliot's point is relevant to Ibsen; but it is perhaps better put as *the more mature the form in which the artist works*. It was this very lack of a mature form which was Ibsen's greatest weakness.

This brings me to the second part of the general revaluation. It is necessary to realise that the naturalist drama which Ibsen created was a legitimate child of the romantic drama in which he began his writing. The making of naturalist drama was, of course, a necessary thing, for the romantic drama had lost its vitality. But the naturalist drama which Ibsen fashioned out of his inheritance retained one of the very causes of the devitalisation. The over-emphasis on "action" and on "character", which had made of them virtually absolute dramatic ends, independent of a larger form, was carried over into naturalism. This was the weakness of the new prose play, and it is a weakness which the successors of Ibsen have exaggerated. Ibsen himself, as he gained experience, tried to overcome the defect. His later work, beginning perhaps with *The Wild Duck*, represents an attempt to achieve a new unity of form. This is the reason, first, for the development of concepts—"symbols", if the word must be retained—such as the wild duck itself, the pistols of Hedda Gabler, "Little Eyolf", and the statue of the Resurrection; and second, for the change in characterisation which may be noted from *Hedda Gabler* on to *Little Eyolf* and *When We Dead Awaken*. Ibsen's purpose was the re-establishment of a total dramatic form, to replace the essential formlessness which had come about as a result of the exaggeration of parts of the former whole.

He never wholly achieved his purpose, perhaps because he retained one of the main forces which had caused the disintegration: the use of representational language. It is significant that his most successful work—*Peer Gynt*—is also the work in which he most fully uses a richer medium of language. But *Peer Gynt* was also an essay in a different kind of form.

The particular revaluations of plays which I have suggested confirm this essential thesis: that Ibsen inherited a drama essentially formless, in any important sense; that this very formlessness limited the success of his refinement of the drama; but that he was always concerned to discover a new and adequate form, and at times came near to achieving it.

Ibsen was a great artist, working in a tradition which was acutely inimical to art. That is the scope of his success and of his failure. It is very unfortunate that incidental aspects of his work should, from the beginning, have been over-valued and widely imitated. The change of emphasis which I have suggested allows us to see his work as a whole, in such a way that elements of it still stand as landmarks in our continuing search for a fully dramatic form. As for the work itself, parts of it—the fifth act of *Brand*, most of *Peer Gynt*, parts of *Emperor and Galilean*, much of *Ghosts* and *Rosmersholm* and *Hedda Gabler*, and again of *Little Eyolf*, *John Gabriel Borkman* and *When We Dead Awaken*—are great positive achievements. It is not the greatness of Shakespeare, or of Sophocles. But it is work as valid and as permanent as our century has. We must remember, in making any final act of valuation, that we are called upon to value something of which we are still a part; something which, more than any other man, Ibsen created: the consciousness of modern European drama.

2

August Strindberg

(i)

"IBSEN," said Bjornson, "is not a man, but a pen." This unfortunate condition is not, of course, without its advantages. It serves at least to protect an artist from his biographers.

The velvet-coated Strindberg, his eyes fixed in "the diabolic expression", his hands burned by the crucibles of his experiments in alchemy; the rages, the passions, the renunciations; the series Siri von Essen, Harriet Bosse, Frieda Ulm; the pose at the window of the Blue Room in Stockholm above the triumphal torchlight procession; these phenomena, confronting us from scores of perfervid, illustrated pages, suggest irresistibly the advantages of being remembered as a mere pen. "Nobody would ever have heard of a Lawrence who was not an artist," wrote Mr. Aldous Huxley, criticising a similar beginning in hagiography. It is, after all, the pen for which we remember Strindberg.

Everyone who knows Strindberg knows that he drew directly on his personal experience in his writing. The biography can readily be used to gloss, but not to explain or judge, the literature. It is time to say, after fifteen wild Decembers, that criticism requires a different discipline. The present essay will be concerned solely with Strindberg as dramatist, and limitation of space is not pleaded as an apology.

(ii)

Strindberg, in a writing life of nearly forty years, wrote almost sixty plays, as well as more than thirty works of fiction, autobiography, politics, and history. By any serious standard this is a very prolific output indeed, and it is understandable that most of us, in England, know only a part of it.

Mention of Strindberg, to the average theatregoer, usually brings as narrowly defined a response as does mention of Ibsen.

With Ibsen the association is feminism, heredity, and the fully-furnished family play—usually *A Doll's House* or *Ghosts*. With Strindberg it is anti-feminism, hysteria, and the play of violent action or declaration—*The Father*, say, or *Lady Julie*, or *The Dance of Death*.

These responses, like the public projections of most artists, contain an element of truth. But Strindberg, like Ibsen, cannot be easily typed; a study of his development shows a variety of dramatic method and purpose, and an immense range of technical experiment, which ought to be appreciated if we are to form anything like a just estimate of his status as a dramatist.

Strindberg was writing plays in his late teens and early twenties, and indeed from this period can be dated the very remarkable history play—*Master Olof*, which he went on revising and rewriting until he was twenty-nine, when it was at last produced in the form in which we now have it. During these years Strindberg had also been trying to become an actor, with very little success.

Master Olof shows in a remarkable degree that quality for which all Strindberg's historical plays may be valued: a freedom from abstraction and from what we may call historicism. Strindberg, like the maturing Shakespeare, took a series of historical events, not so much for their own sake, as for their potency to recreate the texture of an experience which the author might also have communicated directly. I mean that Strindberg took such stories as those of Master Olof, Gustavus Vasa, and Eric XIV, partly because they were the legends of his own history, but mainly because when communicated with his unique vigour and immediacy they became an embodiment of tangible contemporary qualities: fidelity, power, intrigue, ambition, and loyalty. The historical events provided an objective dramatic discipline.

His next important play is one of a group of three written in his early thirties: the fairy play *Lucky Peter's Travels* (1882). This play invites comparison with Ibsen's *Peer Gynt*, which had been written some fifteen years earlier. *Lucky Peter's Travels* is inferior, verbally, to *Peer Gynt*; but it shows that remarkable power of dramatic visualisation which was to be so important in the later, more experimental, work of *The Road to Damascus*, *Dreamplay*, and *Ghost Sonata*. Realism of scene is firmly set aside; the travels of Peter, the boy who achieves his manhood through a magical insight into the nature of power, are rendered with a virtuosity of scene that was quite beyond the theatre of Strindberg's own day. Here is one characteristic scene movement:

> Transformation. The landscape changes from winter to summer; the ice on the brook disappears and the water runs between the stones; the sun shines over all.

It is obvious that Strindberg was using the form of a play with little thought of immediate dramatic production. Like Ibsen, after an early attempt to come to terms with the ways of the contemporary theatre, and finding them at length only shackles on his genius, Strindberg drew strength from an older and broader dramatic tradition, and let the theatre, for a while, take care of itself. But the "demands of the new time" soon began to exert their pressure.

In the '80's the new time began to extend its demands for reform to the stage also. Zola declared war against the French comedy, with its Brussels carpets, its patent-leather shoes and patent-leather themes, and its dialogue reminding one of the questions and answers of the Catechism. In 1887 Antoine opened his *Theatre Libre* in Paris, and *Therese Raquin*, although nothing but an adapted novel, became the dominant model. It was the powerful theme and the concentrated form that showed innovation, although the unity of time was not yet observed, and curtain falls were retained. It was then I wrote my dramas: *Lady Julie, The Father,* and *Creditors.*[1]

Now Strindberg was, perhaps, in revolt against the same things as was Zola,[2] against the "patent-leather themes" of the romantic drama. But his own ideas for reform were different, and the experiments into which his ideas led him represent a unique and quite separate dramatic form. His position is more

---

[1] *Memorandum to the Members of the Intimate Theatre, from the Stage Director* (Stockholm, 1908).

[2] What Zola thought of Strindberg is fairly indicated by the following letter:

> Votre drame (*Fadren*) m'a fortement interessé. . . . Vous avez écrit une oeuvre curieuse et interessante, ou il y a vers la fin surtout, de très belles choses. Pour être franc, des raccourcis d'analyse m'y gênent un peu. Vous savez peut-être que je ne suis pas pour l'abstraction. J'aime que les personnages aient un êtat civil complet, qu'on les coudoie, qu'ils trempent dans notre air. Et votre capitaine qui n'a pas même de nom, vos autres personnages qui sont presque des êtres de raison, ne me donnent pas de la vie la sensation complète que je demande. Mais il y a certainement là, entre vous et moi, une question de race.   Dec. 14, 1887.

AUGUST STRINDBERG

justly represented by the opening paragraph of his *Preface* to *Lady Julie* (1888).

Dramatic art, like almost all other art, has long seemed to me a kind of *Biblia Pauperum*—a bible in pictures for those who cannot read the written or printed work. And in the same way the dramatist has seemed to me a lay preacher, hawking about the ideas of his time in popular form—popular enough for the middle classes, who form the bulk of theatrical audiences, to grasp the nature of the subject, without troubling their brains too much. The theatre, for this reason, has always been a board school, for the young, for the half-educated, and for women, who still retain the inferior faculty of deceiving themselves and allowing themselves to be deceived : that is to say, of being susceptible to illusion and to the suggestions of the author. Consequently, in these days when the rudimentary and incompletely developed thought-process which operates through the imagination appears to be developing into reflection, investigation, and analysis, it has seemed to me that the theatre, like religion, may be on the verge of being abandoned as a form which is dying out, and for the enjoyment of which we lack the necessary conditions. This supposition is confirmed by the extensive theatrical decline which now prevails through the whole of Europe, and especially by the fact that in those civilised countries which have produced the greatest thinkers of the age—that is to say, England and Germany—the dramatic art, like most other fine arts, is dead. In some other countries, however, it has been thought possible to create a new drama by filling the old forms with the contents of the newer age; but, for one thing the new thoughts have not yet had time to become sufficiently popular for the public to be able to grasp the questions raised ; moreover, party strife has so inflamed people's minds that pure, disinterested enjoyment is out of the question. One experiences a deep sense of contradiction when an applauding or hissing majority exercises its tyranny so openly as it can in the theatre. Lastly, we have not got the new form for the new contents, and the new wine has burst the old bottles.

The Father (1887) and especially *Lady Julie* (1888) are attempts at such a new form. By this time, of course, Ibsen's prose plays were widely known. Although Strindberg was in many ways openly contemptuous of Ibsen—he called him "that famous Norwegian blue-stocking"—Ibsen's established practice was a very definite part of Strindberg's new dramatic consciousness.

The substance of *The Father* is the conflict of man and woman in the specific instance of a battle for control of their child. The woman, Laura, drives her husband, the Captain, even to insanity, in order to gain absolute control of their daughter. Her main weapon, allied to interference with his work and talebearing of his growing madness, is an induced doubt as to whether the child is really his:

CAPTAIN: Have you never felt ridiculous in your rôle as father? I know nothing so ludicrous as to see a father leading his child by the hand along the street, or to hear him talking about his children. "My wife's children," he should say . . . My child! A man has no children. It is women who get children, and that's why the future is theirs, while we die childless.

And the battle?

CAPTAIN: Laura, save me, save my reason. You don't seem to understand what I say. Unless the child is mine I have no control over her, and I wish for none. Isn't that the one thing you want? Isn't it? Or perhaps there's something else. Do you want to have sole power over the child and at the same time have me to maintain you both?

LAURA: The power, yes! What has all this life-and-death struggle been for, except the power?

CAPTAIN: For me, not believing in a life after death, the child was my idea of immortality, perhaps the only idea that has any real expression. Take that away and you cut off my life.

LAURA: Why didn't we separate in time?

CAPTAIN: Because the child linked us, but the link became a chain . . .

LAURA: Do you remember that it was as your second mother I came into your life? . . . You were too big a child, or perhaps not wanted at all.

CAPTAIN: Yes, it was something like that. My father and mother didn't *want* me, and thus I was born without a will. So I thought I was completing myself when you and I became one, and that is why you got the upper hand . . .

LAURA: . . . That is why I loved you as if you were my child. But whenever you showed yourself instead as my lover, you must have seen my shame. Your embraces were a delight followed by aches of conscience, as if my very blood felt shame. The mother became mistress! . . . That is where the mistake lay. The mother, you see, was your friend, but the woman was your enemy, and love between the sexes is strife. And don't imagine that I gave myself to you. I didn't give, I took—what I wanted. . . .

CAPTAIN: We, like the rest of mankind, lived our lives, unconscious as children, filled with fancies, ideals and illusions. And then we woke. Yes, but we woke with our feet on the pillow, and the man who woke us was himself a sleepwalker. When women grow old and cease to be women, they get beards on their chins. I wonder what men get when they grow old and cease to be men. Those who had crowed were no longer cocks but capons, and the pullets answered the call. So when sunrise should have come we found ourselves among ruins in full moonlight, just as in the good old days. It was nothing but a little morning sleep, with wild dreams; and there was no awakening. . . .

LAURA: . . . Now at last you have fulfilled your part as the—unfortunately—necessary father, and breadwinner. You are no longer needed, and you can go. You can go, now that you have realised that my brain is as strong as my will—since you won't stay and acknowledge it.

(*The Captain rises and throws the lighted lamp at Laura, who walks backwards through the door.*)

So this, some have said, is naturalism! It is necessary to look a little more closely at what Strindberg understood by the term:

Naturalism, (he wrote) is not a dramatic method like that of Becque,[1] a simple photography which includes everything, even the speck of dust on the lens of the camera. That is realism; a method, lately exalted to art, a tiny art which cannot see the wood for the trees. That is the false naturalism, which believes that art consists simply of sketching a piece of nature in a natural manner; but it is not the true naturalism, which seeks out those points in life where the great conflicts occur, which rejoices in seeing what cannot be seen every day.

Strindberg's point is clearly relevant to *The Father*. The experience with which the play deals is intended as a "revealed truth"; it is obviously, in this form, not an "everyday experience." The principal distinction is the articulacy of the exposition. And this is not merely an articulation of the imperfect conversation of everyday people. The characters are *not persons*, but, as Strindberg put it, and as, in another reference, D. H. Lawrence put it, elemental. The articulacy

[1] Henri Becque, author of *Les Corbeaux, Souvenirs, La Parisienne*, etc.

is not that of real persons' conversation made more explicit, but rather an articulation of the author's discovery of certain facts about relationship.

But one must be concerned to distinguish between this method in a play like *The Father* and in a novel, say, like *The Rainbow*. In *The Rainbow* the characters are virtually impersonal media for the expression of Lawrence's reading of experience, an expression which is supplemented by direct commentary and analysis. It is otherwise in this kind of play. Although, essentially, Laura and the Captain are simply conventions of the author's statement (so that it would be irrelevant to ask whether a woman like Laura could really exist, or whether she would reveal herself as she does in speech) the framework of these conventions remains the simulation of the mechanism of actual existence—a naturalism akin to that of Becque. So that, in performance, bodied forth by naturalistic actors, in the fully-furnished atmosphere of an everyday home, the characters inevitably aspire to personality, and are so communicated. This is the inescapable tension of such drama. The characters lose their quality as conventions in the general unconventionality of the presented drama. Strindberg, more definitely than Ibsen in his *The Doll's House—Wild Duck* period, assumes the conventionality of his characters. He rejects the formal carpentry of the well-made play which Ibsen so persistently retained. *The Father* is "formless" and is played out at a single level. But while this permits more adequate expression of the central experience (compare the speeches of Laura and the Captain with those of Nora and Torvald), the very formlessness, the absence of "theatricality" only reinforces the illusion that this is a life-mechanism. And this is an illusion which limits and perhaps destroys the achievement of the essentially unrealistic literary expression.

Strindberg realised this, and in *Lady Julie* he attempted to fashion new conventions. The "new wine had burst the old bottles"; or, more precisely, the old bottles had soured the new wine.

In the present drama I have not tried to do anything new—for that is impossible—but merely to modernise the form in accordance with what I imagined would be required of this art from the younger generation. . . . In regard to the character-drawing, I have made my figures rather characterless, for the following reasons:

The word "character" has, in the course of the ages, assumed various meanings. Originally, I suppose, it signified the dominant characteristic of the soul-complex, and was confused with "temperament." Afterwards it became the middle-class expression for the automaton. An individual who had once for all become fixed in his natural disposition, or had adapted himself to some definite rôle in life—who, in fact, had ceased to grow—was called a "character". . . . This middle-class conception of the immobility of the soul was transferred to the stage, where the middle-class has always ruled. A "character" on the stage came to signify a gentleman who was fixed and finished: one who invariably came on the stage drunk, jesting, or mournful. For characterisation nothing was required but some bodily defect—a club-foot, a wooden leg, a red nose; or the character in question was made to repeat some such phrase as "That's capital," "Barkis is willin'", or the like. . . .

This analysis of characterisation remains a central text for the study, not only of the later romantic drama, but also of the naturalist drama. Strindberg, however, sees the function of the naturalist author differently:

I do not believe in simple characters on the stage. And the summary judgments on men given by authors: this man is stupid, this one brutal, this one jealous, etc., should be challenged by naturalists, who know the richness of the soul-complex, and recognise that "vice" has a reverse side very much like virtue. . . .

(The "richness of the soul-complex" is certainly the serious author's concern, but he may frequently be able to express it through just such summary judgments as Strindberg rejects, since his concern is the general structure of experience rather than portraiture.)

. . . My souls (characters) are conglomerations from past and present stages of civilisation; they are excerpts from books and newspapers, scraps of humanity, pieces torn from festive garments which have become rags—just as the soul itself is a piece of patchwork. Besides this, I have provided a little evolutionary history in making the weaker repeat phrases stolen from the stronger, and in making my souls borrow "ideas"—suggestions as they are called—from one another.

In so far as this method of characterisation is concerned, Strindberg's theory was at this time in advance of his practice.

Julie and Jean are not "characters", it is true; one could define them in Strindberg's terminology as "souls", as "elemental." Julie is the aristocratic girl, fixed in the conscience of inherited debt, consumed by romantic ideals of honour, and in practice a predatory "half-woman." Jean, the valet, by contrast, is "on the up-grade"; "sexually, he is the aristocrat"; he is adaptable, has initiative, and hence will survive. When they meet, when they clash sexually, it is Julie who goes to pieces. Their love-act has no meaning:

> Love, I think, is like the hyacinth, which must strike root in the dark *before* it can produce a vigorous flower. In my play, it shoots up, blossoms, and runs to seed, all at the same time, and that is why the plant dies quickly.

The clash of Julie and Jean is, then, a convention to express a fact which Strindberg has perceived in relationship. And although the relationship is specific, it is hardly personal. The "drama is enacted by symbolic creatures formed out of human consciousness." But Strindberg's definition of his method of characterisation ("my souls . . ." (above)) hardly seems relevant to his practice in this play, although it is certainly relevant to his later, expressionist, pieces. It is true that Jean, as the stronger, imposes his ideas on Julie, the weaker, but this is rather the specific situation than an instance of the general method of the play's development.

> Finally, as to the dialogue: I have rather broken with tradition in not making my characters catechists who sit asking foolish questions in order to elicit a smart reply. I have avoided the mathematically symmetrical construction of French dialogue and let people's brains work irregularly, as they do in actual life, where no topic of conversation is drained to the dregs, but one brain receives haphazard from the other a cog to engage with. Consequently my dialogue too wanders about, providing itself in the earlier scenes with material which is afterwards worked up, admitted, repeated, developed and built up, like the theme in a musical composition.

Strindberg was right, of course, as Ibsen was right, in rejecting the vapid artifice of French romantic dialogue. But what he proposes to substitute is not a controlled, literary medium, but, at first sight, simply haphazard conversation. In his last phrase, it is true, the idea of a verbal theme—what came later to be called "contrapuntal dialogue"—is stated, and Strindberg's use of this method is important in such pieces as *Dreamplay* and *Ghost Sonata*. But it would be extravagant to see in the dialogue of *Lady Julie* an example of this method. In such passages as the following, phrases that have been used earlier are repeated, but only as a means of argument—the one casting the other's words back in a reversal of a previous situation:

JULIE: So that's the sort of man you are. . . .

JEAN: I had to invent something: it's always the pretty speeches that capture women.

JULIE: Scoundrel!

JEAN: Filth!

JULIE: And now you've seen the hawk's back.

JEAN: Not exactly its back.

JULIE: And I was to be the first branch. . . .

JEAN: But the branch was rotten.

JULIE: I was to be the signboard at the hotel. . . .

JEAN: And I the hotel.

JULIE: Sit inside your office, lure your customers, falsify their accounts.

JEAN: *I* was to do that.

JULIE: To think that a human soul could be so steeped in filth.

JEAN: Wash it then.

JULIE: You lackey, you menial, stand up when I'm speaking.

JEAN: You mistress of a menial, you lackey's wench, hold your jaw and get out. Are you the one to come and lecture me on my coarseness? No one in my class has ever behaved so coarsely as you have tonight. Do you think any servant girl attacks a man as you did? I have only seen that sort of thing among beasts and fallen women.

In this passage, at least, we are back to something very like the "catechism."

The prose of *Lady Julie* is effective, not so much by pattern, as by force. It has a vigour wholly consonant with the dramatic speed of the action: (although this vigour is hardly conveyed by the orthodox English translations; the idea that the prose could be better translated in "American" than English is probably just). From the first words:

JEAN: Lady Julie's mad again tonight, absolutely mad.

to the closing scene where Jean sends Julie out to suicide:

> JULIE: I am asleep already—the whole room seems like smoke.
> And you look like an iron stove, a stove like a man in
> black clothes with a tall hat. And your eyes are like coals when
> the fire is going out, and your face is a white patch·like the
> ashes . . . it's so warm and lovely . . . and so light—and so
> peaceful.
>
> JEAN: (*putting the razor in her hands*) There is the broom. Now go,
> while it's light—out to the barn—and . . . It's horrible. But
> there's no other possible end to it. Go!

the language has the explicit, calculated violence of the whole
dramatic method; but it is always the rush of passionate statement rather than the patterned verbal theme which Strindberg,
in the *Preface*, seems to have in mind.

The whole virtue of *Lady Julie* is its speed. In this, Strindberg's new formal devices play their part:

> In order to provide resting-points for the public and the performers
> without allowing the public to escape from the illusion, I have
> introduced three art-forms, all of which come under the heading
> of dramatic art, namely, the monologue, the mime, and the
> ballet: all of which, too, in their original forms, belonged to
> ancient tragedy, the monody now becoming the monologue, and
> the chorus the ballet.

Most impressive is the "ballet" where the peasants sing a
Midsummer Eve drinking song while Jean and Julie are alone
in the bedroom. Kristin's mime is less successful; it has the air
of simple defiance of normal theatrical practice, and serves
little dramatic purpose. Strindberg, it seems, felt the need of
formal devices of this kind, but felt it theoretically rather than
practically. It is interesting to note that he considers the
possibility of the actor working independently, being encouraged to improvise in these interludes. But in *Lady Julie*,
where so much energy is concentrated for a clear single effect,
it seems vital that a singular control should be retained. Only a
dramatist writing for a specific company would be wise to allow
this improvisation, of which Strindberg's description "creative
art" could be misleading.

Strindberg suggests other experiments in performance:

> As regards the scenery I have borrowed from impressionist
> painting its symmetry and its abruptness. . . .

(backcloth and furniture are set diagonally);

> Another perhaps not unnecessary novelty would be the abolition
> of footlights . . . Would not the use of sufficiently powerful side-
> lights . . . afford the actor this new resource—the strengthening of
> his powers of mimicry by means of the face's chief asset—the play
> of the eyes?

He would like to

> turn the stage into a room with the fourth wall missing

but thinks this might be premature.

Strindberg's *Preface*—and the partial exemplification of its
theories in *Lady Julie*—are very interesting evidence of the
disturbance produced in the mind of an original and serious
dramatist by the state of the stage of his day—where dramatic
conventions had virtually disappeared under the weight of
theatrical conventions, and where conventionalism, as a result,
conveyed only the idea of false artifice. If parts of the *Preface*
now fall a little coldly on our ears, it is because we have seen
"experimental drama" come to mean no more than theatrical
experiment, and are as far as ever from significant *dramatic*
conventions. But the *Preface* retains a genuine interest, in spite
of its having become, consciously or unconsciously, a major
document of the "experimental theatre." Perhaps at this point
it will suffice to quote Strindberg's own judgment (in *An Open
Letter to the Intimate Theatre*—1909) :

> As the Intimate Theatre counts its inception from the successful
> performance of *Lady Julie* in 1906, it was quite natural that the
> young director should feel the influence of the Preface, which
> recommended a search for actuality. But that was twenty years
> ago, and although I do not feel the need of attacking myself in
> this connection, I cannot but regard all that pottering with stage
> properties as useless.

This comment should be everywhere reprinted with the
Preface.

After *Lady Julie* Strindberg wrote a series of naturalist plays,
which gained him considerable success in the new theatres of
Paris and Berlin. There is *The Stronger*, played by two people,
only one of whom speaks. There are *Creditors*, *Comrades*, and
Playing with Fire. The dramatic aim is constant: to find the
crisis, the moment of struggle, and to reveal normal experience
in its light. The virtue of all these plays is the intensity of the

revealed experience, the unforgettable power of a savage insight into motive and situation. The limitation, as in *The Father* and *Lady Julie*, is the incongruity between the bared, elemental experience of crisis and the covering apparatus of seen and spoken normality. The reduction to elements foreshadowed in the proposed conventions for *Lady Julie* is never, on the surface of the plays, achieved. It is this failure, a failure of convention, which led to the critical error of dismissing Strindberg as wild and abnormal, and to the further error of a search for an explanation in his autobiography. The elemental characters of Heathcliff and Catherine in *Wuthering Heights* are acceptable, to those who will read the novel as it is, because of the strict conventional form on which the novel is built. But Strindberg's interpretation of naturalism as the moment of crisis was caught up in the incongruous naturalism of the general dramatic movement; was communicated in the even texture of normality. It was necessary for Strindberg to try yet again; his attempt was the wholly new dramatic form of *The Road to Damascus* (1898).

(iii)

In a note on a list of his works Strindberg writes of this new period:

> The great crisis at fifty: revolutions in my mental life, wanderings in the desert, devastation, Hells and Heavens of Swedenborg. Not influenced by Huysman's *En Route*, still less by Paladan, who was then unknown to the author ... but based on personal experiences.

The Road to Damascus has already been extensively quarried, by Swedish critics, for its autobiographical deposits.[1] Their yield is not impressive. One can relate the Lady, at various periods of the play, to Frieda Uhl or Harriet Bosse; the Woman to Siri von Essen; the first scene to Dorotheenstrasse, Berlin; the café to "Zum Schwarzen Ferkel"; the mountain village to Klam. None of these discoveries advances comprehension of the work in any respect. But one can understand why critics should have been reluctant to write of the play itself, which is always strange, and at times bewildering.

---

[1] See especially *Strindberg's dramer*, Martin Lamm, 2 vols. (Stockholm, 1924-6). Also *August Strindberg*, Lind-af-Hageby Paul (1913); and Introduction to *The Road to Damascus* (Cape) by Gunner Ollen.

AUGUST STRINDBERG

The first critical point to be made may be indicated by an extract from Strindberg's prefatory note to *Dreamplay*:

> In this Dream Play, as in his earlier work, *Till Damaskus*, the Author has tried to imitate the disjointed but apparently logical form of a dream. Anything may happen: everything is possible and probable. Time and space do not exist: on an insignificant groundwork of reality imagination spins and weaves new patterns: a mixture of memories, experiences, unfettered fancies, absurdities and improvisations. The characters are split, doubled and multiplied: they evaporate and are condensed; are diffused and concentrated. But a single consciousness holds sway over them all— that of the dreamer.

The Road to Damascus will not be understood unless this method is realised. The whole construction is subject to the dream form which Strindberg has described, although the particular "method" of the dream is different in each of the three parts of the play. Each part of the work is as long as a normal play; and each part is a separate work in the sense that *Burnt Norton* or *East Coker* is a separate poem; although the full richness of the work, as in *Four Quartets*, only emerges from the series.

The Road to Damascus, as the title implies, is a drama of conversion. Each part ends with the Stranger's conversion but the Second and Third Parts begin again with his unbelief; the conversion at the end of each part increases in conviction until at the end of the play it is final. Thus the First Part ends with the Lady inviting the stranger to the church:

LADY: Come.
STRANGER: Very well. I'll go through that way. But I can't stay.
LADY: How can you tell? Come. In there you will hear new songs.
STRANGER: It may be.
LADY: Come.

The last words of the Second Part are:

STRANGER: Come, priest, before I change my mind.

At the end of the Third Part, the Stranger is buried so that his resurrection may come:

TEMPTER: Farewell.
CONFESSOR: Lord! Grant him eternal peace.

III

CHOIR: May he be illumined with everlasting light!
CONFESSOR: May he rest in peace!
CHOIR: Amen!

The way, the road to Damascus, is in each part a different way. In the highly formal pattern of the First Part, it is, in a sense, the "Round about" of Ibsen's Peer Gynt.

It is played in seventeen scenes, of which the first eight represent a progression to the climax of the ninth, which is then succeeded by eight scenes which correspond, in reversed order, with the opening eight. Thus the play begins and ends at a street corner, and passes through and through again a Doctor's House, a hotel room, a beach, a road, a path in a ravine, a kitchen, and a room known as the "Rose Room." The climax is played in a convent, which the Stranger believes is an asylum, and in which appear shadowy likenesses of persons whom we have encountered in the other scenes. At the beginning of the return journey, the Stranger speaks of his loss of consciousness in the convent:

I lay watching my past life unroll before me like a panorama, through childhood, youth . . . And when the roll was finished it began again. All the time I heard a mill grinding.

In the beginning the Stranger is waiting outside the Post Office for a letter containing money with which he can pay his debts. He will not ask for it. Similarly, he will not enter the church:

. . . I feel I don't belong there . . . That I'm an unhappy soul and that it's as impossible for me to re-enter as to become a child again.

He goes "round about"; the panorama is unrolled, stretching back to childhood. When he returns he goes in to ask for the letter. It had been awaiting him:

STRANGER: I feel ashamed of myself. It's the money.
LADY: You see. All these sufferings, all these tears, in vain.
STRANGER: Not in vain. It looks like spite, what happens here, but it's not that. I wronged the Invisible when I mistook . . .
LADY: Enough! No accusations.
STRANGER: No. It was my own stupidity or wickedness. I didn't want to be made a fool of by life. That's why I was.

The whole exploration of identity, and the quest for knowledge, was fruitless, but inevitable. Salvation, the money to pay his debts, was there at the starting-point; but the Stranger could not take it. He suggests a reason for this:

> It's whispered in the family that I'm a changeling. . . . A child substituted by the elves for the baby that was born. . . . Are these elves the souls of the unhappy, who still await redemption? If so, I am the child of an evil spirit. Once I believed I was near redemption, through a woman. But no mistake could have been greater. My tragedy is I cannot grow old; that's what happens to the children of the elves. . . .
>
> LADY: We must see if you can't become a child again.
>
> STRANGER: We should have to start with the cradle; and this time with the right child.
>
> LADY: Exactly.

It is, in fact, the elves ("that fairy story") who determine his "round-about" search for self-knowledge and redemption. They represent his unbelief, and press him on in an attempt to know. They even represent him to himself as a Liberator.

The Liberator goes out, creating the chimeras with which he will fight. He tries to rescue Ingeborg from the "Werewolf" who holds her prisoner: her husband, the Doctor. But the "Werewolf" is one of his own past victims: a schoolfellow whom he had allowed to be punished for one of his own misdeeds. In taking the punishment for the Stranger's sin, the Doctor has in a way become part of the Stranger himself. This is the type of the dream figure: the apparent person, of separate appearance, who is in fact only a mask for an aspect of the Dreamer's life. There are other masks: the Beggar, who like the Stranger bears the brand of Cain; the Housebreaker, a man with the Stranger's past, now being buried in a parody of celebration; and Caesar, the lunatic, who is in the Doctor's charge—the Stranger had been nicknamed Caesar at the school at which he betrayed the Doctor. The search is for identity. The central figure seeks to identify the Stranger who is himself.

The conventional nature of the drama should be clear; the characters are not persons, but symbolic figures enacted out of a single consciousness. Ingeborg, whom the Stranger will not see as a person ("I should prefer to think of you like that: Impersonal, nameless . . . Eve") is the essential context of this inward search for identity:

> STRANGER: You sit there like one of the Fates and draw the threads through your fingers. But go on. The most beautiful of

sights is a woman bending over her work, or over her child.
What are you making?

LADY: Nothing. Crochet work.

STRANGER: It looks like a network of nerves and knots on which
you've fixed your thoughts. The brain must look like that—from
inside.

When she has read his "terrible book", she tells him:

My eyes are opened and I know what's good and evil, as I've
never known before. And now I see how evil you are, and why I
am to be called Eve. She was a mother and brought sin into
the world. Another mother brought expiation. The curse of
mankind was called down on us by the first, a blessing by the
second. In me you shall not destroy my whole sex. Perhaps I
have a different Mission in your life.

When the Stranger leaves Ingeborg, the central crisis is
upon him. In what he takes to be a convent (but which he
suspects later is a hospital or an asylum) he confesses, and
wakes to find himself cursed by the whole company of his
relations: by the mourners, by the Beggar, by the madman
Caesar, by the Werewolf, by the wife and children he has
abandoned, by the Lady, by her parents, by his own parents,
and by the Confessor. None of these main figures is exactly
real; all that can be perceived is a resemblance. The "doom-
session" is convened by the Stranger himself. He is sent, under
the curse, back along his way.

At the opening of the Second Part the Stranger's sight, like
that of Saul, remains blinded; his conviction of the powers
which assailed him leads him only into an attempt to exorcise
them by magic: to call down the lightning and to "upset the
table of the money-changers" by the alchemist's gift of gold.
There remains a hope of salvation in the child which Ingeborg
bears,

the being . . . who can wipe out the darkness of the past and
bring light.

But the child is threatened by the werewolf. Here again, the
"Werewolf" Doctor, and the lunatic Caesar, are no more than
aspects of the Stranger: the Doctor, in particular, is part of the
Stranger through their succeeding relationships with Ingeborg,
and more fundamentally, through their common past.

The climax of the Second Part is the banquet given in the

AUGUST STRINDBERG

Stranger's honour: given, as he thinks, by the Government in honour of his discovery of gold, but in fact given by the Drunkard's Society. The gold which promised salvation is merely dross, and the Stranger becomes convinced that he is finally damned. Even the birth of his child is too late to save him:

Because I have slain my brother.

(This phrase, and the reiteration of the Stranger's brand of Cain, a brand which the Beggar also bears, is to be understood in relation to the substitution by the elves. The Stranger—the child of the elves—has slain himself, the real child.)

STRANGER: The crime I committed in this life was that I wanted to set men free.[1]

BEGGAR: Set men free from their duties, and criminals from their guilt. . . . You're not the first and not the last to dabble in the Devil's work. . . . But when Reynard grows old, he turns monk—so wisely it is ordained—and then he's forced to split himself in two and drive out Beelzebub with his own penance.[2] . . . You'll be forced to preach against yourself from the house-tops. To unpick your fabric thread by thread.

At this point the time-sense, as might be expected in the dream-structure, has yielded to a simultaneity of past and future. The unpicking of the fabric is already well under way. The Stranger goes for comfort to the Dominican who had cursed him. The Dominican is also the Beggar, and the first lover of Ingeborg. The Stranger can take no comfort:

Over these only was spread a heavy night, an image of darkness which should afterward receive them; yet were they unto themselves more grievous than the darkness.

The Third Part opens with the Stranger being led by the Confessor

along this winding hilly path that never comes to an end.

He seeks

death without the need to die—mortification of the flesh, of the old self . . .

[1] In his capacity (in a recurring phrase in the work) as 'an intelligent man at the end of the nineteenth century.'
[2] This must be related, in this context, to the 'dualism' of Saul and Paul.

115

Because:

> One knows nothing, hardly even that one knows nothing; that
> is why I have come so far as to believe.
> LADY: How do you know you can believe, if belief's a gift?
> STRANGER: You can receive a gift, if you ask for it.
> LADY: Oh yes, if you ask, but I've never been able to beg.
> STRANGER: I've had to learn to. Why can't you?
> LADY: Because one has to demean oneself first.
> STRANGER: Life does that for one very well.

When they cross the river towards the monastery, his debts
begin to fall away. The Confessor tells Ingeborg:

> The evil in him was too strong; you had to draw it out of him
> into yourself to free him. Then, being evil, you had to suffer the
> worst pains of hell for his sake, to bring atonement.

It is the Stranger's ideal of redemption through woman.
But at the last cross-roads the Tempter appears, with the
Stranger's own phrases:

> Do you know why sin has been oppressing you for so long?
> Through renunciation and abstinence you've grown so weak
> that anyone can take your soul into possession. . . . You've so
> destroyed your personality that you see with strange eyes, hear
> with strange ears, and think strange thoughts. You've murdered
> your own soul.

At a village trial, the Tempter absolves all guilt by disputing
as far as the final cause. But with the support of Ingeborg, the
Stranger rejects this temptation, and reaches the Monastery.
Here, in the picture-gallery, he meets a succession of "two-
headed men": Boccaccio; Luther; Gustavus Adolphus;
Schiller; Goethe; Voltaire; Napoleon; Kierkegaard; Victor
Hugo; von Stollberg; Lafayette; Bismarck; Hegel.

> Hegel, with his own magic formula. Thesis: affirmation. Anti-
> thesis: negation. Synthesis: comprehension. . . . You began life
> by accepting everything, then went on denying everything on
> principle. Now end your life by comprehending everything. . . .
> Do not say: either—or. But: not only—but also. In a word, or
> two words rather; Humanity and Resignation.

With the last disputation:

> STRANGER: What is loveliest, brightest? The first, the only, the
> last that ever gave life meaning. I too once sat in the sunlight on

a veranda, in the Spring—beneath the first tree to show new green, and a small crown crowned a head, and a white veil lay like morning mist over a face . . . that was not that of a human being. Then came darkness.

TEMPTER: Whence?

STRANGER: From the light itself. I know no more.

TEMPTER: It could only have been a shadow, for light is needed to throw shadows; but for darkness no light is needed.

STRANGER: Stop. Or we'll never come to an end.

the Confessor and the Chapter appear in procession, and wrapping him in the shroud, cry

May he be illumined with everlasting light!
May he rest in peace!
Amen!

Even at the end, the idea of the changeling ("a face . . . that was not that of a human being") is intermittently retained. But the shadow came from the light; and the secret of identity will not be discovered by seeking among the images of darkness. The search is necessary because of the condition, but it brings only anguish: "they were unto themselves more grievous than the darkness." The search leads away from redemption, which waits at the point of origin when one can "become as a little child." Yet—and this is the tragic paradox —to become as a little child seems to demand the search. In the end there is only submission, the absolute redemption by submission to the light.

I have traced the theme of *The Road to Damascus*, in this summary way, because it is necessary to assert that the play is a controlled realisation of a theme. The orthodox "explanation" of it is in terms of Strindberg's recent insanity, and of his obsessions. But this is a failure of reading, rather than of the dramatist. The more closely one examines the work (having set aside prejudices about autonomous characters and representational form) the more one sees the firmness of its pattern, and its pervading relevance. In my account of the play I have, necessarily, omitted a mass of detail in order to isolate the main theme. But the whole substance of the work is controlled by this theme; and its strangeness, when the pattern is accepted, is seen, not as obsession, but as a powerfully original realisation of deeply considered experience. That Strindberg has formulated his drama with elements of his personal experience is true;

but these elements are placed so firmly in the larger scheme of the work that they are, in fact, transmuted; and so beyond the reach of biographical explanation.

The drama is enacted in scenes of strange power, achieved by Strindberg's new method: the breakdown of autonomous "characters"; the elaboration of a pattern of verbal themes; and complete rejection of the representational stage for a kaleidoscope of imaged expressionist scenes. If the scenic imagery is taken within the read work, the whole becomes a drama of rich and controlled complexity. The only limitation of the work, as I see it, is a heritage of the nineteenth-century divorce of drama and literature. Strindberg has rejected the stage and theatre of his time, because it is no medium for such experience as he wishes to handle. But then, in effect, he produces a play, and an unpresentable play (an emasculated version, of course, could be provided). The new element of scenic imagery is not integrated with the words of the play, but is left in the form of stage directions. Thus the play can only be satisfactorily read; it cannot be spoken. An Elizabethan dramatist would have taken the imagery into the speaking words of the play. Strindberg does not. At the height of his great powers, in his rejection of the limitations of naturalism, he remains the victim of naturalism; his drama is the epitome of the fatal theatrical dissociation.

(iv)

The years at the turn of the century were a period of great production for Strindberg. In 1899 came *Advent*, *There are Crimes and Crimes* (an interesting "normal" play with close thematic affinities to *The Road to Damascus*) and the historical plays *Saga of the Folkungs*, *Gustavus Vasa*, and *Eric XIV*.

"Light after darkness," he writes of this time. "New production, with Faith, Hope and Love regained—and absolute certainty." Among five plays produced in 1901 the most important are *Easter* and *The Dance of Death*. *The Dance of Death* has often been placed among the greatest of Strindberg's work. This is a judgment which I cannot support. The play, which might be described as a restatement of the theme of *The Father*, has moments of terrible power: the vampire scene between Kurt and Alice, for example, and the mime of the Captain's dissolution which precedes it. The sword-dance—the "dance of death"—is magnificent theatre. But the speed which sustained the near-melodrama of *The Father* is absent. In the first part of the work one remains satisfied; the merciless clarity of the revelation of married conflict compels assent. It is the mood of savage farce; and the theme of the Captain's decay—"Cancel, and pass on"—is sustained by a verbal pattern which, superimposed on the representational language, removes the absolute limitations of naturalism. But the Second Part is less acceptable. It resembles nothing so much as a middle-period "family-drama" of Ibsen, although it lacks Ibsen's power of concentration. It is an attempt, doubtless, at objectivity; what Strindberg called "absolute certainty" seems to have driven him in this direction. But the effect of the dance of death on the younger generation has a curiously second-hand air which is very uncharacteristic of Strindberg. The new kind of well-made play which Ibsen had fashioned was ready to Strindberg's hand whenever his essential tension slackened; but in it he seems ill at ease.

Easter ("the school of suffering" Strindberg noted) is the nearest to Ibsen of any of his plays. Aspects of it remind us alternately of *The Wild Duck* and of *A Doll's House*. Eleonora is first cousin to Hedvig, although her function is at once larger and more impressive. The bankrupt house, under the shadow of the father's ruin, is a social formulation of guilt in the manner of *John Gabriel Borkman* or again of *The Wild Duck*. Ellis has a function similar to, if less equivocal than that of Hjalmar. Lindkvist, the "giant" who holds power over the family, is at first a villain in the recognisable dress of Krogstad. *Easter* has more plot, in the conventional sense, than any of Strindberg's plays. The action follows the habitual course: exposition; hint of danger; accumulation of danger; resolution. It begins in the shadows and goes out in sunlight. A morality of conduct is made explicit.

Easter is a play of fragmentary beauty and power. Eleonora, the strange child, is the Christ-agent in this singular passion and resurrection:

ELEONORA: We ought not to possess anything that binds us to earth. Out on the stony paths and wander with wounded feet, for the road leads upwards, that is why it is so toilsome. . . . If we are not to weep in the vale of sorrow where then shall we weep? . . . You would like to smile all day long, and that is why you've suffered. . . . Most of it will clear away as soon as Good

Friday is over, but not everything. Today the birch, tomorrow
Easter eggs. Today snow, tomorrow thaw. Today death,
tomorrow resurrection. . . .
. . . Look at the full moon. It is the Easter moon. And the sun,
you know, is still there, although the light comes from the moon.

The atmosphere of the play—the Easter birch, the stolen
flower, the moonlight—is summed up in the scene as the play
ends, where Eleonora strips off the days of the calendar and
throws them into the sunlight:

See how the days pass. April, May, June. And the sun shines on
all of them. . . . Now you must thank God, for he has helped us to
get to the country. . . . You may say it without words, for now the
clouds are gone and it will be heard above.

In theatrical terms—and *Easter* is a typical piece of the
naturalist theatre—this is always effective. At times, the
realisation of the theme of resurrection through suffering—a
constant subject with Strindberg at this period—seems
adequate. But ultimately one cannot overlook the incongruity
of such emotion with the neat social melodrama which is its
framework. *Easter* remains constantly on the edge of a merely
sentimental "soulfulness." The play is a contradiction of
experience and convention.

Strindberg turned again to experiment, both in the style of
the fantasy of *Lucky Peter's Travels* (see *The Nightingale in
Wittenberg*) and in the remembered manner of *The Road to
Damascus*. The most important work of this latter kind is
Dreamplay, the technique of which Strindberg explicitly
related to *The Road to Damascus*. At the point of technique, I
would say, the relation ends. In the earlier, larger play the
dream-method is a means of serious analysis of the experience
of "identity." Except for certain sections of the Third Part
(which was written at a later period than the first two, and in
the same period as *Dreamplay*) there is little or no discursiveness.
But *Dreamplay* is abstract and discursive from the beginning.
It is based on the familiar idea of the Goddess who descends
to earth to discover the truth about the suffering of mankind.
A fantasy in these terms, where the unifying consciousness of
the dreamer is not so much the substance of the play as its
machinery, is rarely satisfying. (Such abstract fantasy has been
significantly popular in the naturalist theatre, and ends usually
in sentimental whimsy like Maeterlinck's *Blue Bird*—which

is not so far from *Peter Pan*.) *Dreamplay* is an astonishing feat
of virtuosity, and its substance consistently tends back to serious
experience, even if it fails to realise it. But the virtuosity is
characteristically restricted to effects of the stage: the Growing
Castle; the fire which reveals a wall of sorrowing human faces;
the trefoil door which holds the secret of life; the linden which
marks the seasons and which on one occasion strips its leaves
to become a coat-and-hat stand. These would be more than
tricks if they were integral to a genuine consciousness. But the
dreamer of this work has, if any, a social consciousness. The
people who assemble and dissolve are old, representative
types: Glazier, Officer, Billposter, Lawyer, Quarantine Officer,
Blind Man, Coalheaver, Poet, Dean. These, like the characters
of *The Road to Damascus* are not persons. But they are not so much
symbolic as deliberately typical. The difference in function is
an adequate measure of the attenuation of experience. Thus,
when Indra's daughter prepares to go back to the heavens,
and asks:

> Have I not learned the anguish of all being,
> Learned what it is to be a mortal man?

one is bound to answer "No." Anguish, futility, martyrdom,
redemption: all are mentioned, none, in convincing terms, is
shown:

POET: Tell me your sorrows.
DAUGHTER: Poet, could you tell me yours without a single dis-
cordant word? Could your speech ever approach your thought?

In *Dreamplay* clearly it could not. One can extract minor
symbolic patterns from the work—there are very many—but
one cannot relate them to the major pattern, for this—in real
terms—does not exist.

> Hush, you must ask no more, and I must not answer. The
> altar is already adorned for the sacrifice; the flowers are keeping
> watch; the lights are kindled; white sheets before the windows;
> fir-twigs in the porch.

With these last words, describing an experience which
Dreamplay is very far from realising, Strindberg sets the scene
for one of his latest and most interesting plays—*Ghost
Sonata*. This work is one of the *Kammarspel*, or Chamber plays,
which Strindberg produced for his own *Intimate Theatre* in

Stockholm. It was written in 1907, and is a summary of the main lines of his development.

Certain major aspects of the dream technique are fundamental to the play: characters are not, or not all, flesh and blood—some can be seen by only one person on the stage. The Ghost Supper, and the cupboarded Mummy, are clearly non-realistic conventions. The unifying consciousness is that of the Student, although this is more loosely conceived than in *The Road to Damascus*. Yet although characters and story, in the usual sense, are rejected, there is no virtuosity of scenic change. The three sets—façade, round drawing-room, Oriental room—are functional, although elements of the scenery serve definable intentions of meaning in the play as a whole.

Ghost Sonata is short, shorter than *Lady Julie*. The dominant person of the first two scenes is the Old Man, Jacob Hummel. The strange world to which he introduces the Student is summed up in the House of the Dead. At the façade appear in turn: the Janitress; the Dark Lady—daughter of the Janitress by the Dead Man, for whom fir is being strewn on the steps; the Colonel, head of the house; his daughter; the old white-haired woman, fiancée of Hummel; the nobleman, son-in-law of the Dead Man. This is the appearance which Hummel arranged: it is not, as we shall see later, entirely accurate. All are seen in the normal way, but the Dead Man who comes to the door in his shroud, and the Milkmaid, from whom Hummel shrinks in horror, are seen only by the Student, who is a "Sunday-child." On the whole façade the Student comments:

STUDENT: I understand nothing of all this. It's just like a story . . .
HUMMEL: My whole life has been like a collection of stories, sir. But though the stories are different, they hang together on a common thread, and the dominant theme recurs regularly.

Within the façade, in the second scene, appearances change. First revealed is the Mummy, who sits in a cupboard behind a papered door

because her eyes cannot bear the light.

She is the original of the statue of the lovely woman who dominates the scene,[1] and mother of the girl whose father is

[1] This is one of many apparent reminiscences of Ibsen in Strindberg's later work. Compare it with Irene in *When We Dead Awaken*. In *The Road to Damascus* the drunkards' banquet is very like the madmen's court in *Peer Gynt*.

assumed to be the Colonel. She sits babbling in her darkness, like a parrot:

Pretty Polly! Are you there, Jacob? Currrr!

The Old Man enters uninvited:

BENGTSSON (*valet*): He is a regular old devil, isn't he?
JOHANSSON (HUMMEL's *attendant*): Fully fledged.
BENGTSSON: He looks like Old Harry.
JOHANSSON: And he's a wizard, too, I think, because he passes through locked doors.

Left alone, the Old Man inspects the statue, and from behind him in the wall hears the cackle of its original. The Mummy enters the room, and it becomes clear that the Young Lady is not the daughter of the Colonel, but of the Colonel's wife (the statue, now the Mummy) and the Old Man. The Colonel in his turn had seduced the Old Man's fiancée, the White-haired Woman, (who sits all day using the window as a mirror, seeing herself from two aspects—the reflection and the outside world, but forgetting that she herself can be seen from outside). Another lover of the Mummy has been the nobleman, who is now to marry the Dark Lady, daughter of the Janitress (who had been seduced by the Dead Man, father-in-law of the nobleman, and whose husband had in consequence been made janitor):

OLD MAN: A pretty collection . . .
MUMMY: Oh God, if we might die! *If* we might die!
OLD MAN: But why do you keep together then?
MUMMY: Crime and guilt bind us together. We have broken our bonds and gone apart innumerable times, but we are always drawn together again.

They are drawn, in Bengtsson's words, to

the usual Ghost Supper, as we call it. They drink tea, don't say a single word, or else the Colonel does all the talking. And then they crunch their biscuits, all at the same time, so that it sounds like rats in an attic. . . . They have kept this up for twenty years, always the same people saying the same things, or saying nothing at all for fear of being found out.

Before the Supper begins, the Old Man strips the Colonel, whose title and rank he shows to be impostures, who is merely

XYZ, a lackey . . . once a cupboard lover in a certain kitchen.

The Supper party assembles:

COLONEL: Shall we talk then?

OLD MAN: Talk of the weather which we know all about; ask one another's state of health, which we know just as well; I prefer silence, for then thoughts become audible and we can see the past; silence can hide nothing, but words can . . . My mission in this house is to pull out the weeds, to expose the crimes, to settle all accounts, so that the young people can start afresh in the house which I give to them. . . . Do you hear the ticking of the clock like a deathwatch in the wall? Can you hear what it says—"It's time", "It's time", "It's time"? When it strikes shortly your time will be up. . . .

But the Mummy interferes; she stops the clock:

I can stop the course of time. I can wipe out the past and undo what is done. Not with bribes, nor with threats, but with suffering and repentance.[1]

She challenges Hummel's right to judge, and, with Bengtsson's aid, exposes his own past, and all his crimes. She reduces him to the cackling of the parrot which had come from her own lips, and then, as the Death Screen is drawn across, sends him to her cupboard to hang himself:

MUMMY: It is finished. God have mercy on his soul.

ALL: Amen.

In the final scene we look for the resurrection. The Student and the Young Lady sit under the cluster of starlike flowers held by the Buddha image in the Oriental room:

LADY: This room is named the Room of Ordeal. It is beautiful to look at, but it is only full of imperfections.

Over the prospect of their marriage broods the immense Cook, who diverts to herself all the vitality of the household, for she is "one of the Hummel family of vampires."

In this house of stagnation and decay, the Student, like Hummel, wishes to lay bare all secrets. But

it is only in a madhouse you say all you think.

There is only one liberator, the Sleep of Death: as the black screen is drawn in front of the girl—

[1] Cf. Eleanora in *Easter*.

AUGUST STRINDBERG

STUDENT: The liberator is coming. Welcome, thou pale and gentle one. Sleep, lovely, unhappy, innocent creature, whose sufferings are undeserved. . . . Sleep without dreaming. . . . You poor little child, you child of this world of illusion, guilt, suffering and death, this world of eternal change, disappointment and pain. May the Lord of Heaven have mercy on you in your journey.

This is Strindberg's consistent conclusion in his later years. In *Ghost Sonata* he realises the persistent pattern in a powerfully concentrated and eminently dramatic form.

(v)

The revaluation of Strindberg which I have proposed rests, essentially, on a realisation of the nature of the experience which he wished to communicate, and on the incongruity with this material of the available dramatic forms. It involves a rejection of pseudo-biographical explanations of madness and obsession; the experience must be accepted for what it is, both in its strangeness and in its power. Strindberg's genius as a dramatist was that he found, against the grain of the dramatic methods of his time, forms of expression which were adequate at least for himself. The work of his later years exercised, as we now know, a great influence in the European drama. But his imitators never reached his own level; too often, the essential conventions became merely startling novelties and theatrical tricks. Thus, Strindberg did not succeed in establishing a general dramatic form capable of his own level of seriousness. But, in his own best work, he created isolated successes of great significance. This achievement, in the difficult circumstances of the drama of our century, is perhaps as much as we have a right to ask.

3

Anton Chekhov

" I regard the stage of today as mere routine and prejudice. When
the curtain goes up and the gifted beings, the high priests of the
sacred art, appear by electric light, in a room with three sides to
it, representing how people eat, drink, love, walk and wear their
jackets; when they strive to squeeze out a moral from the flat
vulgar pictures and the flat vulgar phrases, a little tiny moral,
easy to comprehend and handy for home consumption; when in a
thousand variations they offer me always the same thing over and
over again—then I take to my heels and run, as Maupassant ran
from the Eiffel Tower, which crushed his brain by its overwhelming vulgarity. . . . We must have new formulae. That's
what we want. And if there are none, then it's better to have
nothing at all."

THIS striking indictment of the naturalist theatre, an
indictment which in fifty years has lost none of its force, is
not, one had better begin by emphasising, Chekhov's own. It
is a speech which he gives to the young writer Constantine
Treplef in *The Seagull*. Chekhov perhaps felt very much in this
way (although from external evidence his literary position
would seem to be more represented in *The Seagull* by Trigorin
than by Treplef), but I do not wish to play the dangerous and
tiresome game of identifications. The outburst, which has a
characteristic late nineteenth-century ring, is better worth
quoting as a first step in the analysis of some of Chekhov's
plays, and as a preface to some remarks on the relation of the
naturalist drama to fiction, and on the "symbolism" which
naturalist dramatists have developed.

"Ibsen, you know," Chekhov wrote to A. S. Vishnevsky,
"is my favourite author." And this affiliation is a point which
the critic can no longer doubt. It is true that in England the
public projections of Ibsen and Chekhov are very dissimilar.
So acute an Ibsenite as William Archer could see nothing in
The Cherry Orchard but empty and formless time-wasting. The
devotees of Chekhov in the little theatres of England, on the
other hand, acclaim his work as "really lifelike and free from

any tiresome moralising."[1] The point is doubtless one which can be settled by analysis. Meanwhile one might hazard a supplementary remark to the sentence quoted from Chekhov's letter: "*The Wild Duck*, you know, is my favourite play"; and imagine Chekhov saying, as Ibsen said of *The Wild Duck*:

> The characters, I hope, will find good and kind friends . . . not least among the player-folk, to whom they all, without exception, offer problems worth the solving.

For the buttress of Chekhov's popularity as a dramatist is his popularity with actors, with "the high priests of the sacred art."

In Ibsen's *The Wild Duck* the crucial point for an evaluation of the play is a study of the function of the title-symbol. The same is true of *The Seagull*, where the "symbol", indeed, has passed even beyond the confines of the work to become the insignia of a new movement in the theatre. Chekhov introduces the seagull in the second act, at a point where Treplef's play has failed, and where his beloved Nina is about to pass from his influence to that of the more famous Trigorin:

> *Enter* TREPLEF *hatless, with a gun and a dead seagull.*
> TREPLEF: Are you alone?
> NINA: Yes.
> *Treplef lays the bird at her feet.*
> NINA: What does that mean?
> TREPLEF: I have been brute enough to shoot this seagull. I lay it at your feet.
> *She takes up the seagull and looks at it.*
> TREPLEF: I shall soon kill myself in the same way. . . .
> NINA: You have grown nervous and irritable lately. You express yourself incomprehensibly in what seem to be symbols. This seagull seems to be another symbol, but I'm afraid I don't understand. I am too simple to understand you.

It is an incapacity—this failure to understand the symbol—which, it becomes clear, the author does not intend the audience to share. Trigorin makes the next point:

> A subject for a short story. A girl—like yourself, say—lives from her childhood on the shores of a lake. She loves the lake like a

---

[1] An incidental reason for this acclaim is perhaps the (erroneous) belief that Chekhov is 'naturalism without politics.' One can understand the comfort.

seagull, and is happy and free like a seagull. But a man comes along by chance and sees her and ruins her, like this seagull, just to amuse himself.

Since this is exactly what Trigorin is going to do to Nina— we are often reminded of this prophecy—the point will doubtless be regarded as subtle. It is a subtlety which stops perhaps a little short of the diabolic—at the deadly.

When Nina has been seduced and abandoned by Trigorin she writes regularly to Treplef:

TREPLEF: Her imagination was a little disordered. She signed herself "Seagull." In Pushkin's "Rusalka" the miller says he is a raven, so she said in her letters that she was a seagull.

And when Trigorin comes on a visit:

SHAMRAYEF: We've still got that thing of yours, Boris.
TRIGORIN: What thing?
SHAMRAYEF: Constantine shot a seagull one day, and you asked me to have it stuffed for you.
TRIGORIN: Did I? I don't remember.

Immediately afterwards Nina returns to see Treplef:

NINA: . . . I am a seagull . . . no, that's wrong. I am an actress. Yes, yes . . . I am a seagull. No, that's wrong . . . Do you remember you shot a seagull? "A man comes along by chance and sees her, and, just to amuse himself, ruins her. . . . A subject for a short story." . . .

As she leaves, the stuffed seagull is brought in and placed on the table, with Trigorin still murmuring:

I don't remember. No, I don't remember.

At this moment Treplef shoots himself. ("I am still adrift in a welter of images and dreams . . . I have been brute enough to shoot this seagull.")

Now in Ibsen's *The Wild Duck* Hedvig, when told to shoot the wild duck, shoots herself. She identifies herself with the bird. In *The Seagull* the story of Nina's seduction and ruin is similarly identified with the bird. In *The Wild Duck* the bird is also used to define other characters and the whole atmosphere of the play. Similarly, in *The Seagull*, the bird and its death, and its stuffed resurrection, are used to indicate something about Treplef, and the general death of freedom which pervades the play. In this comparison, I am not attempting to prove plagiarism. All authors steal (it is only, it seems, in an industrial society, that this has been reckoned as wrong), and a good trick is always worth playing twice. I am trying, rather, to assess the function and validity of the device. The function is surely clear. The seagull emphasises, as a visual symbol—a piece of stage property—the action and the atmosphere. It is a device for emotional pressure, for inflating the significance of the related representational incidents. After *Ivanov* (1887) and *The Wood Spirit* (1888), which had both failed, Chekhov, we are told by Princess Nina Andronikova Toumanova,

> for seven long years gave up the stage, although the search for a new dramatic form unceasingly occupied his mind. He meditated upon a realistic play in which he could introduce a symbol as a means of communicating to the audience his deeper and inner thoughts.[1]

This is the frank orthodox description of the form. The symbol, as we now know, came to hand biographically, and Chekhov commented on the seagull which his friend Levitan had shot:

> Another beautiful living creature is gone, but two dumbbells returned home and had supper.[2]

In the play the symbol is illustrative, and the centre of emotional pressure. I have described it as "inflating the significance of the incidents", which may seem to beg the question. But this very characteristic naturalist device is clearly a substitute for adequate expression of the central experience of the play in language. It is a *hint* at profundity. At a simple illustrative level it is precise. The correspondences, as we have seen, are established explicitly and with great care. At any other level, and at the symbolic level at which it is commonly assumed to operate, it is essentially imprecise; any serious analysis must put it down as simply a lyrical gesture.

The Seagull is a very good example of the problem with which the talented dramatist, in a predominantly naturalist period, is faced. The substance of his play is settled as a representation of everyday life; and the qualities which Chekhov saw in everyday life were frustration, futility, delusion, apathy. This weary atmosphere, moreover, was characterised by an inability to

[1] *Anton Chekhov*, p. 118 (Cape, 1937).
[2] Letter to Suvorin, April 8, 1892.

speak out—an inability of which almost every notable writer in the last seventy years has complained. Major human crises are resolved in silence, or are indicated by the slightest of commonplace gestures. "Let us," Chekhov wrote to Suvorin, "just be as complex and as simple as life is. People dine and at the same time their happiness is made or their lives are broken."[1] Fidelity to the representational method, therefore, compels the author to show people dining, to depict their conversation in minor commonplaces. But if he is seriously concerned with experience, he cannot leave matters in this state. Either one or more of his characters may—for some reason—have an ability to speak out, to indicate the underlying pattern. (In Ibsen this emerged in his tendency to speechmaking, which found its apotheosis in *An Enemy of the People*.) In *The Seagull*, Trigorin, particularly, and Treplef, who are both writers, and Russian writers, possess this faculty. Even then the author may not be satisfied; a total pattern has to be indicated, for since the characters are conceived as absolute, as "real persons", their statements may be merely personal and idiosyncratic. Here, in the final attempt to resolve the difficulty, is introduced such a device as that of the seagull, which is related to the widespread development in the naturalist theatre of the use of stage properties or settings to indicate the essence of the work. But this is a poor substitute for the concrete and precise realisation of the central experience of a play which is achieved in more formal drama by conventionally exact speech. Rejection of convention, in the interest of character-drawing and lifelike speech, is the root of the difficulty. The elaboration of substitute devices is an attempt to escape from the limitations which in the interest of naturalism have been voluntarily self-imposed.

Now certainly, Chekhov's representation of living action is impressive. The structure is more finely and more delicately constructed than that of any of his contemporaries. The same method achieves, in his fiction, very valuable results. But the method, I would say, is ultimately fictional. In the bare, economical, and inescapably explicit framework of drama the finest structure of incident and phrase, left to itself, appears crude. The convention of impersonal analysis which (as in Jane Austen) supplies richness in fiction is impossible in drama. The miniatures are left suspended; there is an air, as in Ibsen's

---

[1] Letter of May 4, 1889. Cf. 'It is in a small room, round the table, close to the fire, that the joys and sorrows of mankind are decided.'—Maeterlinck, *The Double Garden*, p. 123.

ANTON CHEKHOV

The Wild Duck, of disintegration, which springs directly from this absence. A gap must be filled, and to the rescue, as before, comes the unifying pressure of a stage device of atmosphere. It is a poor compromise. The characters, which in fiction remain impersonal, aspire to personality by the conditions of dramatic presentation. Delineation degenerates to slogan and catch-phrase, to the mumbled "and all the rest of it" with which old Sorin ends his every speech in *The Seagull*. For of such is a character built. The just comment is Strindberg's, in the *Preface to Lady Julie*:

> A character on the stage came to signify a gentleman who was fixed and finished; nothing was required, but some bodily defect —a club-foot, a wooden leg, a red nose; or the character in question was made to repeat some such phrase as "That's capital", "Barkis is willin'", or the like.

The red noses of farce seem a long way from Chekhov, but the crudity, in literary terms, is finally of the same order.

Chekhov is one of the most skilful of modern dramatists, and consequently he reveals more than anyone else the limitations and weaknesses of the modern dramatic *form*. A crucial point is the method of revelation of character and the relation of such revelation to the central experience of the play. At times it is simply speechmaking—there is more of this in Chekhov's drama than his admirers would willingly allow. Now speech-making in a play can serve useful dramatic ends. It is at its best in genuine rhetoric, which as Mr. Eliot has pointed out (in his essay *Rhetoric and the Poetic Drama*) is a device of great effect when it

> occurs in situations where a character in a play *sees himself* in a dramatic light.

I think there is a hint of this in Ibsen's treatment of Stock-mann in *An Enemy of the People*, although it is overborne by the general forensic. There are hints of it also in Chekhov: perhaps in Arcadina in *The Seagull*, and occasionally in Treplef; at moments in Irina and Olga in *The Three Sisters*; in Astrov in *Uncle Vanya* and Madame Ranevsky in *The Cherry Orchard*. But I have not myself been able to adduce a single wholly convincing example. Of other, less valid kinds of rhetoric there is, however, no lack.

When a character in a play makes a direct appeal to us, we are either the victims of our own sentiment, or we are in the presence

131

of a vicious rhetoric. This dramatic sense on the part of the characters themselves is rare in modern drama. In sentimental drama it appears in a degraded form, when we are evidently intended to accept the character's sentimental interpretation of himself. In plays of realism we often find parts which are never allowed to be consciously dramatic, for fear, perhaps of their appearing less real.

Mr. Eliot's categories, though of great general value, are too rigid for Chekhov. There is no modern dramatist whose characters are more consistently concerned with explicit self-revelation. All his plays might be described as plays of confession. But purposes differ:

TREPLEF: Who am I? What am I? Sent down from the University without a degree through circumstances for which the editor cannot hold himself responsible, as they say; with no talents, without a farthing, and according to my passport a Kiev artisan; for my father was officially reckoned a Kiev artisan although he was a famous actor. So that when these actors and writers in my mother's drawing-room graciously bestowed their attention on me, it seemed to me that they were merely taking the measure of my insignificance; I guessed their thoughts and felt the humiliation.

(*The Seagull*)

UNCLE VANYA: I am intelligent, brave, and strong. If I had lived normally I might have become another Schopenhauer, or Dostoevsky.

(*Uncle Vanya*)

OLGA: I'm always having headaches from having to go to the High School every day and then teach till evening. Strange thoughts come to me, as if I were already an old woman. And really, during these four years that I have been working here I have been feeling as if every day my strength and youth have been squeezed out of me, drop by drop. And only one desire grows and grows in strength. . . . To Moscow, as soon as possible.

(*The Three Sisters*)

SHIPUCHIN: As I was saying, at home I can live like a tradesman, a *parvenu*, and be up to any games I like, but here everything

ANTON CHEKHOV

must be *en grand*. This is a Bank. Here every detail must *imponiren*, so to speak and have a majestic appearance.

(The Anniversary)

GAYEF: I'm a good Liberal, a man of the eighties. People abuse the eighties, but I think I may say that I've suffered for my convictions in my time. It's not for nothing that the peasants love me. We ought to know the peasants, we ought to know with what . . .
ANYA: You're at it again, Uncle.

(The Cherry Orchard)

Treplef and Olga are outlining their explicit situation; their speeches are devices of the author's exposition, which, because of the large number of characters he handles, is frequently awkward and tedious, as in *The Three Sisters*. There is also, with Olga and Treplef, a sentimental vein (with real persons it would be called self-pity) which depends on their explicitness. While retaining the manner of conversation, they are doing more, or attempting more, than conversation can ever do. In Uncle Vanya, this has become the full sentimentality, as it is also in Gayef. But in Gayef, the device is satiric. We are evidently *not* "intended to accept the character's sentimental interpretation of himself." Shipuchin is a more unequivocal comic figure, but then *The Anniversary*—a short piece—is a less equivocal play: it is farce without strings. One's doubts about even the best of Chekhov's plays are doubts about the strings.

His own attitude to his work is interesting. Of *The Seagull* he writes "it turned out to be a novelette. I am more dissatisfied than contented, and, upon reading my newborn comedy am convinced once more that I am not a playwright." He called *The Cherry Garden* "not a drama, but a comedy, sometimes even a farce"; "the last act is gay, the whole play is gay, light"; "why on the posters and in the advertisements is my play so persistently called a *drama*? Nemirovich and Stanislavsky see in it a meaning different from what I intended. They never read it attentively, I am sure." In the middle plays, like *The Three Sisters*, there is a clear unity of mood, what Chekhov himself called "that grey dawdle." In *The Seagull* and *The Cherry Orchard* considerable emotional agility is necessary: there is a quick intermittent movement of farce and pathos. Or at least that is the usual view. My own question is whether Chekhovian farce and pathos are emotionally distinguishable, whether both in fact do not proceed from the same limited expression. The local point for analysis, in all the plays, is the practice of self-dramatisation by characters, as I have briefly exemplified it above. The key play is, of course, *The Cherry Orchard*, where Chekhov's particular method is most richly employed.

Under the shadow of a Russia which is passing away (the movement is expressed in the figure of the cherry orchard—a characteristic lyrical symbol) a group of characters is revealed. They are all, in a sense, *nedotepa*, which is a keyword in the play.[1] The elements of method which we have already noted are fully employed. There is a good deal of what I would call "red-nose" characterisation: Gayef, with his continual billiards phrases:

> Till the cherry orchard was sold we were all agitated and miserable; but once the thing was settled finally and irrevocably, we all calmed down and got jolly again. I'm a bank clerk now; I'm a financier . . . red in the middle!

Then there is Trophimov, self-dramatised as the "perpetual student." Epikhodov, whose nickname slogan is "twenty-two misfortunes", talks in sentimental officialese:

> Undoubtedly, perhaps, you may be right. But certainly if you regard the matter from that aspect, then you, if I may say so, and you must excuse my candour, have absolutely reduced me to a state of mind.

He is never separated from his guitar, on which he accompanies his love-songs. Gayef, it is true, is less limited than Epikhodov; he is the occasion for some very acceptable comedy, and is a relief in the very sense that in him is satirised the tendency to speechmaking about which one remains uneasy throughout the play. For it is blindness to assume that—however it may be placed by the author—there is no didacticism in *The Cherry Orchard*. Trophimov's speech in the second act, on

---

[1] *Nedotepa* offers particularly difficult translation difficulties. It is a word invented in this play by Chekhov, and now established in the language. It is derived from *ne*—not, and *dotyapat*—to finish chopping. Applied to people its general significance is clear. English versions have variously offered: 'job-lot'; 'those who never get there'; botchment.' In English idiom 'half-chopped' would be literal, and 'half-baked' probably the best translation. But it seems certain that the word is bound up in this context with the *chopping* down of the cherry orchard, for an effect one can apprehend.

a theme which constantly recurs in Chekhov's plays and which seems, from his letters and conversation, to have been also a personal belief—

> At present only a few men work in Russia. The vast majority of the educated people that I know seek after nothing, do nothing, and are as yet incapable of work.

—this indictment is set by design against the declaration of Lopakhin, the son of a serf, a figure of the new Russia, the man who will take over the cherry orchard and chop it down to build villas:

> I work from morning till night. . . . When I work for hours without getting tired I get easy in my mind and I seem to know why I exist. But God alone knows what most of the people in Russia were born for. . . . Well, who cares?

As Chekhov constructs this microcosm for us—the stupid, sentimental, generous Madame Ranevsky, the juggling, isolated Charlotte, the ineffectual Pishtchik—we assent. Our first glance confirms the impotence and the subsequent decay. The expository method is masterly of its kind. But there grows, implacably, a profound uneasiness, an uncertainty about the emotional quality of what is at the very heart of the work. It is the process, though infinitely more complicated, of one's evaluation of Galsworthy: a mastering suspicion of the emotional integrity from which the satire proceeds, a growing conviction that the author remains attached, by strings which in performance extend to and operate on us, attached to something lovable, something childlike, something vague; attached, in the human sense, to a residue of unexamined experience which for one reason or another cannot be faced, and to which, accordingly, renouncing his control, the author must submit. But to take the play beyond naturalism, to make it something more than an entertaining, but limited, collection of human sketches, this unexamined experience would have to be faced and understood. The formal indictment comes, it is true, readily enough, in the last words of Firs—

> There's no strength left in you; there's nothing, nothing. Ah, you . . . nedotepa!

or, more fully, in the speech of Trophimov:

> Your orchard frightens me. When I walk through it in the evening or at night, the rugged bark on the trees glows with a dim light,

and the cherry-trees seem to see all that happened a hundred and two hundred years ago in painful and oppressive dreams. Well, we have fallen at least two hundred years behind the times. We have achieved nothing at all as yet; we have not made up our minds how we stand with the past; we only philosophise, complain of boredom, or drink vodka. It is so plain that, before we can live in the present, we must first redeem the past, and have done with it; and it is only by suffering that we can redeem it, only by strenuous, unremitting toil.

Chekhov leaves it, in the end, to just such formal statement, for at this point he reaches the limit of his form. He turns back to inconsequence, to the elaboration of his portrait of impotence. The haphazard (though controlled) nature of the progress of his play is certainly pleasantly acceptable after the crudities of ordinary naturalist drama, after "the flat vulgar pictures and the flat vulgar phrases, a little tiny moral easy to comprehend and handy for home consumption." But Chekhov only refines the form, he does not overcome it. All that is inaccessible to the form, all that is inaccessible to him, lingers and pervades, creating an acute self-consciousness. The dramatist is self-conscious—admitting his limitations and then shrugging his shoulders—in exactly the same way (for it was this which produced them) as are his characters. It is a consciousness of vague charm, of the hoped-for significance of the silent, imprecise gesture that is made when nothing can be said:

> If ever the news reaches you that I have come to an end, give a thought to the old . . . horse, and say, "Once there lived a certain Simeonof—Pishtchik, Heaven rest his soul." Remarkable weather we're having. . . . Yes.
> (*He goes out deeply moved.*)

It is, moreover, in practical terms, a consciousness of the audience, who are certain to become, in Mr. Eliot's phrase, "victims of their own sentiment." It is the consciousness of the naturalist theatre.

The seagull remains figured on the grey curtains of the Art Theatre in Moscow. Chekhov complained of Stanislavsky's naturalism frequently in his life, and seems to have realised the inevitability of the failure of the attempt at "complete, psychologically-justified, illusion." But in the drama he was of Stanislavsky's camp, and of the camp too of the decadent naturalism, which, in Russia and elsewhere, succeeded him. Perhaps no man is more completely characteristic of the naturalist theatre than Chekhov. He had all its virtues and its talents, in a measure, indeed, amounting to genius. But also he had its limitations. The result is that

> when the curtain goes up and the gifted beings, the high priests of the sacred art, appear by electric light, in a room with three sides to it, representing how people eat, drink, love, walk and wear their jackets,

Chekhov himself, for all his reservations, is highly placed among the questionable deities.

4

Bernard Shaw

(i)

THE Thing, which was foretold in the Metabiological
Pentateuch, almost Happened. In 1950, Shaw, the
younger contemporary of Ibsen, the contemporary of Strindberg and Chekhov, the elder contemporary of Synge and
Pirandello, was still with us. The man, whom we all respected,
and whose death, in spite of all his irreverence to death, was
strangely moving, had outlived his epoch. In a very proper
paradox, the great purveyor of iconoclasm had become, in his
great age, one of the most unassailable of popular ikons.
"Greater than Shakespeare" scandalised in its day; "Shaw is
not great" is today a wider scandal.

The social context of his reputation is responsible for much
that in other terms would be inexplicable. Shaw was the great
literary figure in a society which was largely uninterested in
literature. Criticism, the very breath of Shaw's own being, was
more or less ineffective in a situation which as much as anyone
Shaw himself confused. Shaw's reputation, it is clear, was less
a literary reputation than, in all senses, literary-political; (was
he not, indeed, a principal designer of the fashion in literary
politics that the shortest cut to greatness is, on every available
occasion, to assume and proclaim it?) From so formidable a
confusion criticism might well—as it often does, quail. But now,
while we honour the memory of the man, the attempt at revaluation of the dramatist had better again be made.

(ii)

The Quintessence of Ibsenism was published in 1891, and became
the prelude to Shaw's dramatic career. Shaw's book, as I have
argued elsewhere, has to do with Ibsen only in the sense that it
seriously misrepresents him; but the book was one of the
forces which produced what was known at the time as the
"new drama"—a movement which was identified with Mr.

138

Grein's Independent Theatre. At this point Shaw's position was intelligent. He was, it is true, preoccupied by the censorship (a preoccupation which his personal encounters with it fully explain) and placed it as the main contributory factor in the decline of English drama. Since the suppression of Fielding's dramatic ambitions, he argued, and the driving of serious authors to the uncensored form of the novel

> the English novel has been one of the glories of literature, whilst the English drama has been its disgrace.

Shaw's analysis of the decline was not even a half-truth; but on the related question of interaction of the drama and the theatre he was surely right. Of the Independent Theatre he wrote:

> Every attempt to extend the repertory proved that it is the drama which makes the theatre, and not the theatre the drama. Not that this needed fresh proof, since the whole difficulty had arisen through the drama of the day being written for the theatres instead of from its own inner necessity. Still, a thing that nobody believes cannot be proved too often.

Shaw's refusal to tolerate the popular heresy that important dramatic reform can come only from "born men of the theatre" is greatly to his credit.

He proposed to re-establish the drama as a literary form, and his arguments in favour of publishing plays are powerful so far as they go. But in fact it was precisely at this point that he surrendered to the illusions and prejudices of the theatre he was attacking.

> The fact that a skilfully written play is infinitely more adaptable to all sorts of acting than available acting is to all sorts of plays (the actual conditions thus exactly reversing the desirable ones) finally drives the author to the conclusion that his own view of his work can only be conveyed by himself. And since he could not act the play singlehanded even if he were a trained actor, he must fall back on his powers of literary expression as other poets and fictionists do.

Shaw's intuition of the acting situation, which offered either a realism which was open to the changing personalities and "interpretations" of successive actors, or on the other hand a simple theatrical virtuosity which was virtually independent of the play—the tradition of the "great actors"—was acute. But

he seemed unable to conceive that things could be otherwise.
He continued :

> So far this has hardly been seriously attempted by dramatists.
> Of Shakespeare's plays we have not even complete prompt copies,
> the folio gives us hardly anything but the bare lines . . . If we had
> . . . the character sketches, however brief, by which he tried to
> convey to the actor the sort of person he meant him to incarnate,
> what a light they would shed, not only on the play, but on the
> history of the Sixteenth Century . . . For want of this elaboration
> . . . Shakespeare, unsurpassed as poet, storyteller, character
> draughtsman, humorist and rhetorician, has left us no intellec-
> tually coherent drama, and could not afford to pursue a genuinely
> scientific method in his studies of character, and society.

What (leaving aside the characteristic assumption of the
"genuinely scientific method") Shaw is complaining about,
is that Shakespeare did not write nineteenth-century novels.
He is apparently incapable of seeing that the "bare lines", as
he calls them, constitute a work of literature that is sufficient
in its own right. Shakespeare's views about his plays would, of
course, be illuminating. But the plays do not suffer because
Shakespeare was not his own Bradley or Verity. What Shaw
calls "literary treatment" is the method of fiction rather than
of drama. And he is completely characteristic in this of the
views of his allies and opponents alike : for what no one seemed
able to believe was that drama is capable of being a self-
sufficient literary form. "Anyone," he asserts

> reading the mere dialogue of an Elizabethan play understands all
> but half a dozen unimportant lines of it without difficulty

(this is a proposition which it would be interesting to test)

> whilst many modern plays, highly successful on the stage, are not
> merely unreadable but positively unintelligible without the stage
> business. Recitation on a platform with the spectators seated
> round the reciter in the Elizabethan fashion, would reduce them to
> absurdity.

About modern plays he is right; but he is so much at one
with the dramatists he has criticised that the only suggestion
for improvement he can make is that

> intellectual meaning and circumstantial conditions must be
> supplied by the author so that actors can understand.

In practice this means reforming the drama by making it
something else. The "mere dialogue" will stay as it is, but
because it is inadequate, the dramatist will turn his text into
a pseudo-novel by supplying descriptions of scenery and
characters, and prefaces on the subject of the drama as a whole,
within which the "lines" will be interspersed. The issue, of
course, is neither novel nor play, but a thing inferior to both.

In *The Quintessence of Ibsenism* Shaw misrepresented Ibsen's
work as avowedly didactic. For the same reason, he admired
Brieux, whom he did not misrepresent. He quickly proclaimed
his own similar intention:

> I must however warn my readers that my attacks are directed
> against themselves, not against my stage figures.

And, having rejected clandestine adultery as a subject, he

> tried slum-landlordism, doctrinaire free-love (pseudo-Ibsenism),
> prostitution, militarism, marriage, history, current politics, natural
> Christianity, national and individual character, paradoxes of
> conventional society, husband-hunting, questions of conscience,
> professional delusions and impostures, all worked into a series of
> comedies of manners in the classic fashion.

From this alone, the character of Shaw's work ought to be
clear. It is the injection of seriousness in the drama, and seriousness means "a genuinely scientific method": "we wanted as
the basis of our plays . . . a really scientific natural history."
Shaw is able to tell us, by naming a problem, what each of his
plays is about; and the phrase is always an adequate explanation. This is his affinity with Brieux, whose stage-manager is
instructed to appear and say to the audience:

> Ladies and gentlemen . . . the object of this play is a study of the
> disease of syphilis in its bearing on marriage;

and with his successor, Mr. Priestley,[1] who appears before the
filmed version of *They Came to a City* to announce

> I have dramatised the hopes and fears of the British public about
> the post-war world.

But against this we must set the fact that there are few
serious works of literature which are so lacking in complexity

---

[1] The keyword of this succession is *magic* (cf. Marchbanks in *Candida*).
The word occurs constantly in Mr. Priestley's writing, and an analysis of its
content (including its commercial uses) would be a just analysis of Mr.
Priestley as writer.

that they can be labelled in this way. Many great works of literature would seem to be concerned with a particular problem, social or individual; but it is not the problem which confers seriousness (or Sir Philip Gibbs would be our greatest novelist); but the author's ability to realise his preoccupation in terms of detailed, fundamental, and fully explored direct experience. One need not go outside the modern period to answer Shaw; Ibsen himself had made the point, if Shaw had been prepared to listen:

> Everything which I have written as a poet has had its origin in a frame of mind and situation in life. I never wrote because I had, as they say, "found a good subject."

What Shaw was concerned to do, when, as he says, he had "found a good subject", must be determined by a closer look at certain of his plays.

(iii)

Widowers' Houses ("slum-landlordism") need not detain us; it is not Shaw at his best. It is a crude intrigue melodrama, mechanically contrived to allow Lickcheese, the rent-collector, to be righteously rhetorical about slums, and to involve everyone on the stage in a condonement of criminality. It is very thin stuff. *The Philanderer* ("doctrinaire free-love") is more interesting, not indeed as a play, but as an element in Shaw: because whenever Shaw had to deal with personal emotion, as in this play he chose to do, certain radical weaknesses appeared. It is important to remember that when he wrote this play, he was already mature in years.

Conventional stage romance is rejected.

> CRAVEN: What the dickens did he mean by all that about passing his life amid—what was it—"scenes of suffering nobly endured and sacrifice willingly rendered by womanly women and manly men"—and a lot more of the same sort? I suppose he's something in a hospital.
>
> CHARTERIS: Hospital! Nonsense! He's a dramatic critic.

Well and good; but what are we offered instead?

> JULIA: (*vehemently and movingly, for she is now sincere*) No. You made me pay dearly for every moment of happiness. You revenged yourself on me for the humiliation of being the slave of your

passion for me. I was never sure of you for a moment. I trembled whenever a letter came from you, lest it should contain some stab for me. I dreaded your visits almost as much as I longed for them. I was your plaything not your companion. (*She rises, exclaiming*) Oh there was such suffering in my happiness that I hardly knew joy from pain. (*She sinks on the piano stool, and adds, as she buries her face in her hands and turns away from him*) Better for me if I had never met you.

The ideology may have shifted, but is the emotional quality of this speech (in all its stated sincerity) distinguishable at any point from the familiar rant of romantic melodrama? "Pay dearly; revenge; slave of your passion; trembled; stab; dread; your plaything not your companion; hardly knew joy from pain": the phrases form the conventional declamatory pattern, leading up to the great theatrical moment with its familiar rhythm: the heroine turns away: "Aha! Better for me . . ." etc.

Shaw was conscious of the mechanism of such moments, as indicated here:

JULIA: (*with theatrical pathos*) You are right there. I am indeed alone in the world.

But what is the difference between that and this:

JULIA: (*with deep poignant conviction*) He cares for only one person in the world and that is himself. There is not in his whole nature one unselfish spot. He would not spend one hour of his real life with (*a sob chokes her: she rises passionately crying*) You are all alike, every one of you. Even my father only makes a pet of me.

One begins to see the point of the stage directions, of the "literary treatment": they indicate whether what is being said is burlesque or high passion. Without them, we would be hard put to it to know.

JULIA: (*exhausted, allowing herself to take his hand*) You are right. I am a worthless woman.

CHARTERIS: (*triumphant and gaily remonstrating*) Oh why?

JULIA: Because I am not brave enough to kill you.

GRACE: (*taking her in her arms as she sinks, almost fainting away from him*) Oh no, never make a hero of a philanderer. (CHARTERIS, *amused and untouched, shakes his head laughingly. The rest look at* JULIA *with concern, and even a little awe, feeling for the first time the presence of a keen sorrow.*)

That is the end of *The Philanderer.* We have been told with great care exactly how to feel and respond. Melodrama has been laughed out of court, and then brought in again by the front door, with drums playing, to be acclaimed as the all-new goddess of genuine feeling. The quality of Mr. Shaw's rejection of the current theatre, and his motives, certainly need to be questioned.

Arms and the Man is a sentimental burlesque, and much of it is very funny. It is negative, like most burlesque, and Shaw owes its success to a wise policy of rejecting romance by statement rather than by example. It is not a policy to which he was to adhere. Because:

> When a comedy is performed, it is nothing to me that the spectators laugh: any fool can make an audience laugh. I want to see how many of them, laughing or grave, are in the melting mood.

In such an interest, it would seem, he wrote *Candida.* This play is generally taken as the major work of his early years; and many of his critics have called it "a little masterpiece." In his Preface to the *Plays Pleasant* Shaw rejects certain of his earlier work (or rather he comes as near rejection as his personality would allow):

> Certainly it is easy to dramatise the prosaic conflict of Christian socialism with vulgar unsocialism.

And he instances *Widowers' Houses.* But

> to distil the quintessential drama from pre-Raphaelitism, mediaeval or modern, it must be shown in conflict with the first broken, nervous, stumbling attempts to formulate its own revolt against itself as it develops into something higher. . . . The eyes of men begin to turn to a new age. Discernible at first only by the eyes of the man of genius, it must be focussed by him on the speculum of a work of art, and flashed back from that into the eyes of the common man. Nay, the artist himself has no other way of making himself conscious of the ray; it is by a blind instinct that he keeps on building up his masterpieces until their pinnacles catch the glint of the unrisen sun. . . . He cannot explain it; he can only show it to you as a vision in the magic glass of his artwork. . . . And this is the function that raises dramatic art above imposture and pleasure hunting, and enables the dramatist to be something more than a skilled liar and pander.

Of this vision, he tells us, he availed himself in *Candida.* The conflict is between Christian socialism and the magic

BERNARD SHAW

vision: personalised in the conflict of Morell and Marchbanks for the love of Candida. What, then, are these pinnacles, on which we may concentrate to the exclusion of the Cockney speculator and Prossy the typist and Lexy the curate.[1]

Here is one important moment:

CANDIDA: Are you ill, Eugene?

MARCHBANKS: No, not ill. Only horror! horror! horror!

BURGESS: (*shocked*) What! Got the 'orrors, Mr. Marchbanks! Oh that's bad, at your age. You must leave it off grajally.

CANDIDA: (*reassured*) Nonsense, papa! It's only poetic horror, isn't it, Eugene? (*Petting him.*)

BURGESS: (*abashed*) Oh, poetic 'orror, is it? I beg your pardon, I'm shore. . . .

CANDIDA: What is it, Eugene?—the scrubbing brush? . . .

MARCHBANKS: (*softly and musically, but sadly and longingly*) No, not a scrubbing brush, but a boat—a tiny shallop to sail away in, far from the world, where the marble floors are washed by the rain and dried by the sun; where the south wind dusts the beautiful green and purple carpets. Or a chariot! to carry us up into the sky, where the lamps are stars, and don't need to be filled with paraffin oil every day.

MORELL: (*harshly*) And where there is nothing to do but to be idle, selfish and useless.

CANDIDA: (*jarred*) Oh, James! how could you spoil it all?

MARCHBANKS: (*firing up*) Yes, to be idle, selfish and useless: that is, to be beautiful and free and happy: hasn't every man desired that with all his soul for the woman he loves? That's my ideal: what's yours? . . .

CANDIDA: (*quaintly*) He cleans the boots, Eugene. . . .

MARCHBANKS: Oh, don't talk about boots! Your feet should be beautiful on the mountains.

CANDIDA: My feet would not be beautiful on the Hackney Road without boots.

BURGESS: (*scandalised*) Come, Candy: don't be vulgar. Mr. Marchbanks ain't accustomed to it. You're givin' him the 'orrors again. I mean the poetic ones.

The kind explanation of all this would be that it is burlesque again; but that it is not, that it is meant to be accepted

---

[1] It is one of Shaw's recurrent techniques to shorten the names of his characters: either his grand personages (like B.B. in *The Doctor's Dilemma*) for an obvious deflationary effect; or his young women (like Savvy in *Back to Methuselah*) for an effect which is perhaps not so obvious.

seriously—as the "magic vision" or as the words of what William Archer called "a real poet on the stage"—is clear from the comment/stage-direction which immediately follows:

> (MORELL *is silent. Apparently he is busy with his letters: really he is puzzling with misgiving over his new and alarming experience that the surer he is of his moral thrusts, the more swiftly and effectively Eugene parries them. To find himself beginning to fear a man whom he does not respect afflicts him bitterly.*)

This, then, is the conflict. I do not know how it is possible to assume that it is a real conflict, an experience, that is to say, which survives serious critical attention. Both attitudes are abstract; and one, at least, is hollow: a modish adolescent romanticism. Conflict of an unresolved kind, however, the passage, like the play as a whole, surely reveals; although it is not the formal conflict. The question is whether the romantic reformism of Morell is anything more than a different aspect of the naïve idealism of Marchbanks: whether the deflation of abstract conventions is not rooted in the same complex as the afflatus of conventional sentiment. One cannot understand, to put it another way, why Marchbanks and Morell should quarrel: they have much in common, and share at least one fundamental characteristic: emotional credulity. Whether, further, they share this with their creator is a matter for investigation.

The famous scene of Candida's choice is not reassuring: the emotional discrimination is again mechanical:

CANDIDA: And you, Eugene? What do you offer?

MARCHBANKS: My weakness! My desolation! My heart's need!

> (. . . MORELL, *whose lofty confidence has changed into heartbreaking dread at* EUGENE's *bid, loses all power of concealing his anxiety.* EUGENE, *strung to the highest tension, does not move a muscle.*)

MORELL: (*in a suffocated voice—the appeal bursting from the depths of his anguish*) Candida!

MARCHBANKS: (*aside, in a flash of contempt*) Coward!

CANDIDA: (*significantly*) I give myself to the weaker of the two.

> (EUGENE *divines her meaning at once: his face whitens like steel in a furnace.*)

And:

CANDIDA: One last word. How old are you, Eugene?

MARCHBANKS: As old as the world now. This morning I was eighteen.... In a hundred years we shall be the same age. But I have a better secret than that. Let me go now. The night outside grows impatient.

(. . . *He flies out into the night. She turns to Morell, holding out her arms to him.*)

CANDIDA: Ah, James!

(*They embrace. But they do not know the secret in the poet's heart.*)

When one is liable to outbursts of inflated sentimentality of this order—where even the significance has to be put in by a stage direction—one is perhaps well advised to cultivate a certain flippancy. From this play onwards, the alternating pattern of Shaw's dramatic career was set.

(iv)

Like Shakespeare. . . . I was a born dramatist. . . . Like Shakespeare, I had to write potboilers until I was rich enough to satisfy my evolutionary appetite . . . by writing what came to me without the least regard to the possibility of lucrative publication or performance. . . . In writing *Back to Methuselah* I threw over all economic considerations. . . .

Of Shaw's later work, *Back to Methuselah* and *Saint Joan* are the landmarks. *Back to Methuselah* was chosen by Shaw himself as his masterpiece: and *Saint Joan*—which, more than any other play, is the basis of his present wide popularity—is hailed on most sides as "the one modern tragedy." For my present purpose, a brief estimate of these two works must complete my examination of Shaw's achievement as an artist; and they are surely sufficiently representative.

The link with *Candida* in *Back to Methuselah* is clear:

THE SHE-ANCIENT: Yes, child: art is the magic mirror you make to reflect your invisible dreams in visible pictures. You use a glass mirror to see your face: you use works of art to see your soul. But we who are older use neither glass mirrors nor works of art. We have a direct sense of life.

This discovery—this direct sense of life—was perhaps the secret in the poet's heart for which the night grew impatient. But is it discovery, or is it rejection?

THE HE-ANCIENT: Look at us. Look at me. This is my body, my blood, my brain; but it is not me. I am the eternal life, the perpetual resurrection. . . .

THE SHE-ANCIENT: It is this stuff (*indicating her body*) this flesh and blood and bone and all the rest of it, that is intolerable. . . .

LILITH: They have accepted the burden of eternal life . . . after passing a million goals they press on to the goal of redemption from the flesh, to the vortex freed from matter, to the whirlpool in pure intelligence that, when the world began, was a whirlpool in pure force.

Now Shaw's play, although it goes back to Eden and forward "as far as thought can reach", must not be exempted from its inevitable conditions on those grounds. It must not, that is to say, in spite of its preface, be accepted as scientific history or prophecy. It is, inevitably, a criticism of life as we know it: but the biology does not matter, the emotional pattern does. The He- and She-Ancients (it is unfortunate that this use of the pronoun prefix is only familiar to us as an appellation for goats) are simply conventions of a dramatic judgment on life as Shaw had experienced it. In the play, creative evolution is merely a device: "I exploit the eternal interest of the philosopher's stone which enables men to live for ever." When this is realised, the nature of Shaw's discovery is clearer; and it does not seem unreasonable to describe it as rejection. For the experiences which Shaw explored in his earlier work raised problems of adjustment which, although the night was impatient, he could not make. And now, as far as his thought could reach, all he could offer was an obliteration of the actual human situation in terms of a fantasy of "pure intelligence." The best comment is that of W. J. Turner:[1]

Was it an insufficiency of vital energy which led to this conservation, this shrinkage into two planes—an instinctive process of self-preservation and of self-development founded upon ambitious vanity—vanity being the isotope of passion? This may explain the peculiar forms of exhibitionism Mr. Shaw has always displayed. Passion needs an object exterior to itself by which the self is enriched. Vanity extends itself objectless in space, and *Back to Methuselah* is such an extension on a tremendous scale. As Lilith says of the Ancients (*alias* Mr. Shaw):

"They press on to the goal of redemption from the flesh, to the vortex freed from matter, to the whirlpool in pure intelligence."

In other words, to vanity—pure unadulterated vanity! . . . Why does Mr. Shaw hate all "matter"—nature, the human body,

[1] In *Scrutinies*, p. 139 *et seq.* (ed. Rickword), Wishart, 1928.

works of art, all *objects*? Because matter fills space and gets in the way of the unlimited extension of Mr. Shaw's thought. Mr. Shaw would fill the whole of space. Such is his vanity.

It only remains to add that this desire to be freed from the body, from this "degrading physical stuff"—is a typical adolescent fantasy. And the persistent desire to substitute some abstract ideal for the tangible facts of human living is a typical process of romanticism. The iconoclast of Romance ends, not merely as its ikon, but as its slave.

But he took a last romantic heroine—Jeanne d'Arc—and in a preface attacked the romancers who had misrepresented her. But

> this, I think, is all that we can now pretend to say about the prose of Joan's career. The romance of her rise, the tragedy of her execution, and the comedy of the attempts of posterity to make amends for that execution, belong to my play and not to my preface, which must be confined to a sober essay on the facts.

"The romance of her rise"; "the tragedy of her execution"; "the comedy of making amends": these stages are a useful framework for an examination of this baffling play. Of the six scenes, the first five are devoted to Joan's rise and military career; the sixth to her trial and execution, and the epilogue to the amends. The successful part of the play is Shaw's characteristic comedy: the deflation of great names—

> Polly! ! You impudent baggage, do you dare call Squire Bertrand de Poulengey Polly to my face?;

explicit satire by statement—

> We were not fairly beaten, my lord. No Englishman is ever fairly beaten;

the unromantic prince—

> If you are going to say "Son of St. Louis: gird on the sword of your ancestors, and lead us to victory", you may spare your breath to cool your porridge; for I cannot do it.

All this is as good as anything he had done in his most amusing plays, like *The Devil's Disciple* and *John Bull's Other island.* The historicism (as in the discussion between Warwick and Cauchon) is perhaps more successful than in any of his work; and the excellent forensic of the trial scene is mature when placed against its forerunners: Lickcheese, Caesar, the brothers Barnabas. But it is clear that Shaw has made all those qualities dependent on the success of his central figure: Joan. Unless she is positively realised, even the successful elements fall in the general disintegration.

Now the ancestry of Joan, in terms of Shaw's work, may be traced to such different figures as Marchbanks and Bluntschli; or may be represented as the projection of the Superman in human terms. (One is not limited, in this genealogy, by differences of sex; with Shaw, these do not greatly matter.) Joan, at one level, is energetic and free from romantic conventions. She shows up the French Court as Bluntschli showed up the Balkan army. And while the play is moving on this general plane, it is successful. Bluntschli, it will be remembered, was left largely negative: what positives he had were those of a successful businessman, to which Shaw, for ideological reasons, would not render any stressed assent. The Ancients are more complex, representing the shift from burlesque to drama. Their positives, as Shaw sees them, are not only political commonsense and freedom from conventional illusions (which Bluntschli shares with the early Joan); but also a rational rejection of physical complexities (a willed "redemption from the flesh") and a yearning towards the ideal of "pure force." Now these latter qualities are also the achieved positives of Marchbanks—the "secret in the poet's heart." They are also— it is by now surely obvious—the positive elements of the creation of Joan.

Joan is Shaw's conception of a Saint (the conventional name for a Superman). With her commonsense about politics and fighting she is merely a sensible country girl, uncorrupted by the romantic Court. But the positives of her inspiration, as Shaw sees them, are her singleness of purpose and her sexlessness. Everywhere in the play, it is this latter fact which is given to account for her control over the army:

> There hasn't been a word that has anything to do with her being a woman.

For Shaw, Joan is a saint because she has subordinated the facts of her person in order to become an uncomplicated instrument of the Life Force, of "Creative Evolution." She represents the ideal of the rejection of those tiresome facts of human behaviour which complicate the conception of Progress. She represents, that is to say, a fantasy.

But the fantasy is heavily disguised, and Shaw uses all his dramatic skill to prevent it being recognised as such. He gives Joan an earthy country accent:

Coom, Bluebeard! Thou canst not fool me. Where be Dauphin?

He gives her a solid peasant background, and an implication of normality. The result is that even those to whom the Ancients are unacceptable find Joan captivating. Yet the disguise is superficial. One remembers Marchbanks:

This morning I was eighteen. (I am) as old as the world now.

He, too, is an Ancient. The genealogy of the Ancients, the composite Ancient of Days, is Marchbanks, the He and She, Saint Joan.

The central fact of Joan, that is to say, is no more positive than that of Marchbanks, and *Saint Joan* as a whole is very far from being a tragedy. It is not that tragedy demands simple positives; but rather that the examination of human failure is given place by its context of fully realised human experience (whether or not the forms of this experience are represented as supernatural). Saint Joan's voices, that is to say, are acceptable: they are recognised human experience. But the full creation of Joan has no direct relation to experience: she is an uncomplicated romantic heroine, a figment.

It remains probable that the attraction of Shaw's play has only indirectly to do with the fantasy of Joan—the knight in shining armour—and most to do with the simple romance of the burning. For she passes to the simple romantic heroine in her relapse, with a very typical speech:

I could let the banners and the trumpets and the knights and soldiers pass me and leave me behind as they leave the other women, if only I could still hear the wind in the trees, the larks in the sunshine, the young lambs crying through the healthy frost, and the blessed blessed church bells that send my angel voices floating to me on the wind. But without these things I cannot live. . . .

These familiar, Dickensian-sentimental phrases are simply

conventional romantic pathos: the mechanical evocations of
nature place Shaw firmly in his period—the nature-poetics of
the late Victorians and Georgians. It is the pathos which
moves on precisely to the

> glow and flicker of the fire . . . reddening the May daylight.

and to the "heartrending sobs" of the Chaplain who has
watched her execution. With the fantasies of "pure force"
superseded, and faced by the human fact of death, Shaw
collapses into melodrama. And when, in the Epilogue, he has
made the point about the mechanics of her canonisation, he
pushes home his advantage with the characteristic appeal to
the sentiment of the audience—the structure of the *play's*
emotion set aside:

> O God that madest this beautiful earth, when will it be ready to
> receive Thy Saints? How long, O Lord, how long?

The rhetoric finds its mark at the pit of the stomach,
hammering the audience into consciousness of an experience.
For Joan's self-pity involves the accepting audience; she has
behaved as we would like to behave (but do not) and the pity of
the world's rejection of her is the pity of the world's rejection
of that imagined element in us. Shaw has redeemed and embellished our fantasies, and we are properly grateful. But for
how long, how long?

(v)

Shaw's dynamic as a dramatist is surely weakening, and it
seems impossible that it can, as a major force, survive the period
of which he was a victim. Respect for his ability to laugh at a
great deal of persistent nonsense will certainly endure; and
respect for his great wit and for his skill in forensic and
burlesque which made the willingness literary fact. But the
emotional inadequacy of his plays denies him major status.
He withered the tangible life of experience in the pursuit of a
fantasy of pure intelligence and pure force. It is what Mr. Eliot
wrote some twenty years ago:

> Shaw *was* a poet—until he was born, and the poet in Shaw was
> stillborn. Shaw has a great deal of poetry, but all stillborn; Shaw
> is dramatically precocious and poetically less than immature.

It is more than that; it is the (perhaps inevitable) surrender of the castigator of romance to all kinds of romantic emotion. In this sense, a comment of his own in another context is apt:

> One hardly knows which is the more appalling: the abjectness of the credulity or the flippancy of the scepticism.

As one might have expected, Shaw himself has the last word.

5

J. M. Synge

(i)

SYNGE is undoubtedly the most remarkable English-speaking prose dramatist of the century, in the same way, and for much the same reasons, that the Abbey Theatre is the most remarkable development in the theatrical history of these islands for some three centuries. Certain aspects of his work, as of the Irish dramatic movement as a whole, offer some of the best material we have for a study of the place of drama in the total culture of a modern society. Such a study is outside my scope, but a more direct literary judgment ought to be offered, both for its own sake, and as a necessary groundwork for the larger study. For the insistent question, as one reviews the commonplaces of recent Irish dramatic history—the use of a surprising, organic language akin in process to poetry, and the foundation of event on the living processes of a community which had not suffered the levelling of industrialism—the insistent question is one of value. Initial respect for the sensibility which lies behind and beyond such facts is very natural, but it is nevertheless tempered by doubts which more recent Irish drama in what would seem to be the same tradition have raised, and by a suspicion which one's intuition of the nature of normal response to the surface of Irish drama has reinforced. Towards a resolution of these doubts only a direct literary judgment can adduce evidence. Synge's plays, that is to say, need evaluation as *texts*, with a temporary suspension of interest in the wider cultural issues, save only those which the texts themselves raise. It seems to me that unless such a discipline is brought to bear on the Irish drama, we are likely to be the victims of a long-played hallucination, of which the ultimate exposure might have serious dramatic consequences.

The body of Synge's dramatic work is small. There are only three full-length plays: *The Well of the Saints*; *The Playboy of the Western World*; and *Deirdre of the Sorrows*; and of these the last is unrevised. *The Tinker's Wedding* is a middle-length piece;

J. M. SYNGE

and then there are the two short plays, *Riders to the Sea*, and *The Shadow of the Glen*. This work was concentrated into a period of only seven years—from 1903 to 1910.

The Preface to *The Tinker's Wedding*, written in 1907, is a convenient document of a part of Synge's attitude to the drama, and of some of his intentions. It may be quoted in full:

The drama is made serious—in the French sense of the word—not by the degree in which it is taken up with problems that are serious in themselves, but by the degree in which it gives the nourishment, not very easy to define, on which our imaginations live. We should not go to the theatre as we go to a chemist's or a dram-shop, but as we go to a dinner where the food we need is taken with pleasure and excitement. This was nearly always so in Spain and England and France when the drama was at its richest—the infancy and decay of the drama tend to be didactic—but in these days the playhouse is too often stocked with the drugs of many seedy problems or with the absinthe or vermouth of the last musical comedy.

The drama, like the symphony, does not teach or prove anything. Analysts with their problems, and teachers with their systems, are soon as old-fashioned as the pharmacopoeia of Galen—look at Ibsen and the Germans—but the best plays of Ben Jonson and Molière can no more go out of fashion than the blackberries on the hedges.

Of the things which nourish the imagination humour is one of the most needful and it is dangerous to limit or destroy it. Baudelaire calls laughter the greatest sign of the Satanic element in man; and where a country loses its humour, as some towns in Ireland are doing, there will be morbidity of mind, as Baudelaire's mind was morbid.

In the greater part of Ireland, however, the whole people, from the tinkers to the clergy, have still a life, and view of life, that are rich and genial and humorous. I do not think that these country people, who have so much humour themselves, will mind being laughed at without malice, as the people in every country have been laughed at in their own comedies.

And in the Preface to *The Playboy of the Western World* (written earlier in 1907) he makes these points about language:

All art is a collaboration, and there is little doubt that in the happy ages of literature, striking and beautiful phrases were as ready to the storyteller's or the playwright's hand, as the rich cloaks and dresses of his time. It is probable that when the Elizabethan dramatist took his ink-horn and sat down to his work

155

he used many phrases that he had just heard, as he sat at dinner from his mother or his children. In Ireland, those of us who know the people have the same privilege. When I was writing *The Shadow of the Glen*, some years ago, I got more aid than any learning could have given me from a chink in the floor of the old Wicklow house where I was staying, that let me hear what was being said by the servant-girls in the kitchen. This matter, I think, is of importance, for in countries where the imagination of the people, and the language they use, is rich and living, it is possible for a writer to be rich and copious in his words, and at the same time to give the reality, which is the root of all poetry, in a comprehensive and natural form. In the modern literature of towns, however, richness is found only in sonnets, or prose poems, or in one or two elaborate books that are far away from the profound and common interests of life. One has, on the one side, Mallarmé and Huysmans producing this literature; and on the other, Ibsen and Zola dealing with the reality of life in joyless and pallid words. On the stage one must have reality, and one must have joy, and that is why the intellectual modern drama has failed, and people have grown sick of the false joy of the musical comedy, that has been given them in place of the rich joy found only in what is superb and wild in reality. In a good play every speech should be as fully flavoured as a nut or apple, and such speeches cannot be written by anyone who works among people who have shut their lips on poetry.

These familiar and valuable passages are worth emphasis for two reasons: first, that they directly present an important issue which is highly relevant to the staple of Synge's plays and to the material of most modern drama; and second—a more weighty reason—because they raise, perhaps unconsciously, certain complex issues of dramatic literature and language on which the final evaluation of Synge must depend.

(ii)

Synge's plays are sometimes grouped into comedies—*The Shadow of the Glen, The Tinker's Wedding, The Well of the Saints*, and *The Playboy of the Western World;* and tragedies—*Riders to the Sea* and *Deirdre of the Sorrows.* I cannot myself agree that this classification is adequate, even as a working guide. *The Shadow of the Glen* and *The Tinker's Wedding* are very similar plays, and they are both comedies of a particular kind: both plays are basically naturalist, and their substantial element is a kind of knockabout farce. *Deirdre* is a fully serious, non-naturalist, tragedy; *Riders to the Sea* is a tragic fragment of which the basic element is naturalism. *The Playboy* is "serious drama—in the French sense of the word"—a satiric comedy of which the elements might seem to be naturalist, but which is not really a naturalist work because of its pervading moral intention. *The Well of the Saints*—to my mind the least successful of Synge's works—offers the same problems of classification as presented themselves to Chekhov; it is perhaps a pathetic comedy not unlike *The Cherry Orchard*.

The diversity is considerable; but it is what one might expect from a writer striking out on new bearings within a very short period: Synge wrote his first play when he was 32, and his last when he was 38.

The three straightforward naturalist pieces belong to his early writing years: the particular quality of all of them is their language. *Shadow of the Glen* takes as its central incident the simulation of death by an elderly husband in order to trap his younger wife with her lover. It is a comic situation which—if perhaps equivocal to persons reared in a stratified urban culture—is very familiar in most rural cultures, and not only the Irish. One finds the same quality in the early English Towneley *Shepherd's Play*, with the groans of the wife of the sheep-stealer with the stolen animal at her breast, in a context of the birth of Christ. "Pagan humour", if one wishes it, although the phrase in connection with Synge has been a little overdone. At its own level the play is very successful, and very well done:

NORA BURKE: (*pouring him out some whisky*) Why would I marry you, Mike Dara? You'll be getting old and I'll be getting old, and in a little while, I'm telling you, you'll be sitting up in your bed—the way himself was sitting—with a shake in your face, and your teeth falling, and the white hair sticking out around you like an old bush where sheep do be leaping a gap.

(DAN BURKE *sits up noiselessly from under the sheet, with his hand to his face. His white hair is sticking out round his head.* NORA *goes on slowly without hearing him.*)

It's a pitiful thing to be getting old, but it's a queer thing surely. It's a queer thing to see an old man sitting up there in his bed with no teeth in him, and a rough word in his mouth, and his chin the way it would take the bark from the edge of an oak board you'd have building the door. . . .

(DAN *sneezes violently*, MICHAEL *tries to get to the door, but before* *he can do so* DAN *jumps out of the bed in queer white clothes, with* *the stick in his hand, and goes over and puts his back against it.*)

MICHAEL: Son of God deliver us!

(*Crosses himself and goes backward across the room.*)[1]

Now this kind of incident is not at all exceptional in naturalist comedy; what distinguishes it from sketches which would get their laugh and be forgotten is its language; Synge's farces are readable. It is the point I have made elsewhere: that the simpler forms of literature do not seem unsatisfactory from a critical standpoint when their language is organically related to the language of more serious literature; when the common language contains the elements of literary precision and complexity. It is Synge's first achievement that he discovered a *community of expression* which made this possible. One might say that *Shadow of the Glen* is less a work of art than an entertainment; but it is the merit of Synge's basic attitude, in contrast to the situation in an industrial culture, that the distinction is unreal and unnecessary.

Synge's language, as he tells us himself, is based on recorded Irish peasant speech; but it is a literary product, which has undergone the normal process of shaping. It is clearly a rich language; and it is also a naturalist language, in that its intention is representational, in accordance with the mood of the play.

The figure of the tramp in the play has a certain importance. Some critics have seen in him a representative of that strangely satisfying acceptance of life which is based on a close living identity with the processes of nature:

You'll be saying one time "It's a grand evening, by the grace of God", and another time, "It's a wild night, God help us; but it'll pass surely."

This attitude is dramatically important in *Deirdre*; but here, as in the other early plays, it is less important as an element of the drama than as an observed element of the life which Synge was recording. Its "meaning" may have been important to

---

[1] It is worth noting that the directions are real stage directions, and not pseudo-fictional comment.

Synge; but importance of that kind is not realised in *Shadow of the Glen*.

The Tinker's Wedding is a two-act play of the same nature. The comedy between the thieving tinkers and the mercenary priest is very good, although it suffers in comparison with *The Shadow of the Glen* in point of concentration and control. The tinker girl's complicated desires for marriage and for a fine life with the "great lads" are of the same order as those of Nora Burke. What weakens the play is the intrusion of a kind of naturalist statement, such as in this speech of Mary Byrne's:

> It's sick and sorry we are to tease you; but what did you want meddling with the like of us, when it's a long time we are going our own ways—father and son, and his son after him, or mother and daughter and her own daughter again; and it's little need we ever had of going up into a church and swearing—I'm told there's swearing with it—a word no man would believe, or with drawing rings on our fingers, would be cutting our skins maybe when we'd be taking the ass from the shafts, and pulling the straps the time they'd be slippy with going around beneath the heavens in rains falling.

There is a false self-consciousness about this descriptive revelation which, in this instance, the language reinforces. For Synge was not yet fully capable of using his language dramatically; he was using it, rather, to add "flavour" to the speeches of a play.

(iii)

Riders to the Sea is a descriptive tragedy which draws its strength from the quality of acceptance which Synge had discovered in the lives of the islanders among whom he had lived. It moves on a limited plane: the inevitability of the conflict between men and the sea, and the inevitability of the men's defeat. When the last of Maurya's sons has been drowned she speaks to herself:

> They're all gone now, and there isn't anything more the sea can do to me. . . . They're all together this time and the end is come . . . May the Almighty God have mercy on Bartley's soul, and on Michael's soul, and on the souls of Seamus and Patch, and Stephen and Shawn; and may he have mercy on the soul of every one is left living in the world. . . . Michael has a clean burial in the far

north, by the grace of the Almighty God. Bartley will have a fine
coffin out of the white boards, and a deep grave surely. What more
can we want than that? No man at all can be living for ever, and
we must be satisfied.

The appropriate comment has perhaps been made by Yeats,
in his reasons for excluding war poetry from *The Oxford Book of
Modern Verse*:

> Passive suffering is not a theme for poetry. In all the great
> tragedies, tragedy is a joy to the man who dies; in Greece the
> tragic chorus danced. When man has withdrawn into the quick-
> silver at the back of the mirror no great event becomes luminous
> in his mind . . . some blunderer has driven his car on to the wrong
> side of the road—that is all.

In *Riders to the Sea* the people are simply victims; the
acceptance is not whole, but rather a weary resignation. Miss
Ellis-Fermor's judgment,[1] that the sea is the only character in
the play, is important. What follows is that only the sea is active.
It is man against the elements, but man only in the simple
exercise of his routine existence. The tragedy is natural, in the
most common sense of that term; it is, further, simply an issue
of observation and record. Again, the language is an imposed
constituent of flavour rather than the essence of the tragedy,
and its discovery. Although the vigour of the speech sharply
distinguishes Synge's play from the habitual pathos of naturalism, the emotion of the work is pathetic rather than tragic.
As with the young men of the island, nothing human lives
there; human conflict and experience are obliterated, alike by
the weight of the natural dangers and by the pressure of the
natural view.

With *The Well of the Saints* Synge returns to a subject which
had been part of his plot, if not of his theme, in *The Shadow of
the Glen* and *The Tinker's Wedding*: the dual nature of the
imagination—its capacity for simple deceptive fantasy, and its
frequent rôle as a liberator. This matter was to be the basis of
the impressive *Playboy of the Western World*. The blind beggars,
Martin and Mary Doul, are sustained in joy and self-respect
by the illusion of their own beauty and comeliness. When their
sight is restored by the holy water of the Saint, their revealed
ugliness comes near to destroying them. But when their sight
fades once more, they achieve a new illusion: of their dignity

[1] *The Irish Dramatic Movement*, p. 169.

in old age, the woman with her white hair, and the man with his flowing beard. They fly in terror from a renewed offer to restore their sight of the real world; although their neighbours realise that their continued blindness, leading them along

a stony path, with the north wind blowing behind,

will mean their death.

The real issue is perhaps related to that which Ibsen handled in *The Wild Duck* or *John Gabriel Borkman*; or indeed in any of his plays where the choice between happiness in illusion, and courage in fact, is the substance of the work. Synge's play has moments of great power, especially in the third act, but it is a very uneven work. The handling of blindness on a representational stage provokes serious dangers of sentimentality, not all of which, in my view, Synge avoids. The scenes of the beggars' realisation of their actual state are painful, as might be expected, but they provoke an acute embarrassment which has less to do with the elements of the situation than with what seems to be a direct appeal to audience or reader. (In this connection Synge's stage directions, which are radically different from those of *The Shadow of the Glen*, are critically important. With so capable a language as he commands, this method of embellishment, which the naturalist playwrights developed because of the inadequacy of their spoken language, and because they were under the spell of fictional rather than dramatic methods, seems curiously unnecessary; but its constant employment suggests an unwillingness to be fully committed dramatically, which confirms one's reaction to the general tone of the play.)

MARTIN DOUL: If it was a queer time itself it was a great joy and pride I had the time I'd hear your voice speaking and you passing to Grianan (*beginning to speak with plaintive intensity*), for it's of many a fine thing your voice would put a poor dark fellow in mind, and the day I'd hear it it's of little else at all I would be thinking.

MARTIN DOUL: (*seizing the moment he has her attention*) I'm thinking by the mercy of God it's few sees anything but them is blind for a space (*with excitement*). It's few sees the old women rotting for the grave, and it's few sees the like of yourself. (*He bends over her.*) Though it's shining you are, like a high lamp would drag in the ships out of the sea.

MOLLY BYRNE: (*shrinking away from him*) Keep off from me, Martin Doul.

F

MARTIN DOUL: (*quickly with low furious intensity*) It's the truth I'm telling you.

It is perhaps difficult to define one's uneasiness at such passages. It might be argued that it is only the stage directions which involve the audience in a kind of pathetic vibration, and that since these would not be heard in performance the objection is only secondary. But it is the spoken language which determines the nature of the dramatist's comments: his language involves the same kind of appeal. For the emotion is not there in the spoken language, nor in the incident it creates; response depends on the invitation to inclusion; depends in practical terms on the gestures of voice and body which the actor is directed to undertake in order to register a comment. The emotion is not in the body of the drama; ultimately it is didactic, embracing both explicit and tacit statement, and subsequent proof by illustration. And that is the basic method of the whole play. The word we are seeking, to describe the technique, is manipulation.

(iv)

The Playboy of the Western World is a brilliantly successful comedy; it is also a serious piece of literature. The reference back is to Molière, to Cervantes, perhaps to Rabelais. Even more certainly the reference back is to Jonson.

Mr. Eliot's brilliant essay on Jonson contains passages which are highly relevant to this one play of Synge. One may say that *The Playboy* is satire; and certainly it produced the effect of relentless satire on the rowsters of the Clan-na-Gael. But

> Jonson's drama is only incidentally satire, because it is only incidentally a criticism upon the actual world. It is not satire in the way in which the work of Swift or the work of Molière may be called satire: that is, it does not find its source in any precise emotional attitude or precise intellectual criticism of the actual world ... The important thing is that if fiction can be divided into creative fiction and critical fiction, Jonson's is creative.

Mr. Eliot's definition may be applied as it stands to *The Playboy*.

Perhaps the most important way in which Synge's play is to be distinguished from the main stream of English comedy is its attitude to character. The lively gang in the shebeen do not form a gallery of individual portraits, displayed to us by the normal processes of revelation; neither is the record of the interplay the process of the comedy.

> Whereas in Shakespeare the effect is due to the way in which the characters *act upon* one another, in Jonson it is given by the way in which the characters *fit in* with each other.

For it is not simply the fantasy of Christy Mahon, trailing the awesome (and bogus) glory of "a man has killed his da", with which Synge is concerned; but with the fantasy of the whole community who are equal makers of his illusion. The characters are an individual world rather than a representative group; the individual existence of each is less important than the common emotional process within which their world is circumscribed. It is, of course, a small world, what Mr. Grattan Freyer has called "the little world of J. M. Synge."[1]

> But small worlds—the worlds which artists create—do not differ only in magnitude; if they are complete worlds, drawn to scale in every part, they differ in kind also. And Jonson's world has this scale. His type of personality found its relief in something falling under the category of burlesque or farce—though when you are dealing with a *unique* world, like his, these terms fail to appease the appetite for definition. It is not, at all events, the farce of Molière; the latter is more analytic, more an intellectual redistribution. It is not defined by the word "satire." Jonson poses as a satirist. But satire like Jonson's is great in the end not by hitting off its object, but by creating it; the satire is merely the means which leads to the aesthetic result, the impulse which projects a new world into a new orbit.

How complete Mr. Eliot's judgment of Jonson's comoedic method may be, this is not the place to argue, but the general distinction he has made is the only possible groundwork for an estimate of *The Playboy of the Western World*.

In modern drama, the point may be made again by reference to *Peer Gynt*, with which Synge's play has several correspondences. Ibsen satirises the folk-fantasy of the Norwegians in much the same mood as does Synge that of the Irish. But Ibsen's satire operates at the level of conscious illustration. His is the backward glance of the essential critic; Synge provides the thing itself. For both methods—one need hardly say— there is adequate room.

[1] In an article of that title, *Politics and Letters*, Spring 1948.

Christy Mahon's illusion of greatness is nourished and raised
to the heights by a community where the mythology of force
(compare the tales they spin of Red Jack Smith and Bartley
Fallon) is dominant; Christy—"a man did split his father's
middle with a single clout"—is an Osiris come to judgment.
But when the revengeful father comes on his trail, the collapsed
hero is as quickly turned to sacrifice. And when the hero does
the famous deed in apparent truth, his shocked spectators learn

that there's a great gap between gallous story and a dirty deed.

But again the deed is not completed:

Are you coming to be killed a third time, or what is it ails you
now?

Yet Christy realises that it is not the deed which made him
glorious, but the telling of the deed, that "poet's talking."
And this he retains. He goes out from the community confident
in his new strength, but he acknowledges that it is the
community which made him:

Ten thousand blessings upon all that's here, for you've turned me
a likely gaffer in the end of all, the way I'll go romancing through
a romping lifetime from this hour to the dawning of the judgment
day.

It is not only Christy who is transformed; the community
itself has made something. Their hero may go from them, but
he is their creation—"the only Playboy of the Western World."
The world of process remains inviolate at the end, as Pegeen
Mike indicates in her final acknowledgement. A new world is
projected into a new orbit.

(v)

A powerful dramatic language is not, ultimately, to be
judged in terms of "reality" or "joy", and it is more than a
question of "flavour." The highest dramatic language is that
which contains within itself the substance of the drama, which
discovers and constructs its emotional structure. Mr. Freyer has
pointed out (in the essay already referred to) that the dominant
characteristic of Synge's language is an abundance of simile
and a complete absence of metaphor or verbal symbolism. The
observation, with reference to the plays up to *Deirdre*, is

generally accurate, and it is most revealing. Synge's enrich-
ment of naturalist language is an important achievement; but,
in general, he does not restore language to the function it
performed in a drama like that of the Elizabethans. (The stock
comparison of his language to the Elizabethans is superficial,
although it is not so unjustified as the similar comparison of the
work of later Irish dramatists.) There is a basic difference of
intention: Synge's similes give flavour to speeches which might
otherwise be "joyless" or "pallid"; the absence of metaphor
distinguishes his work from genuine poetic drama. His language,
as in all representational drama, is a parallel element with the
action; in poetic drama the language *is* the action.

Deirdre of the Sorrows was left unrevised when Synge died;
and this is a very real loss, because there are signs that in this
play Synge was working towards a dramatic method which is
genuinely poetic; he was leaving representation behind.

As it stands, the play is slight, and suffers from a disturbing
singleness of level. Its stained-glass quality is perhaps related
to its theme, on which an earlier comment by Synge himself is
relevant:

> No personal originality is enough to make a rich work unique,
> unless it has also the characteristic of a particular life and locality
> and the life that is in it. For this reason all historical plays and
> novels and poems ... are relatively worthless. Every healthy mind
> is more interested in *Titbits* than in *Idylls of the King*.

As a generalisation, this is hardly adequate; but as a description of the source of the strength of his own early work it is
obviously true. It describes the particular quality of his genius,
and explains the singleness of level in *Deirdre*. Yeats tells us
that Synge was not interested in the Heroic Age until he wrote
Deirdre. Perhaps the choice was wrong. But in depriving him of
many of the sources of his earlier strength, and in making
naturalism impossible, *Deirdre* perhaps occasioned the discovery to Synge of resources which might have made him, if
he had lived, a very great dramatist indeed.

The first words of the play show an interest that is no longer
primarily representational:

> OLD WOMAN: She hasn't come yet, is it, and it falling to the
> night?
> LAVARCHAM: She has not . . . It's dark with the clouds are
> coming from the west and the south, but it isn't later than the
> common.

This use, as it will appear, of nature symbolism, which is very characteristic of Elizabethan drama, is a new element. There is a prescience related to the messengers' speech to Macbeth:

Nothing affeared of what thyselfe did make,
Strange images of death;

Lavarcham's words may be compared with Duncan's observations as he arrives at his murderer's castle.

The darkness is a constant element throughout the progress of the tragedy, and is present in the last words of the play:

LAVARCHAM: Deirdre is dead, and Naisi is dead; and if the oaks and stars could die for sorrow, it's a dark sky and a hard and naked earth we'd have this night in Emain.

The whole substance of the tragedy, that inevitability of the destruction wrought by beauty:

LAVARCHAM: I'm in dread so they were right saying she'd bring destruction on the world—

is summed up, in closely related imagery, in the speech of Deirdre herself:

Who'd fight the grave, Conchubor, and it opened on a dark night?[1]

Around the poles of the "dark night" and the "grave" the play revolves.

What we all need is a place safe and splendid,

says Conchubor early in the play, attempting to persuade Deirdre to become his queen. But Deirdre rejects him for Naisi, although she is conscious that it is

for a short space only,

and she is able to say in the end

It was the choice of lives we had in the woods, and in the grave we're safe surely.

The speeches of Deirdre and Naisi at their first meeting:

DEIRDRE: It should be a sweet thing to have what is best and richest, if it's for a short space only.

NAISI: And we've a short space only to be triumphant and brave.[1]

[1] For a penetrating commentary on these passages see Chapter One of William Empson's *Seven Types of Ambiguity* (Chatto, 1930 and 1947).

initiate the pattern which is completed near their death:

NAISI: There's nothing, surely, the like of a new grave of open earth for putting a great space between two friends that love.

DEIRDRE: If there isn't, it's that grave when it's closed will make us one for ever, and we two lovers have had great space without weariness or growing old or any sadness of the mind.

And the same pattern is the basis of the fears of the second act:

OWEN: Three weeks is a long space, and yet you're seven years spancelled with Naisi and the pair.

DEIRDRE: Three weeks of your days might be long, surely, yet seven years are a short space for the like of Naisi and myself.

OWEN: If they're a short space there aren't many the like of you. . . .

DEIRDRE: Am I well pleased seven years seeing the same sun throwing light across the branches at the dawn of day? It's a heartbreak to the wise that it's for a short space we have the same things only.

Deirdre's definition of wisdom is related to the persistent reference to "knowledge":

CONCHUBOR: Isn't it a strange thing you'd be talking of Naisi and his brothers, or figuring them either, when you know the things that are foretold about themselves and you? Yet you've little knowledge, and I'd do wrong taking it bad when it'll be my share from this out to keep you the way you'll have little call to trouble for knowledge, or its want either.

DEIRDRE: Yourself should be wise surely.

CONCHUBOR: The like of me has a store of knowledge that's a weight and terror.

But his knowledge pales at the last besides Deirdre's magnificent affirmation of her choice:

Draw a little back with the squabblings of fools when I am broken up with misery. I see the flames of Emain starting upward in the dark night; and because of me there will be weasels and wild cats crying on a lonely wall where there were queens and armies and red gold, the way there will be a story told of a ruined city and a raving king and a woman will be young for ever. . . . I have put away sorrow like a shoe that is worn out and muddy, for it is I have had a life that will be envied by great companies. . . . It was the choice of lives we had in the clear woods, and in the grave we're safe surely. . . . I have a little key to unlock the prison of Naisi you'd shut upon his youth for ever. . . . It was sorrows were fore-told, but great joys were my share always; yet it is a cold place I must go to be with you, Naisi, and it's cold your arms will be this night that were warm about my neck so often. It's a pitiful thing to be talking out when your ears are shut to me. It's a pitiful thing Conchubor, you have done this night in Emain; yet a thing will be a joy and triumph to the ends of life and time.

This speech is genuine drama; it is that rarest of situations, a character conscious of her own dramatic importance, in the same way as in the earlier magnificence of her entrance dressed as a Queen:

I am Deirdre of the Sorrows.

The points to which I have drawn attention are not adequate for a full critical estimate of the play. But my argument is that this method is a new departure in Synge, as in the modern drama as a whole. The language is no longer confined to "flavouring", but uses metaphor and verbal symbolism for strict dramatic ends. *Deirdre* may not altogether succeed; but it approaches those permanent levels of great drama which seem to be accessible only when a dramatist subordinates all else to the exploration of a major experience, through a lan-guage which the experience alone determines.

(vi)

The Playboy of the Western World is a great prose play, an example of a rare and mature kind of comedy. *The Shadow of the Glen* is a minor play of notable integrity. *Deirdre of the Sorrows* is an impressive experiment in prose tragedy controlled by a strict verbal theme. Synge's achievement, in his short space, is notable; the more so when one distinguishes it from the general cultural movement of which it forms a part. It is important to emphasise the very real differences of level in his work, and to estimate accurately both the virtues and the limitations of his dramatic language. The account which I have suggested makes Synge a somewhat different figure from the name in the usual list of regional dramatists. His work is small in compass, but it is, if not in itself major drama, at the very least an important re-discovery of major dramatic possibilities.

J. M. SYNGE

NOTE

I have argued that Synge must not be relegated to the status of a regional dramatist, and that it is necessary, in considering the Irish dramatic movement, to make very careful discriminations of quality. The point at which discrimination is most necessary is that of language. The language of the plays of Sean O'Casey, the best Irish dramatist of the generation which followed Synge, is, for example, widely praised in terms that certainly require scrutiny. The usual adjective is "colourful", and it is not often that a reviewer fails to make a subsequent reference to "Elizabethan richness." It is worth considering the question of "colour" in a little detail.

In his detailed descriptions of stage settings (cf. the packet of meat sandwiches in *The Silver Tassie*); in his introductions of characters (a random description—"It is a face in which is the desire for authority without the power to attain it"—is clearly fictional rather than dramatic); and in his directions about speech ("impatiently, but kindly"; "plunging out into the centre of the floor in a wild tempest of hysterical rage"), O'Casey works within the normal naturalist tradition. His method of establishing character also is a normal one. Consider, for example, Fluther, in *The Plough and the Stars*, where the method is that defined by Strindberg in the Preface to *Lady Julie*. The trick is done by the use of stock phrases, "such as 'Barkis is willin'' and the like"; for Fluther, things are "derogatory" or "vice-versa." The habit—at a conservative estimate one or other of the words appears in one in three of his sentences—becomes very irritating, although one can imagine its kind of success. Each word on its own for a time one accepts, as in

> It's only a little cold I have. There's nothing derogatory wrong with me.

or

> When . . . he has a few jars up he's vice-versa;

but the insistence is so great that by the time one has reached

> Nothin' derogatory'll happen to Mr. Clitheroe. You'll find now, in th' finish-up, it'll be vice-versa.

a large part of the effect created by the dialect has been dissipated. Naturalist caricature is a particularly degenerate art;

as appears again with the speech of the English soldiers in the same play:

> Ow, hoi fink hit's nearly howver. We've got 'em surrounded, hand we're clowsing hin hon the bloighters. Ow, hit was honly ha little bit hof ha dawg foight.

But it is not in these aspects of his work that O'Casey's distinctive accent appears. When colour and richness are in question, it is to phrases like these that we are directed:

> Is a man fermentin' with fear to stick th' showin' off to him of a thing that looks like a shinin' shroud?

> . . . I'll not stick any longer these titthering taunts of yours, rovin' around to sing your slights an' slandhers, reddenin' th' mind of a man to th' thinkin' and sayin' of things that sicken his soul with sin!

> There's the men marchin' out into th' dhread dimness o' danger, while th' lice is crawlin' about feedin' on th' fatness o' the land! But yous'll not escape from th' arrow that flieth be night, or th' sickness that wasteth be day. . . .

> . . . in dhread any minute he might come staggerin' in covered with bandages splashed all over with th' red of his own blood an' givin' us barely time to bring th' priest to hear th' last whisper of his final confession, as his soul was passin' through th' dark doorway o' death into th' way o' th' wondherin' dead. . . .

> It would take something more than a thing like you to flutther a feather o' Fluther.

Speech of this kind depends on a few simple tricks: on alliteration, which frequently over-rides or dictates the sense (one would hardly call the first example precise); on simple word-play, as in the last example, and on a few keywords which are surprisingly recurrent, and which carry "poetic" associations: *shining, dread, darkness, death, shroud*. As comic abuse, such language is frequently effective: it has some similarity with the sub-scenes of clown-abuse in many Elizabethan plays. But it can rarely carry any literary weight: when it aims to convey some positive emotion it is too frequently open to Fluther's description:

> Blatherin' an' when all is said, you know as much as th' rest in th' wind up!

There is a certain adjectival drunkenness: when bullets smash glass, they must be described as

tinklin' through th' *frightened* windows.

When real impressiveness is sought, the dramatist draws on rhythms and phrases which are already charged with emotional associations: in the third example above the insertion of the Biblical phrase is characteristic. Essentially, this is a device of the same kind as O'Casey's use of songs in his play-structures. In *The Plough and the Stars* Bessie Burgess dies singing *I do believe, I will believe, that Jesus died for me*. Nora is led away in her distraction to the singing of *Lead Kindly Light*, and the final emotion of the play is expressed in a song:

And although our 'eart is breaking,
Make it sing this cheery song:
Keep the 'owme fires burning . . . etc.

The distance between the language of O'Casey and the language of poetic drama is considerable; but perhaps a more significant distance is that between his language and that of Synge. It is not a simple difference of status between the two as writers, although Synge's sensibility is clearly the finer; it is also a change in the language of society, a change from the speech of isolated peasants and fishermen, where dignity and vitality of language were directly based on an organic living process, to the speech of townsmen, normally colourless and drab, containing the undiscriminated rhythms of the scriptures, popular hymns, and commercial songs, which, when it wishes to be impressive, must become either drunken or hysterical, and end in extravagance. When O'Casey brings on two of his people with the note

Emotion is bubbling up in them, so that when they drink, and when they speak, they drink and speak with the fullness of emotional passion.

he is at once diagnosing the secret of his impressive language and blustering about it, for the point is that the men are simply drunk. To speak, as townsmen, in the way they do, they would have to be. Colour, that is to say, needs to be artificially infused, just as O'Casey takes care to relieve the drabness of contemporary clothes with one or two characters appearing in fancy dress (Peter, in *The Plough and the Stars*, wears the green and white uniform of the Foresters). The test surely is in crisis.

The point which seems to confirm my analysis of the nature of O'Casey's language is the routine nature of the words which pass between Jack and Nora Clitheroe as he goes to his death in the fighting:

> My Nora; my little beautiful Nora, I wish to God I'd never left you.
> It doesn't matter, not now, not now, Jack. It will make us dearer than ever to each other. Kiss me, kiss me again.

This, confined to sobriety, is simply the language of the novelette. One would not say that of the crisis of the action, which shows the distraction of Nora after the premature birth (and death) of her baby during the absence of her husband in the fighting. She enters singing scraps of a song which we have heard her husband singing to her:

> Th' violets were scenting th' woods, Nora,
> Displaying their charms to th' bee,
> When I first said I lov'd only you, Nora,
> An' you said you lov'd only me.

She is

> clad only in her nightdress; her hair, uncared for some days, is hanging in disorder over her shoulders. Her pale face looks paler still because of a vivid red spot on the tip of each cheek. Her eyes are glimmering with the light of incipient insanity. . . .

But perhaps this is enough, and the reference back has been established: it is the crisis of so many final acts, this reminiscence of Ophelia (or perhaps even more of Victorian paintings of Ophelia).

> No, not there, Jack . . . I can feel comfortable only in our own familiar place beneath th' bramble tree. . . . We must be walking for a long time, I feel very very tired. . . . Curious mist on my eyes. . . . Why don't you hold my hand, Jack. (*Excitedly*) No, no, Jack, it's not. Can't you see it's a goldfinch. Look at th' black-satiny wings with th' gold bars, an' th' splash of crimson on its head. . . .

Here is colour again, the colour of random association and popular reminiscence. The vigorous, "realistic" naturalism ends, as so often, in the maudlin emotionalism of the popular song or the sentimental print.

Again, in *Red Roses for Me*, the keypoint for analysis is O'Casey's handling of colour: colour in the fantasy of Dublin—violet, gold, crimson, mauve:

> the men looking like fine bronze statues, slashed with scarlet;
>
> (the old woman) showing a fresh and virile face, and garbed in a dark-green robe, with a silvery mantle over her shoulders;
>
> (the men again) like bronze statues, slashed with a vivid green;

and colour in the language, the "colourful" language of a hundred reviews:

> There's th' great dome o' th' Four Courts lookin' like a golden rose in a great bronze bowl! An' th' river flowin' below it, a purple flood, marbled with ripples of scarlet; watch th' seagulls glidin' over it, like restless white pearls astir on a royal breast;
>
> She gives no honour to gold; neither does her warm heart pine for silks and satins from China and Japan, or the spicy isles of Easthern Asia;
>
> I do listen, but I am drifting away from you, Mother, a dim shape now in a gold canoe, dipping over a far horizon.
>
> We've gone a long way in a gold canoe, over many waters, bright and surly sometimes sending bitter spray asplash on our faces, forcing forward to the green glade of united work and united rest beyond the farther waves;
>
> She chatters red-lined warnings and black-bordered appeals into my ears night and day, and when they dwindle for lack of breath, my father shakes them out of their drowsiness and sends them dancing round more lively still, dressed richly up in deadly black and gleaming scarlet.

But it is surely a mechanical habit, this repetition of the names of colours, and particularly of vivid colours, and it is only the careless ear that will be tricked into believing that the language is made vivid because its subjects are often so. The method, like the "dim, dreary and dhread" of *The Plough and the Stars*, involves an aggregation of words charged with conventional "poetical" responses. In theatrical terms, the process is represented by the laying of fancy dress over modern clothes: in *Red Roses* the characters are rehearsing a Shakespeare performance and a minstrel show. Like the "bright green silk doublet over which is a crimson velvet armless cloak bordered with white fur", the words and rhythms of popular sentiment are accumulated in an attempt to overlay a dramatic substance which is limited and essentially inarticulate. O'Casey has recorded, both consciously and unconsciously, the inadequacies of naturalism, while retaining what is vigorous of its limited authenticity. Such achievement, however, is an impasse, and attempts to escape from it by an aggregation of colour are likely to prove even less successful.

6

Two Social Plays

(i) The Weavers, by Gerhart Hauptmann

THE writer of *Michael Kramer*, of *The Beaver Coat* and *Drayman Henschel*, of *Ulysses' Bow* and *The Sunken Bell* and *Iphigenia in Delphi*, cannot be set down as a mere representative of a single dramatic type. Hauptmann's work is as various as that of Strindberg, and, although deficient in power in such a comparison, is of undoubted force. I wish to treat him here, however, solely as the author of *The Weavers*. In this play Hauptmann made a significant innovation in naturalist drama; the dramatic methods of his plays in other moods can, it seems to me, be more usefully examined in the work of other authors.

The naturalism of *The Weavers* is not new in theory. By 1892, when the play was written, the idea of the absolutely realistic treatment of a particular segment of life was a commonplace among dramatists and critics. The work of Ibsen and Strindberg and Dumas *fils*, to mention only the most influential names, had, in its different ways, brought to maturity the naturalist drama of the family, of personal relationships. *The Weavers* was different; not only did it go outside the bourgeois world in which the earlier naturalists had commonly moved; it went also outside the limited group of persons, or the family, and attempted to deal with a community. Further, it was not merely a community, in the older sense, with which Hauptmann was concerned, but a *class*. There had been earlier attempts at the dramatic treatment of working people, but none with this particular emphasis, and none of comparable power.

The action of *The Weavers* is the gathering and final eruption of a revolt among the pauperised fustian weavers of the Eulengebirge, in the 1840's. It is action, rather than plot; and this is the first of Hauptmann's major innovations. *The Weavers* is the first important example in naturalist drama of a method of realistic treatment which is fully emancipated from the ideas of plot of the older romantic drama. Strindberg's domestic plays, it is true, had abandoned plot as Ibsen had learned to understand it; but the abandonment went along with an intensification of experience and characters which was already an essential rejection of naturalism in its popular sense. Hauptmann maintains the traditional realism, but of plot and situation, in the normal definition, *The Weavers* is almost entirely bare. The one possible exception is the accidental killing of Old Hilse, which ends the play; this is very like the ironic coincidence of the intrigue drama. In general, however, *The Weavers* is a deliberate chronicle, without surprise, without uncertainty, without complication, except in so far as these are generated by the collective action of the weavers. The diverse and complex interaction of individuals, on which the romantic plot rested, is set aside here for the determinism of the operation of a class. The first act shows the weavers bringing their work for sale, and sets them in contact with their employer, his manager, the cashier, and a regular apprentice. The second act draws the circle tighter, concentrating on a pauper weaver's home. The third act moves out again, into the wider community at the inn, bringing the weavers into contact with a commercial traveller, a joiner-employer, the innkeeper, the policeman, a smith, and a ragman. The fourth act begins from the other side, in the home of the employer, where the parson is a guest, and where a superintendent of police is called to deal with the rioting weavers; it ends with the weavers taking possession of the house. The fifth act moves the revolt to another village, and its action is set in the house of another weaver, as the rebel weavers approach to continue their destruction of the employers' houses and the factories, led by the returned soldier; it ends with the weavers fighting the soldiers who have been sent to put the revolt down. Through the whole play, within this chronicle framework, the mainspring of the action is not a matter of persons, but of the revolt of the body of weavers, springing from their poverty.

This is an authentic dramatic theme, and Hauptmann's treatment of it, with its concentration on a general movement, is a convincing artistic decision. If one compares *The Weavers* with an almost exactly contemporary "social" play, *Widowers' Houses*, Hauptmann's method is seen to have a clear advantage over that of Shaw; *The Weavers* does not need a Lickcheese. If the theme of a play is the social condition of a body of people, Hauptmann's method is probably the most successful that can, within naturalism, be devised. The moving power is the event, the action, the class articulate in revolt; where this is so, situation, plot, "spokesman" characters are forms which cannot express the new theme. *The Weavers*, in this respect, is the perfect expression of its substance, and it is a very considerable achievement.

But one cannot, within dramatic forms as we know them, articulate an entire class upon the stage. This was what Hauptmann was trying to do, and it is here that one must make distinctions of success. There are two methods used in the play: first, the isolation of a smaller, representative group, the isolation of persons; this may be seen in the Baumert family, in Becker, in the Hilse family. And second there is a method that one can perhaps best define as choral, which is the method of the first act. The first method is in the main tradition of naturalism; it is successful because the characters are not required to be anything but weavers, preoccupied with a crushing poverty and with the defences against it. It is a method, however, which challenges comparison with the novel. Hauptmann works with the characteristic fictional aids of description of scene and person, and with the commentary description of speech. The acts are convincing and powerful, but one is always aware in them of the essential limitation of the method; it is not only that one is aware of the fuller substance of the novel proper, in dealing with such material; one is aware also of the dependence of the dramatic effect upon visual elements which the drama itself cannot finally control. In this sense, the method of the first act is more fully dramatic. The coming of a number of weavers to sell their webs; the creation on the stage of this group—"the weavers"; the interaction of the group *as a whole*, through the successive bargainings, with the employer and his creatures; the speech which is less the speech of individual workers than a pattern of speech of the whole group: in these and similar ways Hauptmann creates in this act a sense of class—the substance of his play—with complete dramatic effect. It is a deliberate impersonal convention for the expression of an essentially impersonal force.

These two methods—the realistic presentation of the lives of workers and workers' families, and the impersonal expression of a class—have both been used in subsequent drama; the former, of course, very much more widely. They are, in fact, both present in a single later play: Sean O'Casey's *The Silver Tassie*. The first method is the most familiar, and if we judge, as I think we must, that it has produced little significant work, it is because most writers who have essayed it have lacked one or both of the two essential elements of Hauptmann's success. They have lacked his conception of action, and have blurred their effects with devices of plot of the older, romantic kind (and hardly anything could be less suitable to such a theme). They have usually lacked also Hauptmann's sureness of language. The success of attempts in the impersonal convention have also been limited by this same failure of dramatic speech.

Hauptmann's language is authentically realistic, and only rarely forced. He is not striving for *effect*, of the usual kind, but is recording. Now it is often believed that recording speech is the simplest of writing tasks; but it demands, in fact, an unusual kind of integrity. I do not say that it is the highest integrity; the greatest dramatic speech is something essentially different from the process of recording. But it requires, nevertheless, an impersonality and a control, which are rare enough. D. H. Lawrence had it, in his working-class novels, and the distinction of those parts of his novels, when compared with the more pretentious kinds of prolet-literature, is significant and marked. Hauptmann had it also, and not only in *The Weavers*. It is a quality, unfortunately, that one cannot represent adequately by quotation; it is a matter of general key and tone. But if one compares *The Weavers* with any of O'Casey's working-class plays, one is struck immediately by Hauptmann's superior discipline. O'Casey is always working for *effect*; he has not the restraint to record, nor has he (I discuss the point in a note in Chapter Five) the means to re-fashion the recorded speech into a full literary medium. Hauptmann's control of recorded speech, and his significantly detailed use of dialect (see *Before Dawn* and *The Beaver Coat*) are the means by which he realises his deliberate chronicle form. It is not that he does not occasionally use speeches, songs and the like—the traditional devices of intensification—but in *The Weavers* these elements are set so firmly in the continuity of recorded speech that they are completely acceptable. The revolutionary song is a proper intensification corresponding to the rising spirit of the weavers; it is not a sentimental accompaniment. The speeches at the inn have a clear difference in kind from Dr. Stockmann's speech at the public meeting in *An Enemy of the People*.

The Weavers, then, is a successful example of a type of drama, in which, if one judged from theory alone, there should be scores of similar successes. It is a successful realistic play because its realism operates at every level of creation—action, persons, and speech, instead of being reserved merely for the convenient elements. If for nothing else (and here one enters on wider and more complex judgments) Hauptmann will be remembered in modern European drama for this rare and particular achievement.

(ii) *Hoppla! Such is Life!, by Ernst Toller*

Toller's plays represent the political mood of expressionism in its most developed form. The essential creative turn towards expressionism had been made by Strindberg, in *The Road to Damascus* and many of the late *kammarspel*. But Strindberg was primarily concerned with the personal consciousness, although in *Dreamplay* he foreshadows the social form. Part of the expressionist movement followed this mode of individual analysis—one of the most striking later examples is Wiene's film *The Cabinet of Dr. Caligari*. But the landmarks of the expressionist theatre are primarily social plays: Kaiser's *From Morn till Midnight*, Capek's *R.U.R.*, Rice's *The Adding Machine*. In England O'Casey built expressionism into a realistic play, in *The Silver Tassie*. Auden and Isherwood united the personal and social modes of analysis in plays like *The Ascent of F6*, which show, among other influences, the very direct influence of Toller.

Masses and Man is perhaps the most striking theme in Toller's drama, but its dramatic method is relatively narrow. The character of Gene in *Hinkemann* is a very powerful creation, and the interpenetration of pity and laughter has considerable effect. *The Machine Wreckers*, a play about the Luddites, is not very successful; among other things, it challenges too close a comparison with Hauptmann's *The Weavers*, and its inferiority in the comparison is clear. *Draw the Fires* is similarly based on a realistic set of events, but modified by expressionist presentation; it is, I think, a much more successful play than *The Silver Tassie*. The best example, however, both of Toller and of expressionism, is none of these, but the play *Hoppla!* which appeared in 1927.

The action of the play passes in Germany in 1927, with a prologue set in 1919. The prologue shows a group of condemned revolutionaries, waiting for execution. At the last moment, the death-sentence is commuted to imprisonment, for all the condemned except one, Wilhelm Kilman, who is secretly released. In the play, Karl Thomas, one of the condemned, is just released from his detention. Kilman, meanwhile, has become Prime Minister, and an enemy of the revolution. The action consists of the exploration and rediscovery of society by Karl Thomas, and ends with his imprisonment on a false charge and with his suicide.

The function of the play, clearly, is the analysis of society, with Karl Thomas as its agent. It is in this analysis that the various expressionist devices serve. The first and most surprising device is the use of film, projected on to a screen on the stage. This is designed to show the larger outline of social events, within which the particular events of the stage action are to be understood. Thus:

On the screen

SCENES FROM THE YEARS 1919-27

Among them Karl Thomas, walking backward and forward in a madhouse cell, wearing the uniform of the institution.

1919: Treaty of Versailles.
1920: Stock Exchange uneasiness in New York—People go mad.
1921: Fascism in Italy.
1922: Hunger in Vienna—people go mad.
1923: German Inflation—people go mad.
1924: Death of Lenin in Russia. Placard. Death of Luise Thomas.
1925: Gandhi in India.
1926: Fighting in China. Conference of European leaders in Europe.
1927: Face of clock. The hands move, first slowly, then more and more quickly. Noises. Clocks.

This is the use as historical outline. Elsewhere, film is used, first to show the present social condition of women, as a prelude to the re-introduction of Eva Berg, one of the revolutionaries; and second, to show the conditions of the workers, as a prelude to an election.

Similar to the use of film is the use of wireless. There are loudspeaker reports of contemporary world events:

Unrest in India.' . . . Unrest in China. . . . Unrest in Africa. . . . Paris. Paris. Houbigant the fashionable perfume. . . . Bucharest. Bucharest. Famine in Rumania. . . . Berlin. Berlin. Elegant ladies delight in green wigs.

At times these wireless reports are reinforced by films of the events which they describe. The wireless is also used in the election, to announce the results of the voting. In other plays,

such as *Hinkemann*, Toller uses newspaper headlines as a similar
background.

> Late night final. Sensational news. New night club opened.
> Stomach dances. Jazz. Champagne. American bar. Late night
> final. Latest sensation. Jews massacred in Galicia. Synagogue
> burnt down. A thousand burnt to death.

Within an outline described in this way, Toller sets his
specific scenes. In *Hoppla!* these range from bedroom to police
court, but the principal are a lunatic asylum and a Grand
Hotel. These are staged on a general structure of a scaffolding
divided into several floors. The hotel, for example, has the
wireless station at the top of the scaffolding, three lines of
rooms below, which are illuminated in turn as the scenes turn
to the various characters occupying them, and at the base the
staff room and the vestibule. The same structure is used for
the prison in which the play ends, with particular cells
illuminated in turn. To observe Toller's method in specific
scenes, we may look at part of the second scene of Act Three,
which is set in the hotel. The first episode is in a private room,
where Kilman, the former revolutionary, is being entertained
by a financier:

> KILMAN: The Service wears me out. People think it means sitting
> in armchairs and smoking fat cigars. Forgive me for being late.
> I had to receive the Mexican Minister.
> FINANCIER: Let's make a start.
> (*They all sit at table. Waiter brings food.*)

The second episode is in the wireless station. Karl Thomas,
who is a waiter at the hotel, listens with the operator to the
world reports that have been quoted. The third episode is in a
Clubroom, a meeting of the Union of Brainworkers:

> PHILOSOPHER X: Listen, Comrade Waiter, young proletarian,
> would you be willing to consummate the sexual act with the
> first attractive young woman you met, or would you first consult
> your instincts on the subject?
> (*Karl Thomas laughs aloud.*)
> CHAIRMAN: This isn't a laughing matter. The question is serious.
> Moreover, we are customers of your employer and you are the
> waiter.
> KARL THOMAS: Oho, first "Comrade Waiter" and now "Keep
> your place." You wish to redeem the proletariat? Here, in the

Grand Hotel, eh? What would happen to you if it were redeemed? Where would *you* be? Back in the Grand Hotel?
Eunuchs!

VOICES: Scandalous. Scandalous.

(*Karl Thomas goes.*)

PHILOSOPHER X: Lower-middle-class idea merchant!

CHAIRMAN: We come now to the second item of the agenda.
Proletarian communal love, and the problem of the intelli-
gentsia. . . .

The fourth episode returns to the financier's entertainment
of Kilman; he is advising the Prime Minister to play the stock
market. A political innocent from the provinces, Pickel, enters
to seek advice, and is sent away. The fifth episode shows a
briefing of journalists for a propaganda campaign; the sixth
a nationalist Count in bed with the daughter of the Prime
Minister—the girl is also a Lesbian. The seventh episode is in
the staff-room: the hotel-porter has had his life's savings
reduced to the price of a box of matches by inflation—he has
turned to gambling. The page-boy complains:

The gentleman in 101 always pinches my bottom.

HEAD WAITER: Never mind. You know which side your bread's
buttered.

Karl Thomas is called with drinks to the Count's room, and
then takes a revolver to answer a call to the room in which the
Prime Minister is being entertained. An intermediate episode
shows the Count preparing a student to assassinate the Prime
Minister for the nationalist cause. The final episode shows
Thomas confronting Kilman:

THOMAS: . . . When we waited together in a common grave we
didn't stand on ceremony. . . .

KILMAN: (*to* FINANCIER) Owing to some romantic episode in his
youth he went off the rails.

The Student, disguised as a waiter, enters the room quietly,
switches off the light, and shoots Kilman over Thomas's
shoulder.

A play like *Hoppla!* requires considerable discrimination in
judgment. A common reaction is to call Toller's political views
extremist, and so dismiss the play. This is inadequate on two
grounds. First, one cannot be sure that the so-called extremism
does not in fact present a more accurate picture of certain

phases of public life than do many so-called moderate views. Second, and more to the critical point, one cannot dismiss a play because one dislikes the views on which it is based; any such judgment is a grave limitation of the enjoyment of literature. And yet *Hoppla!*, and Toller's other plays, leave one essentially dissatisfied. The expressionist devices of spectacle are striking, but they come to seem essentially external, the visual elements particularly so. The panorama unrolls, but increasingly one has the impression that it *shows* nothing. It ought, according to Toller's intention, to show the social background, but the substance of the devices has so much the element of *cliché*, and the techniques involved—the newspaper headline, the wireless announcement, the newsreel—are in themselves so much the embodiment of simplification, that one comes to feel that the whole expression is commonplace and superficial. But here again one must be careful of one's terms. There is a place in literature—a place which includes work of very high value—for the expression of the commonplace, and for work which is deliberately superficial, of the surface, in intention. The condition of success in such work, however, is not only power of expression, but also consistency of treatment. Once a different order of experience is touched upon the convention tends to disintegrate. As to consistency, Toller is frequently successful, but there is at the root of his art a profound doubt:

> In my political capacity, I proceed upon the assumption that units, groups, representatives of social forces, various economic functions have a real existence; that certain relations between human beings are objective realities. As an artist, I recognise that the validity of these "facts" is highly questionable.[1]

And again:

> The plays collected in this volume are social dramas and tragedies. They bear witness to human suffering, and to fine yet vain struggles to vanquish this suffering. For only unnecessary suffering can be vanquished, the suffering which arises out of the unreason of humanity, out of an inadequate social system. There must always remain a residue of suffering, the lonely suffering imposed upon mankind by life and death. And only this residue is necessary and inevitable, is the tragic element of life and of life's symboliser, art.[2]

[1] *Masses and Man: A Note to the Producer.*
[2] Introduction in *Seven Plays by Toller* (The Bodley Head).

The recognition is important; and it puts Toller, as a man, in a very different category from the usual "social realists." But one cannot feel that he ever resolved the tension which the recognition implies, or expressed its irresolution, in his art. The intelligent doubt, the personal reservation, remains in the social plays, not as an element of communication, but as an almost sardonic disintegrator. The simplification which the social view involves seems at times, in *Hoppla!* in *Hinkemann*, in *Transfiguration*, a deliberate, virtually hysterical attempt to repress the profounder consciousness. The very real hysterical element in Toller does not reside in the violence and clarity of his political views, but rather in this attempt to repress a part of the pattern of his experience, which has too much vitality to be simply and easily neglected.

The power of *Hoppla!* and of the other plays is primarily a spectacular power. The language is as deliberately general and unspecific as the visual panorama. Its method is essentially that of the slogan; it very rarely has any power to surprise or, in its own right, to convey emotion. It is a slogan summary of experience, and too many of the slogans are too familiar even to interest. This is especially so in his deliberately expressionist episodes, such as those in the hotel; it is true also of his longer single scenes, where he writes in an explicit kind of naturalism. Hinkemann's whole experience is summed up in his saying:

The world has lost its soul and I have lost my sex

—the slogan again.

It is very common, in England, to be patronising about the expressionist experiment, and to remind readers that it was mainly *German* expressionism, which presumably settles its inferiority. It depends where you criticise from. When expressionist drama is set against poetic drama, or against the very best of the naturalists—Ibsen, Chekhov, Synge—it is true that it must be judged inferior. But when it is set against the cosy, standardised naturalism which still occupies so many of our stages, it is seen as a real attempt at vitality and seriousness. The trouble was—and it is here that expressionism may be seen as an integral part of the development of modern drama— that it served to confirm the impoverishment of dramatic *language*, and sought its reforms in the substitute devices of spectacle.

7

Luigi Pirandello

(i)

WHEN they advance into the theatre, these six characters in search of an author, wearing light masks which leave eyes, mouth and nostrils free, surrounded by "a tenuous light . . . the faint breath of their fantastic reality", the central assumption of the naturalist method in drama has at once been finally realised, and finally questioned. The concept of the absolute existence of characters in a play has been set tangibly on the stage; the phrase which the characters bring with them is the echo of Ibsen's description of his aim, fifty years earlier, "the perfect illusion of reality."

Sei Personaggi in cerca d'Autore is Pirandello's best known and most challenging play. Its very title, in newspapers and in similarly professional organs of outraged sanity, is a byword for the excesses of experimental art. Sanity, however, can be as elusive as any author. The whole experimental basis of Pirandello's interesting play is in fact the most universal and most orthodox prejudice of modern drama. Pirandello saw that it was a prejudice, an assumption; that was all.

> When a character is born, he acquires at once such an independence, even of his own author, that he can be imagined by everybody even in many other situations where the author never dreamed of placing him.

This speech, from the character "The Father" in Pirandello's play, is the whole basis of the experiment; but it might equally have come, not from this supposed extreme of eccentricity in drama, but from the speeches of five eminent popular writers, one after the other, at a literary luncheon.

A company of actors is rehearsing a play, an illusion of reality, in its theatre. While they are engaged in preparing certain aspects of the illusion, other aspects of it—six created characters—enter and interrupt. The resulting contrast between these various stages in the process of dramatic illusion, and the relation of this process to its context of reality, is the material of Pirandello's play.

In the course of the play's development, many of the problems peculiar to the naturalist method are illustrated and discussed. There is the question of the relation of the created character of the author to its acted embodiment on the stage. When the characters have described themselves and their situation, the company begins to represent and act them:

"THE FATHER": Yes, sir, but believe me, it has such a strange effect when . . .

MANAGER: Strange? Why strange? Where is it strange?

"THE FATHER": No, sir; I admire your actors—this gentleman, this lady; but they are certainly not us.

And again:

"THE FATHER": Look here, sir, our temperaments, our souls . . .

MANAGER: Temperament, soul, be hanged! Do you suppose the spirit of the piece is in you? Nothing of the kind!

"THE FATHER": What, haven't we our own temperaments, our own souls?

MANAGER: Not at all. Your soul, or whatever you like to call it, takes shape here. The actors give body and form to it, voices and gesture. . . . The actor here acts you, and that's an end to it.

"THE FATHER": I understand. And now I think I see why our author who conceived us as we are, all alive, didn't want to put us on the stage after all. I haven't the least desire to offend your actors. Far from it. But when I think I am to be acted by . . . I don't know whom . . .

The issue could not have been better put, whatever conclusions Pirandello may draw from it.

Then there is the question of the degree of experience which can be communicated through drama of the type assumed. "The Step-daughter" wants the play to concentrate on her great situation, when she is about to be taken by her step-father:

Ah well, then let's take off this little frock.

The Manager will not have it quite like that:

Truth up to a certain point, but no further.

"The Step-daughter" comments angrily:

What you want to do is to piece together a little romantic sentimental scene out of my disgust.

LUIGI PIRANDELLO

But "The Father" has quite a different play in view. He wants
to get at his complicated "cerebral drama", to have his famous
remorses and torments acted.

The Manager steps in and explains:

On the stage you can't have a character becoming too prominent
and overshadowing all the others. The thing is to pack them all
into a neat little framework, and then act what is actable. I am
aware of the fact that everyone has his own interior life which he
wants very much to put forward. But the difficulty lies in this fact:
to set out just so much as is necessary for the stage, taking the other
characters into consideration, and at the same time hint at the
unrevealed interior life of each. I am willing to admit, my dear
young lady, that from your point of view it would be a fine idea if
each character could tell the public all his troubles in a nice
monologue or a regular one-hour lecture.

Here, once again, the statement of the limitations of
naturalist drama in the communication of experience, and its
distinction from a dramatic method in which "a nice monologue" is perfectly possible, is as clearly made as one could
wish.

The issue is related to the question of speech. When "The
Step-daughter" is talking with her procurer, the actors cry:

Louder! Louder please!
Louder? Louder? What are you talking about? These aren't
matters that can be shouted at the top of one's voice.

And again, when "The Father" tries to analyse his situation,
the Manager protests:

I should like to know if anyone has ever heard of a character who
gets right out of his part and perorates and speechifies as you do.
Have you ever heard of a case? I haven't. . . . Drama is action,
sir, action, and not confounded philosophy.
All right, I'll do just as much arguing and philosophising as every-
body does when he is considering his own torments.
If the drama permits.

The naturalist drama, of course, does not permit. But if the
Manager has not heard of such a case, the European drama of
two thousand years has. The fact of the possibility of a different
dramatic method, within which all the problems raised in *Six
Characters in Search of an Author* could be satisfactorily negotiated,

is the one piece of evidence which Pirandello does not explicitly include in his analysis. Because of its exclusion, it is possible to respond to the play in such a way as to surrender to the contradictions which it analyses. The relation of this possibility to Pirandello's drama in general I shall come to discuss. But one can say of *Six Characters in Search of an Author*, if one reads it from an understanding of general dramatic possibilities, that it is, in its way, conclusive. A competent analysis of naturalism could be outlined by attention to this play alone. As drama, it is perhaps best described as a brilliant aside on a method of play writing which, as it moved further into the area of serious experience, was increasingly demonstrating its inadequacy.

(ii)

Pirandello's experiments in drama were part of a general movement in the Italian theatre. Its starting-point was the revolt against romantic drama, which had been the general pattern of European dramatic reform. The romantic drama had a very firm hold in Italy, and the revolt was correspondingly extreme. Its initiation may be dated with the production of a play by Luigi Chiarelli, in 1916. The title of the play, *The Mask and the Face (La Machera e il Volto)*, became a slogan for the general movement which followed. Chiarelli's intention was to "expose" the romantic drama, to pull off the mask of its conventional morality, and reveal the actual form of the life which it concealed. But the mood was not that of the French realists, exposing deliberately unromantic material. The complication of the intrigue action, the nature of the dramatic situations, was largely retained. But the play was given a grotesque twist in resolution, confounding the romantic morality. For both these reasons—the retention of complicated intrigue, and the grotesque resolution—the new method came to be known as the *Teatro del Grottesco*. It went back, in the nature of its action, to the native Italian tradition of the *commedia dell' arte;* its resolution came from the deliberate experimental innovation and flouting of convention of the futurist movement in art.

Chiarelli's play is a parody, a grotesque caricature, of the romantic drama. Its characters are puppets, who are manipulated into the conventional complication, and then jerked violently into a mocking, anti-romantic resolution. This puppet

nature of the characters, going back as it does to the Pulcinella
and Arlocchino of the *commedia dell' arte*, is an essential element
of Pirandello's dramatic method. It provides him with the
means of manipulation which is essential to the realisation of
his fantasies. It involves, also, a dependence on certain highly
skilled methods of acting, including the capacity for improvisation which was the central method of the *commedia dell' arte*. In
the *commedia dell' arte* each actor was regularly assigned to a
particular masked part, of which he had all the stock phrases
and gestures at his command. An author then provided a framework of plot, and the actors improvised its realisation, on the
basis of the stock characters whose convention they com-
manded. In addition to the conventional characters there were
stock *lazzi*, pieces of stage business, to represent the acting of
the recurrent stock situations.

Now Pirandello was very much the dramatic author, with
his insistence on "the book", the text. He was, for that reason,
an absolute opponent of the idea of the "producers' theatre",
which was one of the characteristic central ideas of the
experimental theatre in Europe generally. In the play *Tonight
We Improvise*, he sets a producer of this kind, Hinkfuss, in
contact with the material of a drama. Hinkfuss has the
characteristic attitude to his function:

> I have a greater rôle than the playwright, for I bring to life what is
> enclosed in the playwright's written work.[1]

He tries to dictate the development of the play, to make a
"production" of it, but the essence of the actual drama breaks
down his schemes, and the characters end by driving him off
the stage.

This is Pirandello's consistent attitude to performance. He
insists on the text, and it is the author who must control its
performance (cf. the Manager's treatment of the Characters
in *Sei Personnagi*). As to the actors, however, they must be
encouraged to improvise, in order to find the best way of
expressing the written drama. When, in 1925, Pirandello
founded a theatre in Rome (in the *Teatro Odescalchi*), his
intention was to develop a technique of acting, a convention
of improvisation one might call it, which would serve to realise
the essential nature of his plays. The theatre failed financially,
and the convention was never established. But Pirandello's

---

[1] Cf. Terence Gray, p. 35 above.

plays remain, in an essential sense, *commedia dell' arte*. They depend absolutely, in performance, on a conventionally stylised method of acting, a subtle realisation of the essential puppetry of characters and action. Anyone who has seen a typically earnest repertory production of *Six Characters in Search of an Author* will surely agree that the play falls to pieces, in performance, because of the normal lack of achievement of any such convention. The plays are not only essentially professional; they require a professional method of a particular and specialised kind.

Now Pirandello's experiments were not, primarily, theatrical, although they required experimental performance of the kind which I have outlined. They were always dramatic experiments aimed at the realisation of a particuiar pattern of experience. The phrase *the mask and the face* indicates one essential element of this pattern. It can be used, of some of his plays, in the sense that it was used by Chiarelli: an exposure of the romantic drama and romantic morality. *Pensaci Giacomini* is a good example of this kind, in which the typical Pirandellian mouthpiece character, Professor Toti, expounds, against the conventions of his bourgeois neighbours, the rightness of his acceptance of his young wife's lover and the consequent *ménage a trois*. Leone Galla, in *Giuoco delle Parti*, similarly attacks the concept of honour which would send him to his death in a duel for the honour of a wife whose infidelity he is willing to accept. "You are the husband," he tells her lover; "you go and be killed."

But the concept of *the mask and the face* is not confined to this apotheosis of the anti-romantic. Its next development is in situations where a character agrees to play a part, for one reason or another, and then finds the mask intolerable. Baldovino, in *Il Piacere dell' Onesta*, is characteristic of this type. The situation is also the basis of the effective acting piece *Ma non e una Cosa Seria*, where the mask of a ridiculous marriage is gradually stripped into seriousness and living acceptance.

A further development is the use of the situation where a character is brought to realise that he has been playing a part, where the mask drops suddenly and he has to negotiate a revealed actuality:

When a man lives, he lives and does not see himself. Well, put a mirror before him and make him see himself in the act of living. Either he is astonished at his own appearance, or else he turns

away his eyes so as not to see himself, or else in disgust he spits at
his image, or, again, clenches his fist to break it. In a word, there
arises a crisis, and that crisis is my theatre.

This is Pirandello's own definition of this particular method,
which has come to be known as the *teatro dello specchio*. The
play *Tutto per Bene* is an excellent example, where the mask
drops, and is then consciously resumed, as the best way to go
on living (cf. Synge's *The Well of the Saints*). Another example
is the well-known *Henry the Fourth*.

Most of Pirandello's plays are dramatised from his own early
novelle. This, if nothing else, would confirm that his experiments
were always concerned with realising his preoccupying
experiences—the nature of reality and of illusion, the facts of
man's conscious rôles and disguises, the difficulty of truth in
the shifting, essentially unknowable, aspects of personality.
That is the experience behind the fantasy of the Six Characters:

> Your reality is a mere transitory and fleeting illusion, taking this
> form today and that tomorrow, according to the conditions,
> according to your will, your sentiments, which in turn are con-
> trolled by an intellect that shows them to you today in one manner
> and tomorrow . . . who knows how? Illusions of reality, represented
> in this fatuous comedy of life that never ends, nor ever can end.

This, then, is Pirandello's material. I have outlined the
nature of his ends, and his consideration of means. It remains
to offer a judgment on the degree of his success. I wish to suggest
a judgment on the basis of the play which has already been
considered, *Six Characters in Search of an Author*, and of two other
plays, *Henry the Fourth*, and the piece which is his most striking
exposition of the problem of truth, *Cosi e (se vi pare)*, which is,
literally, *So it is (if you think so)*, and which is usually translated
as *Right you are (if you think you are)*.

(iii)

Pirandello is a naturalist writer, in the sense which Strindberg had defined:

> I do not believe in simple characters on the stage. And the
> summary judgments given on men by authors: this man is stupid,
> that one brutal, this one jealous, this one stingy, etc., should be

challenged by naturalists, who know the richness of the soul-complex and recognise that "vice" has a reverse side, very much like virtue.

Pirandello's drama is the most striking challenge that has been made to such "summary judgments." Either he turns the judgment upside down, in an explicitly anti-romantic drama comparable to Shaw's *Arms and the Man*. Or he creates situations which imply that judgment is impossible, and the attempt at judgment mere impertinence or curiosity. The first method is worth a little emphasis, because it defines one aspect of Pirandello very well. You have not got away from summary judgments, you have not ceased to be curious or impertinent, if you merely assert a solution based upon a different morality. The morality of *Pensaci Giacomino* is as artificial as anything in the romantic drama; the dismissal of the jealous wife Beatrice in *Il Berretto a Sonagli* is either a summary joke or summarily vicious. What Strindberg had in mind, when he talked of the "richness of the soul-complex", was not simply the creation of a series of anti-romantics. He was concerned with a method of drama which should not require a type of characterisation which *abstracted* from the complexity of experience. Pirandello's experiments, in contrast, are so many squibs under the feet of conventional morality. There is an important difference in seriousness and preoccupation, even if Strindberg could not wholly succeed.

The level of Pirandello's exploration of "life" and "truth" may be judged from the entertaining *Cosi e (se vi pare)*. He does not create so much an authentically complex situation, by which the shallowness of commonplace judgments may be revealed, as a deliberate (and brilliant) theatrical exception. The situation of Signor Ponza, Signora Frola, and the lady who may be either Ponza's first wife and Signora Frola's daughter, or Ponza's second wife and not Signora Frola's daughter, is not so much complex as confused. In order to sustain the demonstration, Pirandello has to invent the obviously theatrical device of the earthquake which has destroyed all the relevant records. One cannot help feeling, in spite of his repeated assertions to the contrary, that discovery of the records would at least have taken us *some way* nearer an understanding. The lady's announcement that she is in fact both alternatives—both daughter and second wife—is an entertaining bathetic twist, but we do not, I imagine, sit up at that point and cry "Ah,

Life!" or "Ah, Truth!", or indeed feel anything except that it is the authentic climax to a pleasantly ingenious diversion. One must be careful not to complain that the play is not something it was never intended to be, but Pirandello's tone, and the tone of many of his admirers, implies seriousness; the key-word is "philosophical." The play is, in fact, an entertaining trick-comedy, of the kind which Mr. Priestley has made familiar in the English theatre; it has no more reference to philosophical seriousness than, say, *I have been here before* or *The Long Mirror*.

Cosi e (se vi pare) is, in fact, simply a twist of the romantic drama. Its *raisonneur*, Luidisi, is in the authentic tradition, presiding over the usual complication of action and situation. The innovation is the negative twist, Luidisi's

> Well, and there, my friends, you have the truth. But are you satisfied? Hah hah hah hah hah hah hah!

Similarly, the conflict between "life" and "the mask" is, in Pirandello's drama, primarily theatrical illusion. In *Six Characters in Search of an Author* the contrast is not between artifice and reality, but between two levels of artifice. The characters, that is to say, cannot represent a reality against which the artificiality of the theatre may be measured; they are themselves (and Pirandello's methods insist on this) products of the theatrical method. They do not provide a convincing life-standard, but rather a different degree of abstraction:

> The Step-daughter is dashing, almost impudent, beautiful. She wears mourning, but with great elegance.

> The Mother seems crushed and terrified as if by an intolerable weight of shame and abasement. She is dressed in modest black and wears a thick widow's veil of crepe. When she lifts this, she reveals a wax-like face.

The Characters provide, as I have indicated, an entertaining exposition of the nature of dramatic illusion, but the status of the play remains that of a brilliant aside, a trick-comedy within the established conventions and limitations. Pirandello's attempts to contrapose illusion and reality are carried out with great skill. His most ingenious device is in *Each in his Own Way* (*Ciascuno a suo modo*), where the inner play is a *pièce a cléf*, the performance of which is commented upon by its supposed audience, which includes the supposedly real persons upon whose lives the inner play was based. The contrast of these varying aspects of characterisation (they are not varying aspects of reality) is striking; but it is significant that the outcome of the action is that the play cannot go on at all.

It is the problem of the "illusion of reality" in the contemporary theatre with which Pirandello is nearly always, at root, concerned. To have contrasted reality with *delusion* (which is what he is always claiming to do) he would have needed to use a dramatic form through which he could have created a conviction (if not a representation) of essential reality and life-experience. But his representations of reality are always of a limited, theatrical kind, so that the conflict loses its full potential power.

His most serious attempt is perhaps *Henry the Fourth*, which is intended as tragedy. There is always, in Pirandello's drama, a *potentially* tragic situation, within the circle of the comedy of illusion. But the nature of the development of the plays is such that the effect of this inner drama is never tragic, but simply pathetic. The laughter of Luidisi and his kind is the dominant emotional tone. *Henry the Fourth* is a play in which the comic element is less stressed; the laughter is quickly and deliberately turned. A gentleman, acting the part of Henry the Fourth in a pageant, fell from his horse; since then, for twenty years, he has continued to act the same part—for the first twelve years under a delusion, for the last eight quite consciously, because he does not see how he can take up his normal life again. The main action of the play is a declaration of his consciousness of the "mask" which he is wearing, and his accusation against a friend, Belcredi, who had caused the fall from the horse. There are degrees of relapse and revelation, and in the end he kills Belcredi. This is the most important point in the developed contrast between mask and face, for he has now committed an act which can only be justified within the former masquerade. It is the deepest interpenetration of actuality and delusion.

HENRY: (*who has remained on the stage, with his eyes almost starting out of his head, terrified by the life of his own masquerade which has driven him to crime*) Ah now . . . yes now . . . inevitably (*he calls his valets around him as if to protect him*) . . . here together . . . here together . . . for ever . . . for ever.

This is one of the greatest moments in the Pirandello theatre, and one can see its force; but one has only to look at it to be reminded of Pirandello's limits, limits that were, in spite of his technical experiments, essentially naturalist. The drama, the reality if you like, cannot be achieved in words. The most dramatic point, Henry's realisation of the "life of his own masquerade", cannot come into dramatic speech. The drama has to be injected, explained, pointed from outside; for if Pirandello had thought the spoken words alone would have the full effect, he would not have bothered with his anxious directions. It is the recurrent limitation of the naturalist drama, the same limitation which has prevented any full impact of the crisis of delusion and uncertainty in so many of his other plays. In *Six Characters in Search of an Author*, "The Father" has an appropriate comment:

> But don't you see that the whole trouble lies here? In words, words. Each one of us has within him a whole world of things, each man of us his own special world. And how can we ever come to an understanding if I put in the words I utter the sense and value of things as I see them; while you who listen to me must inevitably translate them according to the conception of things each one of you has within himself. We think we understand each other, but we never really do.

It is, indeed, here that the whole trouble lies: in words. Absolute communication there may never be, but "The Father's" observation is really the unanswerable case for a conventional dramatic language, a convention of expression and understanding. Pirandello had confounded the "illusion of reality", as naturalism had attempted it. The drama needed a new start, with radically different methods and aims.

8

Jean Anouilh: A Comment

THE use of myth or legend as a basis for the play or novel of contemporary life is an important development of twentieth-century literature. The best known example in general literature is, of course, James Joyce's *Ulysses*. T. S. Eliot, reviewing *Ulysses* in *The Dial*, described the method as follows:

> In using the myth, in manipulating a continuous parallel between contemporaneity and antiquity, Mr. Joyce is pursuing a method which others must pursue after him. They will not be imitators, any more than the scientist who uses the discoveries of an Einstein in pursuing his own, independent, further investigations. It is simply a way of controlling, of ordering, of giving a shape and a significance to the immense panorama of futility and anarchy which is contemporary history. It is a method already adumbrated by Mr. Yeats, and of the need for which I believe Mr. Yeats to have been the first contemporary to be conscious. It is, I seriously believe, a step toward making the modern world possible in art.

In the drama, the method has been used in verse plays by Yeats and, implicitly, by Eliot; in prose plays, by Synge and O'Neill. It is not always easy to distinguish the method from certain types of historical play; Ibsen's *Emperor and Galilean* clearly has much in common with the method. The distinction is always a matter of purpose; the method exists where a writer uses myth or legend or historical story as the form for the expression of his experience, rather than as material in itself.

In the prose drama, the most important use of the method has been in France. Cocteau has used it in his *Orphée* and in *La Machine Infernale*. Sartre uses the Orestes story as a basis for his *Les Mouches*. Other examples of the method are Maurice Druon's *Megarée*, and Thierry Maulnier's *La Course des Rois*. The most interesting use of myth, however, is, it seems to me, not to be found in the writers I have mentioned, but in the work of Jean Anouilh, who has written a *Eurydice*, an *Antigone*, and a *Medée*. Anouilh's achievements are an important extension of the modern drama, and his exemplification of the success of the method has a considerable bearing on future developments.

In *Antigone*, which appeared in 1944, the characters of the myth appear in their own right, but the myth is used as a form of expression of contemporary experience. This does not mean that the myth is offered as an analogy of the times, although it would be possible to construct such a relation. It is not the analogy which is important, but the form, and the experience which the form embodies.

Antigone is played in "a neutral setting", which indicates the purpose of the use of the myth. Its most striking achievement is its easy adoption of conventions which stem from the Greek drama, and their flexibility in terms of the modern stage. The play begins with all the characters on the stage, in an informal group. Prologue detaches himself from the group, and steps forward:

Voilà. Ces personnages vont vous jouer l'histoire d'Antigone.

It is as easy and confident as that, and yet immediately the whole necessary convention for the dramatic method of the play is established. Immediately, Prologue is able to accomplish all the necessary exposition of characters and situation. He points out the various characters of the group:

Antigone, c'est la petite maigre qui est assise là-bas, et qui ne dit rien. Elle regarde droit devant elle. Elle pense. Elle pense qu'elle va être Antigone tout à l'heure. . . . Il n'y a rien à faire. Elle s'appelle Antigone et il va falloir qu'elle joue son rôle jusqu'au bout. . . . Et depuis que ce rideau s'est levé, elle sent qu'elle s'éloigne à une vitesse vertigineuse de sa sœur Ismene, qui bavarde et rit avec un jeune homme, de nous tous, qui sommes là bien tranquilles à la regarder, de nous qui n'avons pas à mourir ce soir.

The convention, both of commentary on the various characters in turn, and of establishment of the play and the characters as action and parts which begin "now that the curtain has risen", is very impressive. By the end of Prologue's speech, the audience has been firmly introduced to the conventional nature of the play, and also to each of the characters:

Cet homme robuste, aux cheveux blancs, qui médite là, près de son page, c'est Creon. . . .

Ce garçon pâle, là bas, au fond, qui rêve adossé au mur, solitaire, c'est le Messager. . . . Il n'a pas envie de bavarder ni de se mêler aux autres. Il sait déjà. . . .

—and to the situation:

Et maintenant que vous les connaissez tous, ils vont pouvoir vous jouer leur histoire. Elle commence au moment où les deux fils d'Oedipe, Etéocle et Polynice, qui devaient régner sur Thèbes un an chacun à tour de rôle, se sont battus et entre-tués sous les murs de la ville. . . .

Prologue steps back out of sight, the characters leave the stage, the lighting changes, and the persons of the play begin to enter, each in his turn in the course of the action. It is very simple, and completely convincing. It gains an immediate dramatic concentration, and the conditions of intensity; it also provides the major resource which the naturalist drama has lacked, that of commentary. Prologue has begun this; it will be continued by Chorus, who enters at several points in the action to continue the form. Not the least of the achievements of this method is that it restores to the dramatist major control of the form of his play.

The main events of the play are foretold by the device of commentary. This is a deliberate choice with reference to the play's nature:

C'est propre, la tragédie. . . . Dans le drame, avec ces traîtres, avec ces méchants acharnés, cette innocence persécutée, ces vengeurs, ces terre-neuve, ces lueurs d'espoir, cela devient épouvantable de mourir, comme un accident. On aurait peut-être pu se sauver, le bon jeune homme aurait peut-être pu arriver à temps avec les gendarmes. Dans la tragédie, on est tranquille. D'abord, on est entre soi. On est tous innocents en somme! Ce n'est pas parce qu'il y en a un qui tue et l'autre qui est tué. C'est une question de distribution. Et puis, surtout, c'est reposant, la tragédie, parce qu'on sait qu'il n'y a plus d'espoir. . . .

The explicit rejection of the romantic drama only echoes the rejections, sixty years earlier, of Ibsen and Strindberg and Hauptmann. But now the rejection had found an alternative form: that is Anouilh's innovation in the prose drama, as it had been Eliot's innovation in *Murder in the Cathedral*.

The drama is played without intervals, and the central scene is the confrontation of Creon and Antigone, when Antigone has persisted in her attempts to bury her brother and has accordingly forfeited her life to the law. The scene is an intense realisation of the experience of choice:

> ANTIGONE: Moi, je n'ai pas dit "oui." Qu'est-ce que vous voulez que cela me fasse, à moi, votre politique, votre nécessité, vos pauvres histoires? Moi, je peux dire "non" encore à tout ce que je n'aime pas, et je suis seul juge. Et vous, avec votre couronne, avec vos gardes, avec votre attirail, vous pouvez seulement me faire mourir, parce que vous avez dit "oui."

As in *Murder in the Cathedral*, the form of the play is not a matter of abstract technical choice, but, in its certainty of what is to come, a finely operative context for the particular experience of choice which the action embodies. The intensity of the form is the intensity of Antigone:

> Nous sommes de ceux qui posent les questions jusqu'au bout.

The inevitability is the inevitability of Creon's conception of order. It does not matter to him which of the bodies lies rotting and which is buried in state; one must rot, so that the citizens may smell the end of revolt. This must be done, for order; the attempt to:

> conduire les hommes.

And Antigone must act as she does, for herself:

> CREON: Ni pour les autres, ni pour ton frère? Pour qui alors?
> ANTIGONE: Pour personne. Pour moi.

And thus the design of the characters and of the action is integral with the design of the play. Chorus enters at the end, reminding the audience of the "tranquillity" which has been enjoined throughout as the mood of watching.

> Et voilà. Sans la petite Antigone, c'est vrai, ils auraient tous été bien tranquilles. Mais maintenant, c'est fini. Ils sont tout de même tranquilles. Tous ceux qui avaient à mourir sont morts. Ceux qui croyaient une chose, et puis ceux qui croyaient le con- traire—même ceux qui ne croyaient rien et qui se sont trouvés pris dans l'histoire sans y rien comprendre. Morts pareils, tous, bien raides, bien inutiles, bien pourris. Et ceux qui vivent encore vont commencer tout doucement à les oublier et à confondre leurs noms. C'est fini. . . .

The dramatic method of *Antigone* is that of the pure legend, used as an objective correlative in the way defined by T. S. Eliot:

> a situation, a chain of events which shall be the formula of that *particular* emotion; such that when the external facts, which must terminate in sensory experience, are given, the emotion is immediately invoked.

The legend may, of course, be modified, as Anouilh has modified that of Antigone, in order that the "situation" and "chain of events" may express more exactly the particular emotion of the dramatist. This modification of the legend is often an interest in itself. In Sartre's *Les Mouches*, for example, it is Orestes' refusal of guilt, Sartre's modification of the legend, which is the main interest. But in Sartre's play one's attention is directed to the philosophical change, and the legend is not so much a *form* as a *case*. The philosophical interest is possibly considerable, but the play is an example of a gain in interest at the expense of intensity. The particular achievement of *Antigone* is the intensity of form, which controls and directs the language.

A great deal of the public attention to Anouilh has been directed to the philosophy of the plays: the particular concept of happiness, and the rejection of what is called in *Antigone* "l'espoir, le sale espoir." The mode of these attitudes to experience is very acceptable to some contemporary groups, and Anouilh, like Sartre, is being widely praised on these grounds. The emphasis is probably right with Sartre, who is fundamentally a melodramatist, and whose opinions are more interesting than the plays which express them. But with the Anouilh of *Antigone*, the emphasis seems to me to be quite wrong; it is the kind of mistake which was made, sixty years ago, with Ibsen. Anouilh's achievement is, like that of Ibsen, the achievement of a dramatist, and not of a philosopher.

Antigone is Anouilh's indisputable success. *Eurydice*, which appeared in 1947, is a different use of legend as form: legend re-created and modified into substantial contemporary terms. The method is even more interesting, but just as there was a decline in intensity in Eliot's similar movement from *Murder in the Cathedral* to *The Family Reunion*, so, it seems to me, is there a decline from *Antigone* to *Eurydice*. It is not the contemporary furnishing of scene and characters which is at fault; indeed this process has greater dramatic potentialities than that of the "pure legend" in a "neutral setting." But the necessary formal conventions, so easily assumed in *Antigone*, are never fully achieved in *Eurydice*; and the absence of Eliot's resource, a verse convention, comes to be felt in the language. The play seems to me to retain too many of the manners of naturalist drama to be able to achieve the intensity and precision which the use of the legend implies. It is, however, a notable experiment and the method is one which I am confident will be taken a great deal further, and with greater success. It is for this reason, even setting aside the outstanding achievement of *Antigone*, that the work of Anouilh seems to me to be the present "growing-point of consciousness" in modern prose drama.

PART II

W. B. Yeats

*The theatre began in ritual and it cannot come to its greatness
again without recalling words to their ancient sovereignty.*

(i)

YEATS fashioned a theatre, giving it life and direction; he
also wrote many plays. Today the theatre which he made
is only a memory, although its name lives for different ends, and
elements of its practice, in one place and another, persist. The
plays live as they always did.

Now Yeats's plays, certainly, are important in their own right;
yet it is still only at a second or third remove that we think of
him as a dramatist. Meanwhile, although the Abbey Theatre
would seem to have lost its distinctive literary purpose, and the
Irish dramatic movement to have yielded its birthright to the
romance of regional naturalism, the example of a theatre called
into being by a literary need is yet so rare, and the practical
discoveries of Yeats of such continuing importance, that they
seem to claim our primary attention. The plays and the
dramatic theories and practices spring, it is true, from the
same source; but their events do not altogether correspond.
Yeats's magnificent creative impetus formed the general
achievement; yet perhaps it will be found in the end that the
particular creation of the plays must properly be judged and
sustained by the wider effort in the theatre and in criticism.

(ii)

Yeats wrote in 1919:

We have been the first to create a true *People's Theatre* and we
have succeeded because it is not an exploitation of local colour,
or of a limited form of drama possessing a temporary novelty, but
the first doing of something for which the world is ripe, something
that will be done all over the world and done more and more

perfectly: the making articulate of all the dumb classes each with its own knowledge of the world.[1]

Certain of these phrases are by now over-familiar, although others—Yeats's rejection of the limited veins of regionalism and naturalism—are characteristic and brave. Since he wrote that judgment, many manifestoes, many reports to shareholders, have talked of a "People's Theatre." The distinction, and it is the important thing about Yeats, is that he saw his opportunity, not in the service of regionalism, not in the interest of a democratic abstraction, but in the *existence* of a living and organic society of Irish peasantry. A drama could be fashioned, not from an idea, but from a language:

> That idiom of the Irish-thinking people of the West ... is the only good English spoken by any large number of Irish people today, and we must found good literature on a living speech, seeing "the difference between dead and living words, between words that meant something years ago and words that have the only thing that gives literary quality—personality, the breath of men's mouths." Falstaff gives one the sensation of reality, and when one remembers *the abundant vocabulary of a time when all but everything present to the mind was present to the senses*, one imagines that his words were but little magnified from the words of such a man in real life.[2]

The social basis of his work, then, was:

> that conversation of the people which is so full of riches because it is so full of leisure, or ... those old stories of the folk which were made by men who believed so much in the soul, and so little in anything else, that they were never entirely certain that the earth was solid under the foot-sole.[3]

Yeats was committed, as any artist must be, to the actual and the contemporary; but elements of continuity in a society with which he had contact extended the immediacy of his experience with the content of a live tradition: his actuality avoided the ephemeral because it was thus sustained by a depth in time; his contemporaneity avoided drabness because it was continually re-creating an achieved richness. Yeats was, in any case, too intelligent to identify living drama with the processes

[1] *A People's Theatre.* Reprinted in *Plays and Controversies.*
[2] *Samhain*, 1904. Reprinted in *Plays and Controversies*, pp. 119-20.
[3] *Samhain.* 1904. *Plays and Controversies*, p. 123.

of naturalism. Here, for instance, is a particularly acute diagnosis:

> Of all artistic forms that have had a large share of the world's attention, the worst is the play about modern educated people. Except where it is superficial or deliberately argumentative it fills one's soul with a sense of commonness as with dust. It has one mortal ailment. It cannot become impassioned, that is to say, vital, without making somebody gushing and sentimental.[1]

This caused him explicitly to reject the new advanced drama:

> Put the man who has no knowledge of literature before a play of this kind and he will say as he has said in some form or other in every age at the first shock of naturalism: "Why should I leave my home to hear but the words I have used there when talking of the rates?"[2]

He called Ibsen—the Ibsen he knew from *Ghosts* and *Rosmersholm* and *A Doll's House*—

> the chosen author of very clever young journalists who, condemned to their treadmill of abstraction, hated music and style.

It was, one must be clear, the methods rather than the intentions of the free theatres with which he disagreed. He could write in 1903:

> We have to write or find plays that will make the theatre a place of intellectual excitement—a place where the mind goes to be liberated as it was liberated by the theatres of Greece and England and France at certain great movements of their history, and as it is liberated in Scandinavia today.[3]

It was representation, the strictly imitative fallacy, against which he set his powers. His protégé Synge could reject "pallid language" and yet largely retain the intentions of representation. Yeats went further: implicitly, he set his face against all those prejudices about the drama which had resulted from its domination by fiction, which was increasingly the only serious literary form. On the question of character, for example:

> One dogma of the printed criticism is that if a play does not contain definite character, its constitution is not strong enough for the stage, and that the dramatic moment is always the contest of

---

[1] *Discoveries*, 1906.   [2] *Discoveries*, 1906.
[3] *Samhain*, 1903. *Plays and Controversies*, pp. 45-6.

character with character. . . . When we go back a few centuries and enter the great periods of drama, character grows less and sometimes disappears. . . .[1]

Of his collaboration with George Moore, he wrote:

Because Moore thought all drama should be about possible people set in their appropriate surroundings, because he was fundamentally a realist . . . he required many dull, numb words. . . .[2]

and, more significantly:

He would have been a master of construction but that his practice as a novelist made him long for descriptions and reminiscences.[2]

The drama has suffered, and suffers, overmuch from this particular influence of the narrative-novel. *Minutiae* of surface personality, alleged detail of place and feature, the exposure of labels of "character", patient carpentry of the exterior illusion, preoccupation with theses and "problems": all these Yeats wished to reject, from a standpoint which was valid to him in his life and in his art:

We lose our freedom more and more as we get away from ourselves, and not merely because our minds are overthrown by abstract phrases and generalisations, reflections in a mirror that seem living, but because we have turned the table of value upside down, and believe that the root of reality is not in the centre but somewhere in that whirling circumference.[3]

(iii)

Poets throughout the century before Yeats had made attempts upon the drama, and one or two of them had tried to come to terms with the theatre. A further measure of Yeats's distinction may be drawn from examining the way he handled this eternally vexatious issue. Once and for all he would not listen to the chorus of producers and actors and their supporters inviting the dramatic poet to come into the theatre to learn his trade from them. In a period of theatrical anarchy he knew better than that; he was not a Tennyson willing to accept the patronage of an Irving. When actors and producers were

---

[1] *The Tragic Theatre*, 1910.   [2] *Dramatis Personae*, p. 63.
[3] *Samhain*, 1904.

required for the new plays, George Moore wanted to import a stock-company of English-trained artists, but Yeats would not agree. He had his own very definite ideas about presentation, and he was not willing to surrender them to the dogmas of the contemporary professional theatre. He discovered, by chance, a company of spare-time, amateur actors, working-men and women, led by two amateur producers, the Fays. By joining to their society the forces of the Irish Literary Theatre, he produced the organisation which was to become the Abbey Theatre. By experiment in service of a dramatic idea, rather than by imitation of past theatrical habits, a new method of presentation was evolved, much of which remains of permanent importance—though it has effected no wide change—today.

It was not that Yeats was opposed to the theatre; a dramatist could hardly be that; but he believed the first condition of significant achievement to be the restoration of the "ancient sovereignty" of words, and that required a theatre in which language should not be subordinate, as throughout the Victorian theatre it had been, to spectacle or the visual elements of acting. So we find him writing:

> I think the theatre must be reformed in its plays, its speaking, its acting, and its scenery. . . . There is nothing good about it at present.[1]

But although Yeats was unwilling to accept the domination of the theatre, he valued drama too much to be able to withdraw from its practice and presentation. With the Fays' company he found something of what he wanted:

> They showed plenty of inexperience . . . but it was the first performance I had seen since I understood these things in which the actors kept still enough to give poetical writing its full effect upon the stage. I had imagined such acting, though I had not seen it, and had once asked a dramatic company to let me rehearse them in barrels that they might forget gesture and have their minds free to think of speech for a while. The barrels, I thought, might be on castors, so that I could shove them about with a pole when the action required it.[2]

He was not prepared to tolerate that element of distraction from the words of the play which forms so large a part of

---

[1] *Samhain,* 1903.
[2] *Samhain,* 1902. *Plays and Controversies,* p. 20.

modern acting (of course with most modern plays one understands why the distraction is necessary), nor that more obvious
distraction which is the work of the stage designer:

> The poet cannot evoke a picture to the mind's eye if a second-rate
> painter has set his imagination of it before the bodily eye.[1]

Starting from such general principles, he learned as he went
along, and was always prepared to experiment, with his plays
as with the presentation, for new dramatic effects. All the time
he was seeking a realised drama which should have the status
of poetry, a rich and penetrating form which should reveal,
not character, but those deeper forces of which character is
merely a lineament. Like Strindberg, he hated the large
mechanical theatre, with its intricate apparatus of illusion. Of
his *At the Hawk's Well* he wrote:

> My play is made possible by a Japanese dancer whom I have seen
> dance in a studio and in a drawing-room and on a very small
> stage lit by an excellent stage-light. In the studio and in the
> drawing-room alone, where the lighting was the light we are most
> accustomed to, did I see him as the tragic image that has stirred
> my imagination. There, where no studied lighting, no stage-
> picture made an artificial world, he was able . . . to recede from us
> into some more powerful life. Because that separation was achieved
> by human means alone, he receded, but to inhabit as it were
> the deeps of the mind. One realised anew, at every separating
> strangeness, that the measure of all arts' greatness can be but in
> their intimacy. All imaginative art remains at a distance, and
> this distance once chosen must be firmly held against a pushing
> world. Verse, ritual, music and dance in association with action
> require that gesture, costume, facial expression, stage arrange-
> ment must help in keeping the door. Our unimaginative arts are
> content to set a piece of the world as we know it in a place by itself,
> to put their photographs, as it were, in a plush or plain frame, but
> the arts which interest me, while seeming to separate from the
> world and us a group of figures, images, symbols, enable us to pass
> for a few moments into a deep of the mind that had hitherto been
> too subtle for our habitation. As a deep of the mind can only be
> approached through what is most human, most delicate, we
> should distrust bodily distance, mechanism, and loud noise.[2]

---

[1] *Samhain*, 1904. *Plays and Controversies*, p. 134.
[2] *Certain Noble Plays of Japan*, 1916.

(iv)

The virtue of Yeats's intention was its opposition to the artificial narrowness of theme which the practices of naturalism seemed to predicate; he wished the drama once again to rest on human integrity, and in particular to attend to those deeper levels of personality which it has been the traditional interest of literature to explore.) The question, turning to his practice, which has to be asked, is the measure of his own distance from the "pushing world." One is concerned, that is to say, with the nature of his withdrawal. The issue is most clearly raised in a passage like this:

> If the real world is not altogether rejected, it is but touched here and there, and into the places we have left empty we summon rhythm, balance, pattern, images that remind us of vast passions, the vagueness of past times, all the chimeras that haunt the edge of trance. . . .[1]

As Mr. Leavis has commented—on another sentence—

> "Reverie" and "trance" are dangerous words;

and Mr. Leavis has gone on to formulate this judgment of Yeats as playwright:

> His resolute attempt upon the drama serves mainly to bring out the prepotence of the tradition he started in. His plays repudiate the actual world as essentially as his incantatory lyrics and his esoteric prose repudiate it. . . . A drama thus devoted to a "higher reality" of this kind could hardly exhibit the dramatic virtues. . . . Mr. Yeats the dramatist, that is, remains the poet who had "learned to think in the midst of the last phase of Pre-Raphaelitism."[2]

Perhaps of many of Yeats's plays one accepts Mr. Leavis's judgment, although it would in any case be difficult to accept the way in which it is put. An "essential . . . repudiation" of the "actual world" is a severe thing to urge against any writer; and the tone of the remark causes one to infer that it is the lack of correspondence with "the natural order" which is the basis of complaint. What the judgment would seem to amount to is that Yeats's spiritual insights were a fraud, and that lack of

---

[1] *The Tragic Theatre*, 1910.   [2] *New Bearings in English Poetry*.

contact with the "actual world" (a phrase as open and questionable as "higher reality") proscribes the "dramatic virtues." One wishes that Mr. Leavis had gone further, demonstrating his judgment on the plays (it is from a few chosen sentences of Yeats, which could be at least balanced by other chosen sentences, that he argues; not from any text). For it would have been useful to have had an informed discussion of the relation of the "dramatic virtues" (which, again, one would like to see some account of) to the degree of abstraction from actual life upon which any dramatist decides. One might take the two earliest plays: *The Countess Cathleen* and *The Land of Heart's Desire*. From the latter one would take some such line as:

Her face is pale as water before dawn

and remark the relation to late Victorian poeticism. But could one go on to reject even these two early plays as undramatic? *The Land of Heart's Desire* is concerned with the conflict between the love of man and the love of the "old Sidhe." This is reduced to the simple story of the spiriting away of Mary, the conflict for her soul between, on the one hand, priest and husband, on the other, the fairy child. Now it is not because it is undramatic that the play fails, nor because it attempts the realisation of a spiritual theme. It fails for the general reason which Mr. Leavis has urged against the early Yeats, an inheritance of stock poetic objects and manners which disintegrates the achievement of representation of the impulse towards the Sidhe. Of this supernatural we are told little more than that

—the faeries dance in a place apart,
Shaking their milk-white feet in a ring,
Tossing their milk-white arms in the air. . . .

That this element is characteristic of the early Yeats, and that it deprives *The Land of Heart's Desire* of serious validity, is certain. But there was always more to Yeats than that. As early as 1904 he himself wrote the best criticism of the play in question:

It has an exaggeration of sentiment and sentimental beauty which I have come to think unmanly. The popularity of *The Land of Heart's Desire* seems to me to come not from its merits but because of this weakness.[1]

[1] *Samhain*, 1904.

And with the earlier play, *The Countess Cathleen*, he had already achieved more than anything in the dramatic-poetic tradition which he had inherited. The form of the play is the re-creation of an old legend, and this might perhaps be taken as immediate proof of the poet's withdrawal into "unreality." But the legend is in fact used, in the full dramatic sense, for the direct realisation of an actual and contemporary experience. Yeats's account of the play's genesis is relevant:

> At first, if it (the play) has psychological depth, there is a bundle of ideas, something that can be stated in philosophical terms. My *Countess Cathleen* for instance was once the moral question: may a soul sacrifice itself for a good end? But gradually philosophy is eliminated until at last the only philosophy audible, if there is even that, is the mere expression of one character or another. *When it is completely life it seems to the hasty reader a mere story.*

This distinct moral preoccupation, which is satisfactorily realised in the play, makes it impossible to describe Yeats's use of the legends of the heroic age as "withdrawal from the actual world." The play is not more than minor, but for its date it is a noteworthy achievement. The incantatory verse of *The Land of Heart's Desire* (which it is interesting to note Yeats cut severely for performance—one wishes the pruning had taken place even earlier) has little in common with the quite successful verse of *The Countess Cathleen*:

> CATHLEEN: There is a something, Merchant, in your voice
>   That makes me fear. When you were telling how
>   A man may lose his soul and lose his God
>   Your eyes were lighted up, and when you told
>   How my poor money serves the people, both—
>   Merchants, forgive me—seemed to smile.
>
> FIRST MERCHANT: I laugh
>   To think that all these people should be swung
>   As on a lady's shoe-string—under them
>   The glowing leagues of never-ending flame.

This is not verse of any great intensity, but it is specifically dramatic in kind.

Through almost all the plays which Yeats wrote up to the time when he adopted the form of the Play for Dancers run certain particular themes, and the greater part are centred on the communication of a spiritual insight, the realisation of a vision of the transcendental. In one aspect this takes the form of the poet-plays, where the act of poetry itself is the foreground of the drama. Thus in *The Shadowy Waters* the poet Forgael says:

> I can see nothing plain; all's mystery.
> Yet sometimes there's a torch inside my head
> That makes all clear, but when the light is gone
> I have but images, analogies,
> The mystic bread, the sacramental wine,
> The red rose where the two shafts of the cross,
> Body and soul, waking and sleep, death, life,
> Whatever meaning ancient allegorists
> Have settled on, are mixed into one joy.

To cast these images into dramatic form is Yeats's particular endeavour; and the effort would have been formidable even within a valid dramatic tradition. Yeats's measure of success very naturally varies. *The Shadowy Waters*, in both of its versions, has moments of tenacity, and its ending, where Forgael gathers round him the hair of Dectora, is impressive:

> Beloved, having dragged the net about us,
> And knitted mesh to mesh, we grow immortal;
> And that old harp awakens of itself
> To cry aloud to the grey birds, and dreams,
> That have had dreams for father, live in us.

But the play as a whole has certain major defects. In a sense they are those of which Yeats spoke when he wrote:

> When I began to rehearse a play I had the defects of my early poetry: I insisted upon obvious all-pervading rhythm.

The rhythm of the action, particularly at the climax between Forgael and Dectora, is over-simple, almost naïve; it is a bad guess at the rendering of dream. The similar celebration of the poet in *The King's Threshold* has an emotional uncertainty and stridency which suggests that the form is perhaps too near the experience to allow of adequate dramatic moulding. The story of the poet who will not eat until the ancient right of poets to sit at the council table has been restored contains perhaps too much—and the wrong elements—of that "pushing world" which is the self. One notes about the play's method an attempt at movement from dialogue to ritual incantation (a technical problem with which Yeats was to continue to grapple and which Eliot was to take up after him) in the chant of the mayor, the old servant and the cripples; but the device serves little more than its own ends, it is not absorbed into the structure of the drama. Of more immediate promise was the evidence of a lively prose speech, Yeats's drawing on the source of vitality in Irish peasant speech from which Synge was drawing his comedies. The small prose plays *Cathleen ni Houlihan* and *The Pot of Broth* are little more than anecdotes, but the latter particularly has a freshness of contact with words which was one of the forces which modified and overcame Yeats's excesses of romanticism. In *Deirdre* there is considerable dramatic success, both in design and speech. One can work back from the brevity of *Deirdre* to a realisation of one of Yeats's intentions in the drama at this time. From the legend, which Synge was to handle in traditional narrative form, he isolates the climax, and from this even he excludes all that can be excluded of conflict and suspense. The play is a lament, a surprisingly consistent abstraction from the play of character and action which is our most familiar form and for which the legend has obvious material. The musicians fulfil the function of a chorus; and within their narrative, which continually leaps forward to the known end with presage of disaster, the persons of Deirdre, Naoise, Cuchulain and Fergus move as if to their appointed places for the final dramatic instant, *the tableau which is the insight*. When Naoise has been killed Deirdre prepares the climax:

Now strike the wire and sing to it a while,
Knowing that all is happy and that you know
Within what bride-bed I shall lie this night,
And by what man, and lie close up to him,
For the bed's narrow, and there outsleep the cock-crow.

The musicians provide the choric commentary:

1ST M: They are gone, they are gone. The proud may lie by the proud.
2ND M: Though we were bidden to sing cry nothing loud.
1ST M: They are gone, they are gone.
2ND M: Whispering were enough.
1ST M: Into the secret wilderness of their love.
2ND M: A high grey cairn. What more is to be said?
1ST M: Eagles have gone into their cloudy bed.

It is for these particular realisations that Yeats strives, a process of continuing refinement of the normal material of drama until the final moment of insight is physically reached. And by insight one does not mean the discovery of anything which could be formulated outside the terms of art. Yeats's search is for pattern. The meaning of *Deirdre* may perhaps be found in the earlier song:

> Love is an immoderate thing
> And can never be content
> Till it dip an ageing wing
> Where some laughing element
> Leaps, and Time's old lanthorn dims.
> What's the merit in love-play,
> In the tumult of the limbs
> That dies out before 'tis day,
> Heart on heart or mouth on mouth,
> All that mingling of our breath,
> When love-longing is but drouth
> For the things come after death;

where the theme is the traditional identity of love and death as a moment outside time, a moment when the torch burns. Yeats is working continually to express this in words; but his parallel effort takes for material the physical stage, and already he is using elements of formal grouping (which were also prominent in *The King's Threshold*) as a means of precise communication. This is an element which had been suppressed in the drama for very many years, and Yeats was to bring it back, in his later work, to intensity.

The most interesting and successful play of this middle period is *On Baile's Strand*, where a word-structure of a particular kind is discovered which Yeats will use again and again. There are formal visual elements—the masks of beggar and fool; but the important conventions are verbal, of chorus and of dramatic metaphor. The outer circle of the play is in the conversation of the Fool and the Blind Man, which is in prose. This conversation accomplishes a skilful exposition, but Fool and Blind Man are more: their incapacities, their energy for deceit and restlessness and vexation, make them the proper setting for the restlessness among the kings which drives Cuchulain to the slaughter of his own son, and then to an insane fight with the sea. In this play Yeats achieves an end for which all important drama in this century has sought, the interpenetration of different levels of reality in an integral and controlled structure. From the outer circle of Blind Man and Fool the play

tightens to the verse in which the tragedy is prepared. Through
the altercation moves a chorus of women, and as Cuchulain
goes out to kill against his instinct, they speak:

> I have seen, I have seen.
> What do you cry aloud?
> The Ever-Living have shown me what's to come.
> How? Where?
> In the ashes of the bowl.
> While you were holding it between your hands?
> Speak quickly!
> I have seen Cuchulain's rooftree
> Leap into fire, and the walls split and blacken
> Cuchulain has gone out to die.
> O! O!
> Who would have thought that one so great as he
> Should meet his end at this unnoted sword.
> Life drifts between a fool and a blind man
> To the end, and nobody can know his end.

And the play moves outward again to the fighting of Blind Man
and Fool, with the noise of the fight to the death of Cuchulain
and his son as background. Cuchulain re-enters and wipes the
blood from his sword with the Fool's feathers; it is the Blind
Man who reveals that the man he has killed is his son. As
Cuchulain runs fighting into the sea, the beggars continue
their thievery.

For its date, *On Baile's Strand* is a remarkable achievement,
and one on which Yeats and others were to build. Among
other facts, one notes the assurance of Yeats's handling of his
legendary material: the outer and inner circles of the play
might be described as the movement from the present and
actual into the living past, and also as the movement from
the lively speech of the poet's countrymen to an authentic
poetry. There was to be very little more romanticism about
the "dim far-off times": what was living from tradition was
to be taken into the present to provide depth for present
analysis. It is a measure of Yeats's increased assurance that he
was able in 1910 to write *The Green Helmet* and to use the
material and manners of his serious drama as a basis for farce.
He has himself described the change:

> To me drama . . . has been the search for more of manful energy,
> more of cheerful acceptance of whatever arises out of the logic of

events, and for clean outlines, instead of those outlines of lyric poetry that are blurred with desire and vague regret.[1]

This was clearly related to changes in certain radical attitudes. One may observe these changes clearly in such a play as *The Unicorn from the Stars* (a later version of *Where there is Nothing*):

MARTIN: I thought the battle was here, and that the joy was to be found here on earth, that all one had to do was to bring again the old wild earth of the stories—but no, it is not here; we shall not come to that joy, that battle, till we have put out the senses, everything that can be seen and handled, as I put out this candle. We must put out the whole world as I put out this candle. We must put out the light of the stars and the light of the sun and the light of the moon, till we have brought everything to nothing once again. I saw in a broken vision, but now all is clear to me. Where there is nothing, where there is nothing— there is God!

This effective theatrical speech loses much of its power in its actual context: *The Unicorn from the Stars* is the nearest thing Yeats wrote to the conventional modern prose play, with its solid material setting for the communication of a particular spiritual experience. More successful is *The Hour-Glass* (which exists in prose and verse texts) where the form is that of a morality or, more exactly, of an interlude. The Wise Man has taught:

There is nothing we cannot see, nothing we cannot touch.

but in the moment before death he acknowledges God's will:

We perish into God and sink away
Into reality—the rest's a dream.

But he is saved from obliteration (as was Peer Gynt) by the faith of the Fool, the only person whose faith has not been destroyed by the Wise Man's rationalism.

It is in a special sense only that it is possible to argue that Yeats "repudiates the actual world"; and I do not think it is possible to argue at all that his experience involves the sacrifice of the "dramatic virtues." For the experience was that which refined his verse and which made him a great poet. To assume that he ended where he began, a slave to sentimental poeticism,

---

[1] *Discoveries*, 1906.

is to ignore the evidence. And the search for dramatic form was a particular refining agent: the discovery of a way to write drama in verse again.

Nor has any poet I have read of or heard of or met with been a sentimentalist. The other self, the anti-self or antithetical self, as one may choose to name it, comes to those who are no longer deceived, whose passion is reality.[1]

(v)

Yeats claimed that his Plays for Dancers were a new art form, and in one sense this is true. They represent an intensification of particular elements of drama which, in the modern period, have been suppressed or minimised, and which it has been the function of verse drama—whether that of Yeats or of Eliot or of such experimenters as Rosenberg—to re-create. These elements were present in Yeats's work before the particular form of the dancer-plays, and have been already remarked: isolation of particular moments from their actual context; physical realisation through verbal and visual design. The five plays are all short. The brevity depends, as Mr. Ronald Peacock has put it, on an "acute judgment of what the method will stand."[2] Yeats's own description of *At the Hawk's Well*, quoted above, could not be bettered as a description of intention. As to method, one remarks the great beauty of the design of such plays as *At the Hawk's Well*, *The Only Jealousy of Emer*, and *Calvary*. The masked musicians are a dramatic tour-de-force: they serve, variously, the purposes of prologue, chorus and orchestra; in *The Cat and the Moon* the first musician speaks for the invisible saint. And the design of the plays is not merely visual. In each case the song, which accompanies the folding and unfolding of the cloth which mark the beginning and end of the play, provides an image which is at the centre of the action into which the play then moves. The most obvious example is that of the heron in *Calvary*; but there are the withered leaves choking the well in *At the Hawk's Well*; the "white fragile thing" of *The Only Jealousy of Emer*; the "fantastic dreams" in a "cup of jade" in *The Dreaming of the Bones*; implicitly the cat and the moon in the play of that name. The plays achieve what dramatists so unlike as Strind-

[1] *Anima Hominis.*   [2] Essay in *The Poet and the Theatre.*

berg and Eliot had demanded; intensity, and disciplined statement. It is doubtless easy to dismiss them as "unreal", to be
glad (as Mr. Peacock is glad) when the homely accents of Irish
peasants can be heard once more as in *The Cat and the Moon*.
But this is perhaps to surrender to naturalist preconceptions
which have blunted our capacity for this kind of experience.
At least, in view of the ancestry of the form (which is not only
the *Nōh* plays of Japan but also the dramatic methods of early
Greek plays and of many of our pre-Elizabethan and even
Elizabethan works) it is to be hoped that no one will press the
charge that they lack the "dramatic virtues."

> Why do you stare like that?
> You had that glassy look about the eyes
> Last time it happened. Do you know anything?
> It is enough to drive an old man crazy
> To look all day upon these broken rocks,
> And ragged thorns, and that one stupid face,
> And speak and get no answer.
>
> Why does my heart beat so?
> Did not a shadow pass?
> It passed but a moment ago.
> Who can have trod in the grass?
> What rogue is night-wandering?
> Have not old writers said
> That dizzy dreams can spring
> From the dry bones of the dead?
> And many a night it seems
> That all the valley fills
> With those fantastic dreams.
> They overflow the hills,
> So passionate is a shade,
> Like wine that fills to the top
> A grey-green cup of jade,
> Or maybe an agate cup.

The verse is not uniformly successful, and is perhaps always
of a higher quality in the songs. But Yeats is concerned with
dramatic *recital* rather than with dramatic representation.
There was much to be done before the inherited narrative
blank-verse became again fully dramatic. Perhaps that task
is not even yet nearly complete. But of the *Plays for Dancers*

it may be said that they first showed poetic drama to be possible again in our century.

(vi)

Yeats's prodigious capacity for development is well known, and many of the experiments of his latest years retain great interest. *The Resurrection* is an expansion of the dancer-play in other interests; it retains much of the beauty of the form, but includes new elements of discussion and celebration. *The Herne's Egg* is an entertaining play with literary affinities to that aspect of *Nōh* technique which Yeats had adopted in his dancer-plays; definition by a single metaphor—here by the herne's egg and the donkey.

Purgatory achieves the old end of physical realisation of a moment of insight, but without obvious stylisation: there is complete isolation of the moment against the scene of a ruined house and a bare tree. The verse has the fine power of Yeats's latest years:

> They know at last
> The consequence of their transgressions
> Whether upon others or upon themselves;
> Upon others, others may bring help,
> For when the consequence is at an end
> The dream must end; upon themselves
> There is no help but in themselves
> And in the mercy of God.

The dancer-play is further varied in *The Death of Cuchulain*, written in 1939, the year of Yeats's death. The mockery of the prologue—spoken by a "very old man looking like something out of mythology"—is succeeded by the isolation of Aoife and Cuchulain, and by the blind man taking the king's head, and Emer dancing in the shadow of the Morrigu. It is "antiquated romantic stuff", but it is alive on the lips of a singer at a contemporary Irish fair, with the eternal question:

> Are those things that men adore and loathe
> Their sole reality? . . .
> What comes out of the mountain
> Where men first shed their blood
> Who thought Cuchulain till it seemed
> He stood where they had stood.

For oneself at least it is necessary to decide whether Yeats's work in the theatre or the actual achievement of the plays is the more important. The latter ought always to be highly regarded, but the former may bear greater fruit. For the moment it is sufficient to acknowledge that he has given us both energy and achievement. Within limits that he set himself, he restored to words "their ancient sovereignty" in the drama.

2
T. S. Eliot

(i)

MR. ELIOT'S creative work in the drama is small in quantity; it is also, one hopes, unfinished. As yet, there are the three major plays—*Murder in the Cathedral*, *The Family Reunion*, and *The Cocktail Party*; the important fragments of *Sweeney Agonistes*; and, though it cannot really be said to count, *The Rock*. On these few works a radical innovation in the European drama has been based, and recognition of their quality and influence is general. Assertion of the importance of Eliot's dramatic experiments, which for some people and in several places and not so long ago was a minor crusade, is now an established and metalled road of pilgrimage. The change is partly due to a recognition of the achievement itself; it is perhaps even more due to "the *susurrus* of popular repetition", and to the perhaps final act of contemporary literary faith, commercial success. In any case, strict critical assessment of the achievement, in the context of modern dramatic development as a whole, is particularly necessary. The plays are no longer isolated successes, but the beginning of a movement; we must try to see where Eliot's influence is taking the drama. Moreover, even the small body of the work contains a wide variety, both of method and of success; the time for proclamation of the work as a manifesto is past; we must be concerned now with precise distinctions and discriminations. The present essay is concerned to review Eliot's plays as experiments in a new dramatic form; to offer some conclusions as to relative success and failure, with regard to performances as well as to texts; and to estimate the degree of gain and its relation to modern drama as a whole.

(ii)

The essentially dramatic nature of Eliot's early verse has been sufficiently demonstrated in the criticism of F. R. Leavis and others. It is only necessary here to recall that this dramatic quality may be seen in three important elements: first, in the attention to a dramatic rather than a prose structure, which may be seen very well in *The Waste Land*; second, in the dramatisation of a consciousness, the dramatic realisation of a mind, to be seen in *Prufrock*, in the Sweeney poems, in *Gerontion*; and, third, in the experiments with dramatic speech, such as the following:

> You do not know how much they mean to me, my friends,
> And how, how rare and strange it is, to find
> In a life composed so much, so much of odds and ends
> (For indeed I do not love it . . . you knew?, you are not blind!
> How keen you are!)
> To find a friend who has these qualities,
> Who has, and gives
> Those qualities upon which friendship lives. . . .

These elements, in the shorter poems, represent, in addition to their particular success, experiments in the two major problems of dramatic technique which Eliot had defined in his criticism: the discovery of "how people of the present day would speak, if they spoke verse", and the discovery of a—

> form to arrest, so to speak, the flow of spirit at any particular point before it expands and ends its course in the desert of exact likeness to the reality which is perceived by the most commonplace mind.

Eliot's first specific experiment in drama, *Sweeney Agonistes*, is known to us only in fragments; and its major importance is its experiment in speech rather than in form. *The Fragment of a Prologue* and *Fragment of an Agon* were designed, Eliot tells us, as part of "an Aristophanic melodrama." The most important formal experiment was to be in the creation of varying levels of consciousness, so that there should be—

> one character whose sensibility and intelligence should be on the plane of the most sensitive and intelligent members of the audience; his speeches should be addressed to them as much as to the other personages in the play—or rather, should be addressed to the latter, who were to be material, literal-minded, and visionless, with the consciousness of being overheard by the former.

Sweeney himself answers to this description; he is carefully shown to be aware of the problem of communication:

> I gotta use words when I talk to you.

He is, moreover, the essential pattern of the action, himself the "meaning" of the play. But in the fragments as we have them, this form is largely inferential; it would have very little clarity if it were not pointed by elements outside the play, the keys of the epigraphs. Orestes' phrase from the *Choephoroi*:

You don't see them, you don't, but *I* see them.

—is a statement of the experience which separates Sweeney and gives him the formal status described above. The sentence from St. John of the Cross embodies a judgment of the whole action and of Sweeney himself. But the fragments are incomplete, not only in themselves, but in their considerable dependence upon these external written aids. Sweeney is a fragment of the Orestes experience, and *Sweeney Agonistes* is a brilliant dramatic aside on the contemporary context of such experience. But it is probable that the fragments will be remembered as important, not for this creation, but for the experiments in language. A form is discovered, not so much in characters and action, and not in any conclusive way in a pattern of experience, but rather in an inclusive ordering of speech. It is in the success of rhythms like these that *Sweeney Agonistes* marks such a notable advance:

DORIS: There's a lot in the way you pick them up.
DUSTY: There's an awful lot in the way you feel.
DORIS: You've got to know what you want to ask them.
DUSTY: You've got to know what you want to know.

SWEENEY: I tell you again it don't apply.
Death or life or life or death,
Death is life and life is death.
I gotta use words when I talk to you,
But if you understand or if you don't,
That's nothing to me and nothing to you.
We all gotta do what we gotta do.

SWEENEY: That's what life is. Just is
DORIS: What is?
What's that life is?
SWEENEY: Life is death.

After such an achievement, although limited by its existence in fragments, Eliot's next experiment in drama is disappointing. *The Rock*, which is described as a pageant play, was written for a charity performance, and Eliot received much collaboration. One would perhaps like to think that his prefatory dis-

claimer of full responsibility is substantial rather than merely
polite; there is indeed a fleeting tone of irony in the courtesy.
But one's surprise is not that he retains only a joint responsibility, but that he retains any. The worst thing in the "book of
words" is the prose dialogue of the modern workmen. In
speeches like—

> . . . people is still born very much the same. There's some new
> notion about time, what says that the past—what's be'ind you—is
> what's going to happen in the future, bein' as the future 'as
> already 'appened. I 'aven't 'ad time to get the 'ang of it yet; but
> when I read about all those old blokes they seems much like
> us . . .

—the hand is the hand of Eliot, but the voice is the voice of Sir
Arthur Pinero and of the Robertson of *Caste*. The tradition is
not the vitality of the popular music-hall, which Eliot had
acknowledged, but rather the debility (a patronising humani-
tarian "charity") of *Punch*.

The verse choruses are more important. The writing of the
final Chorus on a base of the *Gloria* of the Mass is a significant
presage of the success of *Murder in the Cathedral*. There is a
brilliant dramatic movement in verse like the following:

The Soul of Man must quicken to creation.
Out of the formless stone, when the artist united himself with stone,
Spring always new forms of life, from the soul of man that is
　　joined to the soul of stone;

and:

In our rhythm of earthly life we tire of light.
　　　　　　　　　　　　　　　　We are
　　glad when the day ends when the play ends; and
　　ecstasy is too much pain.
We are children quickly tired: children who are
　　　　　　　　　　　　　　up in the
　　night and fall asleep as the rocket is fired;
　　and the day is long for work or play.
We tire of distraction or concentration, we sleep
　　and are glad to sleep,
Controlled by the rhythm of blood and the day and
　　the night and the seasons.
And we must extinguish the candle, put out the light
　　and relight it;
Forever must quench, forever relight the flame.

But these are isolable passages of intensity, drawing attention to themselves rather than to any total form in the work as a whole. In deference to the received temporal sequence of the pageant play, there is no integral creation of form. The incompleteness permits an enormous variation of level, and the corruption of "the past—what's be'ind you" comes to dominate. *The Rock*, indeed, is a case of "versifying the drama", for local effect; Eliot's substantial work was to move in a quite different direction, towards the discovery of a dramatic method which should have the status of poetry.

(iii)

Murder in the Cathedral is Eliot's most assured dramatic success. It has a completeness which springs from the perfect matching of material and form; and a certainty of communication which depends on the use of a living convention of action and speech. A play written for performance in a cathedral, which explicitly invites the collaboration of its audience in the celebration of the martyrdom of an archbishop, assumes the inheritance of Christian ritual so easily that we are likely to overlook the actual process of the convention. A continuity of traditional form was available to the poet because of the subject of the play, and Eliot exploits this continuity to great effect. It is not simply that the story of the martyrdom of Becket was already almost universally known, although this strengthened the invitation to participation. The use of traditional form is most important as an assured convention for both speech and action.

The best dramatic conventions are usually those which the audience do not recognise as conventions; which they accept and assume so completely that their participation is immediate. The chorus, for example, is one of the most difficult conventions to establish in modern drama. Where it is based simply on a lost tradition it has to fight against its own unfamiliarity. Eliot uses the chorus in *Murder in the Cathedral* in part according to Greek practice, as an expository device:

> Seven years and the summer is over
> Seven years since the Archbishop left us,
> He who was always kind to his people.

If he had had to depend on this function, it is doubtful whether he could have established any substantial degree of communication. But the function is merged in a larger method, for which the tradition still lives; the chorus becomes a link between ritual and believers; chorus is choir, the articulate voice of the body of worshippers:

> Forgive us, O Lord, we acknowledge ourselves as type of the
> common man,
> Of the men and women who shut the door and sit by the fire. . . .
> We acknowledge our trespass, our weakness, our fault; we
> acknowledge . . .

The dramatic possibilities of this function of the chorus may have been suggested to Eliot by the Greek drama, but the dramatic realisation is in terms of the Christian ritual, the accepted, familiar relationships of priests, choir, and congregation. Thus a convention of choral speech, which is of great dramatic value, not only is not an unfamiliar barrier, but is the actual convention of participation. The convention is more; it is the actual form of the play. It embodies one of the principal dramatic movements, from the early—

> For us the poor there is no action,
> But only to wait and to witness—

through the median—

> In our veins our bowels our skulls as well—

to the final—

> . . . the blood of the martyrs and the agony of the saints
> Is upon our heads—

a movement from passivity to surrender to participation.

This is one element of the ritual tradition, and it is powerfully reinforced by the use of verse rhythms based on Christian hymns, as here on the *Dies Irae*:

> The agents of hell disappear, the human, they shrink and
> dissolve
> Into dust on the wind, forgotten, unmemorable, only is here
> The white flat face of death, God's silent servant.

The formal language is acceptable because of its context and its familiar rhythms, and this acceptance extends itself to the degree of formalisation in the language of the play as a whole. There are other structural elements which permit dramatic experiment while appearing familiar to the audience. Here, for example, is an exchange of dialogue based on the responses:

> SECOND PRIEST: Your Lordship will find your rooms in order as you left them.
> THOMAS: And will try to leave them in order as I find them.

The sermon, a familiar and natural form of direct address, gives the dramatist a convention for soliloquy, which, in any other terms, might have been impossible.

The action of the play has great formal beauty of design, but it is not a design that has to be imposed on the audience; it is a formal movement, a succession of balances, which springs naturally from the fundamental relationships within the ritual. It is indeed "a form to arrest the flow of spirit" and to communicate it; but its design does not seem contrived, because the audience is from the beginning within the formulation. Its correspondences are as clear as those of a morality play, and similarly acceptable; for both depend upon the same originating form within the church.

The verse of the choruses is an obvious success. Its movement is an exciting realisation of a kind of dramatic experience which the theatre had entirely lost:

> Here is no continuing city, here is no abiding stay.
> Ill the wind, ill the time, uncertain the profit, certain the danger.
> O late late late, late is the time, late too late, and rotten the year;
> Evil the wind and bitter the sea and grey the sky, grey, grey, grey.
> O Thomas return, Archbishop; return, return to France.
> Return. Quickly. Quietly. Leave us to perish in quiet.
> You come with applause, you come with rejoicing, but you come bringing death into Canterbury:
> A doom on the house, a doom on yourself, a doom on the world.

> We do not wish anything to happen.
> Seven years we have lived quietly,
> Succeeded in avoiding notice,
> Living and partly living.

The most important dramatic advance of verse of this kind is that language reasserts control in performance. The problem of performance is the application of these rhythms, within which all the visual elements of performance are contained and prescribed. This is perhaps Eliot's most important general achievement. There is the same control over character. The persons

are individualised so far as is necessary, but they are contained
by the total pattern. The device of character permits a full
communication of consciousness, because speech is not limited
to representation, but is made fully articulate within the
dramatic form:

> They speak better than they know, and beyond your under-
> standing.
> They know, and do not know, what it is to act and to suffer.
> They know, and do not know, that action is suffering
> And suffering is action. Neither does the agent suffer
> Nor the patient act. But both are fixed
> In an eternal action, an eternal patience
> To which all must consent that it may be willed
> And which all must suffer that they may will it,
> That the pattern may subsist, for the pattern is the action
> And the suffering, that the wheel may turn and still
> Be forever still.

The achievement of *Murder in the Cathedral* is dramatic
pattern, a pattern which "is the action." Only at times is this
completeness threatened, perhaps most notably in the Sermon
and in the speeches of the Knights. In the Sermon, when one
comes to phrases like these—

> A martyrdom is always the design of God, for His love of men, to
> warn them and to lead them, to bring them back to His ways. It is
> never the design of man . . .

—one feels that the "meaning" which they bear is perhaps a
crude addition to the fully dramatic communication which is
the total action. It is natural self-explanation by Becket, and
natural exposition; but it lacks the intensity of the play as a
whole. Similarly, the speeches of the Knights to the audience
can be theoretically justified, as a dramatic device to indicate
the speciousness of their reasoning; and the tone is an
interesting variation in the movement of the play. But there is
a distinctly Shavian element of "knowing comedy" which
seems to me essentially sentimental.

Yeats criticised the play adversely on the grounds of lack of
clarity in the creation of Becket; this was surely a defect of
reading, induced perhaps by his antipathy to the theme.
Another criticism, made by Mr. Ronald Peacock, suggests that
the historical context should have been made more plain. But
the centre of the play is not the particular death of Becket; the

death serves as an expression of the permanent experience of martyrdom. When Yeats complains that "nowhere has the author explained how Becket and the King differ in aim" he is becoming involved in a similar distraction from the essence of the play—which is the "design" of martyrdom, in favour of incidental political elements in its context. "I cannot find that the Bishop played any such prominent part in the struggle between the King and the Earl as Ibsen assigned to him", wrote William Archer of *The Pretenders*. It is strange to find critics sympathetic to poetic drama falling into the same blunder, confusing history with a situation that defines an experience. The concentration on Becket, so that everywhere he dominates the play, either by direct presence or in the words of others, is an inevitable dramatic choice. And the context of the martyrdom is similarly set aside, as the drama tightens:

> It is not in time that my death shall be known;
> It is out of time that my decision is taken
> If you call that decision
> To which my whole being gives entire consent.
> I give my life.

It is in this very concentration that *Murder in the Cathedral* is dramatically important. I have suggested certain minor reservations, on the Sermon and on the speeches of the Knights; and I would add a recurring doubt about the explicit relation of Becket's martyrdom to the contemporary situation of the Church. This relation is made with great tact and persuasion, but it is made, it seems to me, in dramatic error. Its sensibility is finer than Shaw's similar process in *Saint Joan* (a play which may very profitably be compared with *Murder in the Cathedral*, as an example of the superiority of Eliot's dramatic form); but it has something of the same "vicious rhetoric", a form of didacticism which perhaps proceeds from a faulty relation between dramatist and audience. The triumph of Eliot's use of the liturgy as a basis of convention concealed within itself this real danger; and I do not think that he entirely avoided it. But one is entering here the difficult country between poetry and belief; and one's judgments are subject to curious obliquities. I retain my sense of this local failure in the play; but even so, and with the other minor reservations, I take *Murder in the Cathedral* as a very great dramatic achievement. It is the best example in the years I have been considering of the discovery of an adequate form for serious drama.

(iv)

The Family Reunion, if not a wholly new start, is a different kind of success. In theme it is related to *Murder in the Cathedral* and, very closely, to *Sweeney Agonistes*. Its difference is indicated in one sense by the label which it has acquired: "a drama of contemporary people speaking contemporary language." The persons of the play, with the important exception of the Eumenides, are certainly contemporary; they are, moreover, characters of the contemporary drama, in distinction from the characters of *Sweeney Agonistes*, whose only near modern relations are the figures of the comic strip. The phrase "contemporary language" is similarly true, but it must not be taken as an antithesis to Eliot's earlier work, for the language of *Murder in the Cathedral* is triumphantly contemporary, in spite of its dependence on traditional forms. Once again, the phrase is best understood in relation to the contemporary drama; in the lower reaches of *The Family Reunion* the small talk (and this is the innovation) is our own.

The scenes of *The Family Reunion* are the familiar drawing-rooms of naturalism. The persons of the play include several "everyday, insignificant characters", such as it was Ibsen's creed and novelty to introduce. These elements are framework rather than structure, however; the play draws a measure of initial acceptance from the familiarity of its surface; from its resemblance, indeed, if I am not mistaken, to the average detective play. But there is a further relation to naturalist method, and particularly to Ibsen. The close-knit family drama; the *incidental* revelations of certain aspects of character; the development through retrospect, so that the present is continually deepened to include the past: these are manners inherited, directly or indirectly, from Ibsen; and perhaps also from the novel. The drama has moved out of the church, and the former continuity and contact is not available. New links have to be forged.

The critical issue is raised sharply by these now notorious lines:

What's the use of asking for an evening paper?
You know as well as I do, at this distance from London,
Nobody's likely to have this evening's paper.

Mr. Martin Turnell commented in *Scrutiny*:
The great dramatic poets of the past wrote their works in verse

because verse could do something which prose could not. Mr. Eliot's choice of verse, however, seems to have been prompted merely by the belief that poetic drama is a good thing and ought to be encouraged. "Contemporary language" can hardly be transposed unchanged into a verse-form; it only becomes effective when it is deliberately stylised as it was in *Sweeney Agonistes*.

The point is important, and it is a pity that Mr. Turnell's formulation is so careless. His first sentence is a somewhat curious version of the past relations of prose and verse; his second sentence is surely "making a sneer do the work of a demonstration." More important, the *unchanged* of the last sentence is grossly unfair to *The Family Reunion*; (how, in any case, is *language* changed in such circumstances?). Yet one could indeed make an anthology of passages from the play, of similar apparent vapidity. No proper critical conclusion could be drawn from them, however, for it is the total verse-form that is important in the play, and everything must be judged as an element of that total form.

Consider an example from the first scene:

> The younger generation
> Are undoubtedly decadent
> The younger generation
> Are not what we were. Haven't the stamina. . . .

This minutely stylised deadness is very characteristic of Eliot's earlier work, and indeed of *Sweeney Agonistes* itself. The organisation of different kinds of statement may be seen very well in an exchange of this kind:

> GERALD: That reminds me, Amy,
> When are the boys all due to arrive?
> AMY: I do not want the clock to stop in the dark.
> If you want to know why I never leave Wishwood
> That is the reason. I keep Wishwood alive
> To keep the family alive, to keep them together.
> To keep me alive, and I live to keep them.
> You none of you understand how old you are
> And death will come to you as a mild surprise
> A momentary shudder in a vacant room.
> Only Agatha seems to find some meaning in death
> Which I cannot find.
> —I am only certain of Arthur and John,
> Arthur in London, John in Leicestershire:
> They should be here in good time for dinner.

The sudden deepening of level with the first line of Amy's speech is the test of Eliot's essential organisation. The verse-form of the whole play must be such that it can, when necessary, be intensified into the statement of a complex experience, while retaining its affinity with the verse of ordinary conversation through which the audience is led into the play. It is a form designed to express the interpenetration of different levels of reality; not merely as a dramatic device, but because this inter-penetration is the condition of experience of the play as a whole. The passage I have quoted seems to me successful in its aim, and it succeeds very largely because the transition of level is not consciously pointed by the author. When attention is drawn to the transition, there is dislocation, because the uncertainty of the convention is revealed. Here, for example:

> AGATHA: When the loop in time comes, and it does not come for
> everybody,
> The hidden is revealed, and the spectres show themselves.
> GERALD: I don't in the least know what you are talking about.
> You seem to be wanting to give us the hump.

This play for laughter as a smooth transition from what is deemed too great an intensity is of the same order as Mr. Granville-Barker's:

> Now shall we finish the conversation in prose?

or Mr. Denis Johnston's:

> Here endeth the first lesson.

There are several such manipulations of tone in *The Family Reunion*, typified perhaps in Aunt Violet's conscious play with the audience:

> I do not understand
> A single thing that's happened.

The failure is perhaps a theatrical timidity, an uncertainty of the audience's acceptance of the convention, so that a need is felt to offer reassuring explanations in naturalist terms. It is a serious corruption of a possible form. When Harry and Agatha, after virtual soliloquies, ask:

> What have we been saying?

the effect is perhaps right; but the interpenetration of levels is most successful when Eliot is confident of his convention, and offers no explanation. When one is launched into a form of this kind, the middle of the play is no place to express technical hesitations.

This kind of failure is what might be expected of Eliot's attempt to come to apparent terms with the methods of the naturalist theatre. Within the total form which he has attempted, the attraction of certain of the superficial elements seems to have been too great. The policeman, for example, is a rather weary caprice, although it is doubtless assumed that the audience will be reassured by having the familiar figure around. Similarly, the chauffeur's exposition of the death of Harry's wife involves an over-familiar piece of business:

You know it is just my opinion, sir,
That his lordship is rather psychic as they say.

It is the familar comic exercise, the *Punch* tradition; a character in the shadow of Mr. Forster's Leonard Bast and Mrs. Woolf's sudden insensitive charwomen. The fault is partly social, a very real corruption of the common language. More relevantly, it is part of the general anxious reassurance of the audience; and the question is not whether the audience is in fact reassured, but whether such reassurance helps the communication of the play. Comic episodes may serve communication, by setting the central experience in relief (it is in this sense that the serious use of comic relief is best understood); they may also, like Mr. Eliot's policeman, simply distract. The experience of *The Family Reunion* is revelation, but the coincidence of the word does not demand that this should involve character-revelation of the familiar naturalist kind. The "inside stories" of the newspapers are revelations, and for spiritual autobiography of the special interview variety one does not need the talent of an Eliot.

I shall have to stay till after the funeral.
Will my ticket to London still be valid?

This is one of Eliot's theatrical aunts; and while it is an amusing appeasement of certain appetites of the contemporary theatre, it is the kind of thing which blurs the significant communication of the play.

The problem which faces the critic is of deciding whether these things are mere blemishes, a minor residue of confusion as to means; or whether they are local indications of some more fundamental disharmony in the play. Harry's experience is the search for redemption, which cannot come while he flies from the pursuing Eumenides, but only when he recognises them and their significance. This he is able to do, with Agatha's help, in a moment of illumination when the past of himself and his family becomes realised in the present. In this revelation his guilt is transformed; the Furies will not continue to pursue him, but he, instead, will—

follow the bright angels.

The series of events which Eliot has created to embody this experience is generally adequate; but there is sometimes the sense of the form being fitted, as a secondary process, to the already realised experience. This is the foundation of the otherwise irrelevant criticism of the uncertainty of the nature of the wife's death; and it is also the reason why Harry's emotions are larger than the facts offered to account for them. Some part of this difficulty is inherent in the nature of the experience, which is of a kind in which the demand for explanatory facts and motives is not valid. But the difficulty is too persistent to be dismissed with a gesture towards the "incommunicable." For one has, as it happens, an immediate basis for comparison, in the *Four Quartets*. The central experience of the poems is similarly "incommunicable", but in fact, in each of the poems, and perhaps particularly in *The Dry Salvages*, there is a convincing achievement of finely resolved emotion beside which *The Family Reunion* pales. The organisation of the *Four Quartets* as a whole is, moreover, an essentially dramatic achievement with a perfect fitting of experience and form. The uncertainties of *The Family Reunion* are a striking contrast with this, and they point the difficulty of the compromise with the theatre.

The Family Reunion, by the general standards of contemporary drama, is nevertheless a success, although limited. Its greatest positive achievement is in certain scenes, of which the middle scene of Part Two is perhaps the best sustained example. If you take a "great scene" from some prose play—say that between Ella and Gunhild in Ibsen's *John Gabriel Borkman* (a play which has certain affinities with *The Family Reunion*)—you will find, when you compare the two, that it is not only Eliot's language which is finer, but that in Eliot the emotions of the drama itself are more intense and more precise. It is in such local achievements that the potential greatness of the dramatic method is most clearly seen, and in the richness and flexibility of such dramatic speech as this:

> Not yet. I will ring for you. It is still quite light.
> I have nothing to do but watch the days draw out,
> Now that I sit in the house from October to June,
> And the swallow comes too soon and the spring will be over
> And the cuckoo will be gone before I am out again.
> O Sun, that was once so warm, O Light that was taken for granted
> When I was young and strong, and sun and light unsought for
> And the night unfeared, and the day expected
> And clocks could be trusted, tomorrow assured
> And time would not stop in the dark.
> Put on the lights. But leave the curtains undrawn.
> Make up the fire. Will the spring never come? I am cold.

(v)

Ten years separated *The Family Reunion* and *The Cocktail Party*, and the new play was awaited with more than ordinary interest. Mr. Eliot's influence was very considerable, and his choice of method was almost certain to have important effects. He might have returned to the deliberately formal pattern of *Murder in the Cathedral*, which had been his most complete success; or he might continue with the experiment of using current theatrical forms and trying to raise them to the status of poetic drama by the use of a flexible overall verse convention, as he had done in *The Family Reunion*. His choice, as we now know, was the latter. *The Cocktail Party* almost entirely abandoned even those elements of ritual which had been retained in *The Family Reunion*: the use of an occasional chorus, of interspersed lyrics, and of "runic" recital. The chorus of *The Family Reunion* had not been very satisfactory: the verse was adequate, but the formal convention depended upon a sudden change of function by the aunts and uncles, who had been set in a deliberate comic characterisation and were required suddenly to become agents of a formal commentary; this was not easy to accept. The lyrics had been used to express certain of the moments of illumination; a good example is given to Mary, beginning:

> I believe the moment of birth
> Is when we have knowledge of death.

The "runes" had been used as a formal ending to each part,
spoken by Agatha:

> Round and round the circle
> Completing the charm
> So the knot be unknotted
> The crossed be uncrossed
> The crooked be made straight
> And the curse be ended.

Unlike the lyrics, the placing of these passages had made
transition into conversational speech unnecessary, and for this
reason they were more successful. This is the only formal device
of the kind retained in *The Cocktail Party*; it is used in the liba-
tion near the end of Act Two:

> ALEX: The words for those who go upon a journey.
> REILLY: Protector of travellers
> Bless the road.
> ALEX: Watch over her in the desert
> Watch over her in the mountain
> Watch over her in the labyrinth
> Watch over her in the quicksand.
> JULIA: Protect her from the Voices
> Protect her from the Visions
> Protect her in the tumult
> Protect her in the silence.

With this exception, *The Cocktail Party* uses no formal devices
which are not already familiar from the average prose play.
Its main formal device is the overall verse convention.

The verse of *The Cocktail Party* is similar in function to that of
The Family Reunion, with its capacity for sudden change of level
from light conversation to conscious statement:

> EDWARD: Celia? Going to California?
> LAVINIA: Yes, with Peter.
> Really, Edward, if you were human
> You would burst out laughing. But you won't.
> EDWARD: O God, O God, if I could return to yesterday
> Before I thought that I had made a decision.
> What devil left the door on the latch
> For these doubts to enter? And then you came back, you
> The angel of destruction—just as I felt sure.
> In a moment, at your touch, there is nothing but ruin.

The function is similar to that in *The Family Reunion*, but the quality of the verse is very different. In the first place, the verse of conversation, particularly at the beginning of the play when the measure needs to be established, is very closely stylised, in the manner of *Sweeney Agonistes*:

PETER: I like that story.
CELIA: I love that story.
ALEX: *I'm* never tired of hearing that story.
JULIA: Well, you all seem to know it.
CELIA: Do we all know it?

or, again:

JULIA: The only man I ever met who could hear the cry of bats.
PETER: Hear the cry of bats?
JULIA: He could hear the cry of bats.
CELIA: But how do you know he could hear the cry of bats?
JULIA: Because he said so. And I believed him.

The device is obvious in print, but in speech it is virtually an unconscious form, since the repetitions on which the rhythm depends are normal elements of conversation.

The second, and more important difference in the verse of *The Cocktail Party* is that it is always, at every level, *statement*, of a deliberate lucidity, and with the minimum of imagery and evocation. In *The Family Reunion* the speech of Harry and Agatha is full of the characteristic imagery of Eliot's general poetry: the corridor, the footfall, the door opening into the garden. The words:

—have often a network of tentacular roots, reaching down to the deepest terrors and desires.

In *The Cocktail Party* the language is never, or hardly ever, of that kind. It is verse of the surface, although not superficial. It is conscious, lucid statement, with a generality which is quite unlike the normal verse of *The Family Reunion*. Here, for example, is a speech which will illustrate the change:

EDWARD: No—not happy; or, if there is any happiness,
Only the happiness of knowing
That misery does not feed on the ruin of loveliness,
That the tedium is not the residue of ecstasy.
I see that my life was determined long ago
And that the struggle to escape from it
Is only a make-believe, a pretence

That what is, is not, or could be changed.
The self that can say "I want this—or want that"
—The self that wills—he is a feeble creature.
He has to come to terms in the end
With the obstinate, the tougher self; who does not speak
Who never talks, who cannot argue;
And who in some men may be the *guardian*—
But in men like me, the dull, the implacable,
The indomitable spirit of mediocrity.
The willing self can contrive the disaster
Of this unwilling partnership, but can only flourish
In submission to the rule of the stronger partner.

The third and fourth lines of this speech are in the recognisable manner of *The Family Reunion* and of much of Eliot's poetry, but the dominant tone in the passage is surely something quite different; it is the deliberate, contained statement to which I have referred. It is a very remarkable achievement, for it is both eminently speakable and also the instrument of complete precision in the expression of feeling. This distinct manner is the main strength of the play; it can be very widely exemplified from the best scenes, those between Edward and Reilly, Edward and Celia, Edward, Lavinia and Reilly, Reilly and Celia. However the play as a whole may be judged, this development of a flexible, lucid verse manner, based very closely on speech and yet capable of the greatest precision and distinction, is unquestionably a major achievement.

The speech of Edward which I have quoted provides one key to the theme of the play: the concept of the *guardian*. The play is concerned with the salvation, not of an individual, but of a group, and the elements of this salvation are the guardians Reilly, Alex and Julia. The word is certainly *salvation*, although for a considerable part of the play one could substitute *cure*. This double sense is an important element of the play, and it is this above all which has caused confusion in the judgments of the play which I have read and heard. The double sense is most clearly expressed in the character of Reilly, who is at once psychiatrist and confessor. Reilly's treatment of Edward and Lavinia is in the familiar psychiatric tone, even if it is never quite orthodox:

I learn a good deal by merely observing you,
And letting you talk as long as you please,
And taking note of what you do not say.

The cure of the delusions and dishonesties of Edward and Lavinia is a cure *within* society:

> . . . my patients
> Are only pieces of a total situation
> Which I have to explore. The single patient
> Who is ill by himself, is rather the exception.

What Reilly does is to bring Edward and Lavinia to knowledge of themselves and their situation, and to forward the process of reconciliation:

> The best of a bad job is all any of us can make of it.

Now this, although the honesty of the analysis is unusual in the contemporary drama, is familiar, and readily acceptable. It is when Reilly comes to deal with Celia that the objections begin to be made:

> The best of a bad job is all any of us can make of it,
> Except of course the saints.

Delusion, irreconcilability, have been seen with the others as part of the habitual mask; health lies in acceptance of the reality. But delusion must be carefully defined; Reilly says to Celia:

> A delusion is something we must return from.
> There are other states of mind, which we take to be delusion
> But which we have to accept and go on from.

This is Celia's case.

> CELIA: It's not the feeling of anything I've ever *done*
> Which I might get away from, or of anything in me
> I could get rid of—but of emptiness, of failure
> Towards someone, or something, outside of myself;
> And I feel I must . . . *atone*—is that the word?

This is not delusion, but:

> —a sense of sin.

It is, as Reilly comments, "most unusual."
Even this might be accepted without cavil, so long as

nothing is done about it. But Celia chooses, not the first way
of "cure", of reconciliation; but the second way, of atonement:

> REILLY: The first I could describe in familiar terms
> Because you have seen it, as we all have seen it
> Illustrated, more or less, in lives of those about us.
> The second is unknown, and so requires faith—
> The kind of faith that issues from despair.
> The destination cannot be described
> You will know very little until you get there;
> You will journey blind. But the way leads towards possession
> Of what you have sought in the wrong place.
> CELIA: . . . Which way is better?
> REILLY: Neither way is better.
> Both ways are necessary. It is also necessary
> To make a choice between them.
> CELIA: Then I choose the second.

The way of atonement need not necessarily lead outside society.
Some who have chosen it—

>   . . . lead very active lives
> Very often, in the world.

But Celia's way leads to isolation and to a terrible death.

Now this is an essential element of the play, and its terms,
it seems to me, are quite clearly stated. It has been frequently
said that Celia's motives are unsubstantiated, that the play
does not prepare us for her decision. It seems to me that this
criticism is a rationalisation, covering an essential antipathy to
the nature of her experience. "Making the best of a bad job"
is a familiar contemporary morality, and much of the play
has moved on this acceptable level. But Eliot seems to have
deliberately provoked the shock of Celia's experience and
decision and death. By making Reilly the guardian of those
who follow both ways, he has achieved, in the most striking
possible way, the realisation of a particular pattern of values.
It does not matter at all, in spite of the insinuations of the newspapers, whether this pattern is "new." It is a little late in
human experience to expect a brand-new "message" in every
serious play; the demand for such a thing is simply an incidental misunderstanding of naturalism. Eliot's basis of values
is not at all new, but it is—and here we return to the proper
material of criticism—both original and particular in its realisation. Celia's experience and decision, and Reilly's acceptance

of the consequence, are shown with great lucidity and power. It is the nature of the experience that has been commonly questioned; its realisation seems to me unquestionable. And the business of criticism, the process of the enjoyment of literature, involves such acceptance as the power of the play enjoins of the values on which it is based. To question the values in themselves is to leave literature behind, and to enter a no-man's land between literature and morality.

I have attempted to describe the success of *The Cocktail Party*, and would continue to insist on this success while making certain reservations. There does not seem to me to be any substance in the complaint and question that it was not realised in the theatre that the play was in verse, and so why was it in verse at all? The verse-form is of the kind which imposes its control at a level which is often below conscious observation. If you try to alter almost any line in the play, you lose something of this form, and the effect could never be the same. Eliot did not want the speech to be recognised as "poetry." [1] He succeeds so completely in this that he is able to make Reilly and Julia say, in verse:

REILLY: Do you mind if I quote poetry, Mrs. Chamberlayne?
JULIA: Oh no, I should love to hear you speaking poetry.

The joke is largely private; but the whole intention is that the audience should listen, not to "poetry", but to speech; the formalisation and intensification achieved by the arrangement in verse is primarily the poet's business. The difficulty, however, arises with the question of character. The other manners of the drawing-room play can be used without compromise; but the form normally involves the creation of characters in the usual theatrical sense: engaging personalities whose every incidental turn is noted. The essential pattern of *The Cocktail Party* is clear, but I find myself feeling that in the matter of this kind of character Eliot has been unable to escape a dangerous compromise. The writing of Julia in the early scenes, for example, seems to me to be too preoccupied by "character" in the theatrical sense, and to provide the wrong kind of "light relief." Much the same may be said of most of the minor characters, and of certain aspects of the most important characters. Eliot is working for acceptance by the theatre audience, and these are his means. It is a difficult question, and the phrase, the Theatre of Character, which

[1] See his answer to Question 9, *World Review*, November 1949.

Eliot has used in connection with *The Cocktail Party*,[1] might well be confusing. In saying that "we should turn away from the Theatre of Ideas to the Theatre of Character" Eliot is probably only saying what he has said before. When he says that "the essential poetic play should be made with human beings rather than with ideas" he is perhaps only emphasising the difference of level of experience which the poetic drama requires, a particularity and immediacy, in opposition to the abstract problems and theses of the naturalist drama. I do not wish to challenge his statement, but the phrase is capable of being misunderstood; and the element of "Character", in the sense of Strindberg's famous definition, complicates matters in *The Cocktail Party*. The point is vital, and the difficulty is best analysed in the context of the contemporary theatre, which is where the confusion has its seat. I have been considering Eliot's plays primarily as texts, with only incidental reference to performance; I now wish to consider some performances of the plays, as the final stage in my assessment.

(vi)

Sweeney Agonistes is a triumphant success in performance; the right degree of distortion is easily attained, and this form is brilliantly sustained by the integral pattern of the verse. *Murder in the Cathedral* is similarly successful. The formal scenes of Cathedral and Hall, and the conventional costumes of Archbishop, priests, and knights, assure an integral visual pattern which harmonises with the verse and experience of the play. The chorus, within this pattern, is completely acceptable; and its brilliant writing for movement controls the action perfectly. In both *Sweeney Agonistes* and *Murder in the Cathedral* the rhythms provide a clear direction of the actors' speech.

The performance of *The Family Reunion* is different. Mr. Martin Browne, whose production I saw, has written that the verse of the play "should impose its discipline naturally on the sensitive actor." I am disposed to agree, but one can only judge by results. It seemed to me that this discipline was only partially observed. Not only was much of the speaking deliberately naturalist in tone, but many habits of naturalist acting—and in particular the actors' consciousness of themselves as acting a "character"—were clearly evident. Gerald and Charles, for

[1] Answer to Question 12, *World Review*, November 1949.

example, were turned into character-studies of the usual kind, and played in character costume. The local effect is always pleasant, but the exaggeration tends to disintegrate the total form of the play. A more serious difficulty arose with the chorus. It is difficult enough at any time, in the contemporary theatre, to move from near-conversation into choral recital. But to pass from consciously "played" conversation, with its characteristic flicks and starts, to the required degree of formality seemed quite impossible. The aunts and uncles stepped into a self-conscious, rather solemn line, turned up their eyes, and recited. It was a very chastening spectacle. The appearance of the Eumenides presented a similar problem. I have no idea how they might convincingly be made to appear, but in the performance which I saw I became suddenly aware, beyond the window embrasure, of a constellation of green headlamps, or signal lights. I am prepared to do without Aeschylus' snakes, and I am aware of the diversity of all such manifestations; but this oddly glowing cluster beyond the curtains seemed to me a little short of adequacy.

I had read, and was familiar with, *The Family Reunion* before I saw its performance; and my general impression was that the uncertainty of convention which I believed I had observed in the text was deepened and emphasised on the stage. With *The Cocktail Party*, the order of acquaintance was, as it happened, transposed. I was very much impressed by the performance, but most of what I judged to be failure in it was in fact removed when I read the text. The level of speaking, for example, was very uneven in the performance. Mr. Alec Guinness, as Reilly, seemed to me to have achieved the exact balance of speech and statement which was required. But his success only emphasised the uncertainty of many of the other players. Julia, Alex, Peter, Lavinia spoke normally without that nuance of emphasis of the measure which Mr. Guinness had achieved with Reilly. Each of these characters seemed always suddenly surprised when they came upon something which did not flip and trip easily into likely conversation. Miss Irene Worth, as Celia, was very much more controlled; but she provided what is to me the most significant example of the difficulty. In her scene with Edward (Act One, Scene Two) she spoke beautifully, and with a completely assured measure corresponding to the verse. Now the emotions of Celia at that point were conveyed completely *by the words*. She had only to speak them for communication to be complete. But in fact, while she spoke, she also "acted"—

very well, as it happened—with her hands and body. The gestures of the hands were not controlled by the movement of the words, but by the movement of the general emotion. Now this is normal naturalist acting, but in this case, when the words were so adequate and so final, the essentially separate "acting" not only did not support the words, but actually distracted attention from them.

It is not a matter of criticism of individuals; the problem is supremely difficult. Everything that Mr. Martin Browne, whose production it was, has said on the matter has convinced me that he has a full understanding of the nature of the problem; and no one will pretend that the solution is easy. What matters, I think, is that the dramatist should limit the opportunities for distraction. Actors and producers will find a way of speaking appropriate to the verse, as they gain experience of the form; and the text will always be there, as a permanent control. But if the dramatist himself engages in diversion, control in performance will be impossible. It is in this sense that I think the "characterisation", in particular of Julia, is a limitation of *The Cocktail Party*'s success. It was very successful "theatre", while it lasted, but it confused the essential condition of the full communication of the play. Character is significant as a convention of expression; as incidental spectacle it is a relatively trivial device. The Theatre of Character and the Theatre of Ideas have, after all, lived in a willing and intimate union for seventy or eighty years; if we need a phrase for the kind of drama which Eliot is attempting to re-create we might speak of the *theatre of experience*.

Eliot cannot be said to have solved all the problems which arose from the decay of romantic drama and from the limitations of the naturalist drama which replaced it. But he has perhaps brought us to a point at which such a solution can be envisaged. It is a very considerable achievement, whatever the immediate future of the drama may be; and in its nature it is beyond the mode of praise.

Note: Mr. Eliot's important lecture, *Poetry and Drama*, was published while this book was in the press. He makes an even more strong case than I have done against the staged Eumenides, and I agree. For the rest, the lecture does not lead me to revise any of the opinions expressed in this essay; but as a contribution to theory, particularly in the *Hamlet* analysis and in the vital distinction of prose from talking, it is of great value.

Some Verse Dramatists

(i) Auden and Isherwood

OF all dramatic work that has received serious critical attention in this century, the three plays written in collaboration by W. H. Auden and Christopher Isherwood— *The Dog Beneath the Skin, The Ascent of F6,* and *On the Frontier*— are the most obviously related to a particular, unmistakable period: the middle nineteen-thirties in England. This fact has limited their more recent appreciation, but the plays have a more than temporary importance, and need examination as examples of a lively and influential form of verse drama.

Before the collaboration with Isherwood, Auden had written two dramatic pieces: *Paid on Both Sides,* and *The Dance of Death.* Certain features of the later plays are prominent in these experiments. In *Paid on Both Sides,* which the author calls a charade, there is the usual mixture of popular songs, slapstick, and serious intentions. As a whole, the piece is obscure; by what, one feels, is a deliberate act of will. Yet much of it is accomplished and original, and its dramatic possibilities are obvious. The achievement of *The Dance of Death,* however, is tenuous. In performance it was exciting to English audiences in its use of various expressionist techniques which are always well suited to satire; and it had much topical interest. More important now is that it was the first production of the Group Theatre, which was later to produce all the joint plays. The first of these was *The Dog Beneath the Skin,* which appeared in 1935.

What is most interesting in the three main plays is the use of mass cultural forms as a dramatic framework. *The Dog Beneath the Skin* opens in the manner of a musical comedy, and this atmosphere, sustained by the frequent songs and choruses in this deliberate manner, persists. And this element is undoubtedly the most successful in the play: the comic invention, though uneven, is frequently brilliant. Here, in the first scene, is the musical comedy technique operating as exposition:

IRIS: And here am I, Miss Iris Crewe,
   I live in Pressan Ambo too,
   The prize at village dances.
   From Honeypot Hall, the haunt of doves,
   In my blue Daimler and white gloves
   I come to take your glances.
CHORUS: With nose and ear and mouth and hair
   With fur and hat and things like that
   She takes our loving glances.

The tradition, of course, is that of burlesque (with a certain minor reference to the self-introduction of the characters in morality plays). And the question one comes to ask of it is to what degree the burlesque formula is used as a simple literary technique. For in the end, if you set out to burlesque a musical burlesque you find that you have written a musical burlesque.

But emphasis is distributed to certain other intentions. In the Chorus which precedes the first scene, we find a characteristic pattern. There is the satiric statement:

   Tourists to whom the Tudor cafés
   Offer Bovril and buns upon Breton ware
   With leather work as a sideline: Filling stations
   Supplying petrol from rustic pumps;

and the affirmative counter-statement:

   Man is changed by his living; but not fast enough.
   His concern today is for that which yesterday did not occur.
   In the hour of the Blue Bird and the Bristol Bomber, his thoughts
     are appropriate to the years of the Penny Farthing:
   He tosses at night who at noon-day found no truth.

One cannot now be blamed for finding this kind of verse, particularly as it appears in affirmation, rather thin. The seriousness has an inescapably casual air, or is as if thrown at one:

   The sky is darkening like a stain,
   Something is going to fall like rain,
   And it won't be flowers.

There remains another element of this play, which is, indeed, formally the central element:

For walk he must the empty
Selfish journey
Between the needless risk
And the endless safety.

The thematic intention of *The Dog Beneath the Skin* is, clearly, the Quest. A young man is elected and sent out in search of the missing baronet who would normally be head of the village:

Would he were here! We badly need him.

One of the rewards for success is marriage with the baronet's sister. Formally, this is close to the Fairy-Story Quest which Mr. Auden himself has recently described:

The rescue of the magical object, the marriage with the princess . . . are of benefit, not only to the hero himself, but to society as a whole; as long as the magical object is in the wrong hands the crops will not grow, the people are unhappy and their future is dark, for there is no heir to the throne.[1]

So the search for Sir Francis Crewe is easily identified with the search for a better society: even when Francis has been found, the Quest continues, led by him:

GENERAL (*shouting after them*): You're traitors to Pressan!
FRANCIS (*shouts back*): Traitors to *your* Pressan, General, not to ours!

The actual quest is, of course, non-individual: it operates, not towards "the centre of dreams", but towards a political commentary. If one seeks its real dramatic antecedent, one arrives at the fourth act of *Peer Gynt*. It is not so much that the mad scene in the English play is strongly reminiscent of the similar scene in the Norwegian, as that, in this part of *Peer Gynt*, and in *The Dog Beneath the Skin*, we find the same method and intention. The method is that of identifiable caricature; the intention topical satire. It seems impossible that the authors did not have Ibsen in mind, especially when the end of the play—the transformation of the respectable villagers into animal faces—provides a further important reminiscence (of *When We Dead Awaken*—"Just the dear old farmyard, Maia.")
Since Ibsen, of course, many new technical devices had been

---

[1] *K's Quest*, W. H. Auden; p. 47 in *The Kafka Problem* (ed. Flores); (New Directions; U.S.A.; 1946). There is more than a suggestion of Kafka in all the plays. The habit of pairs of attendants is perhaps coincidence.

discovered—particularly by Strindberg and the German expressionists—and some of these are effectively used (in, for instance, the animal transformation just referred to). And further, the authors' very considerable talent for comic verse makes the play much more lively than, in abstract, it sounds. Such scenes as those in the Nineveh Hotel (Act III, Scene 2), and especially the figure of Destructive Desmond, retain their brilliance. But everywhere, one feels, it is no more than a local success which is being registered. The play becomes a revue, and the choruses which are clearly intended to stabilise the many evaluations take on increasingly the character of a hectoring compère:

> But already like an air-bubble under a microscope-slide, the film of poverty is expanding
> And soon it will reach your treasure and your gentlemanly behaviour.
> Observe, therefore, and be more prepared than our hero.

And then the edges between scenes and choruses become ragged. One is confronted with passages like these:

(i) Men are falling through the air in flames and choking slowly in the dark recesses of the sea to assuage our pride. Our pride!

(ii) Sons, see your aged father who has taught you to reverence truth and purity: see him caught as the house collapses, his skull smashed like an egg before your eyes by a falling beam.

(iii) O lion, O sun, encompass me with power,
Feed lion, shine sun, for in your glory I flower,
Create the huge and gorgeous summer in an hour.

(iv) Where time flows on as chalk stream clear
And lovers by themselves forgiven
The whole dream genuine, the charm mature
Walk in the great and general light
In their delight a part of heaven
Its furniture and choir.
—To each his need: from each his power.

(v) Our sails are set. O launch upon love's ocean,
Fear has no means there of locomotion
And death cannot exhaust us with his endless devotion.

(vi) There you see! I knew it! You don't like me. None of them like me. Wherever I go I see it.

(vii) I was fascinated and horrified by you all. I thought such obscene, cruel, hypocritical, mean, vulgar creatures had never existed before in the history of the planet.

I think it would be difficult to estimate, from the tone of these passages alone, their respective intentions. About the first, a reservation has been made for the rhetoric, but the context clearly indicates that the intention is positive. Yet in what sense is it distinguished from the next extract, which is from the hysterical speech of the leader of Westland to the madmen? Similarly, the third and fifth extracts are spoken by the tailor's dummy in the seduction scene at the Nineveh Hotel; but the fourth, which lies between them without any clear disparity, is from the concluding chorus of the play and contains, presumably, the most positive note of all. The sixth extract is from the self-pitying sentimentality of the financier; but the seventh, which is irresistibly reminiscent of it in tone, comes from the final, and positive, speech of Francis. Whether its tone is not also the basis of the whole satire of the play is an open question.

The Ascent of F6, which appeared in 1936, is more substantial than either of the two other joint plays, and is probably the authors' most considerable achievement. Thematically, it has many links with *The Dog Beneath the Skin*. The central figure, the climber Ransom, is clearly involved, when he attempts the peak F6, in a kind of quest. And like the search for Francis, the ascent of F6 has more than individual, has also social, implications. Ransom is able to say near the end:

F6 has shown me what I am

and the general emphasis is on this kind of discovery, on self-knowledge. Yet the context of the ascent, beside having immediate political point, is also a search for the salvation of society. Ransom's final settlement with his mother and brother on the last stages of the ascent represents a highly individual experience; but at the same time the brother is the Dragon and Ransom the liberator.

Let the eye of the traveller consider this country and weep.

It is to end the despair of society that the liberator has also come.

The reward for slaying the dragon is normal:

The princess' cheek burns red for your love.

Ransom's reward, however, is also salvation, achieved through discovery of his mother, who is the demon-figure at the peak. The discovery is death and solitude.

In much of the play the authors are concerned with one of the main tasks of the serious dramatist—the creation of myth. Parts of this achieved work are valuable. Yet the limitation is certain, and proceeds from the attempt at universality, where significance is sought by the direct imposition of comment rather than by growth from within the dramatic body. And this tendency in the structure finds confirmation in the substance, where the process of experience is more often the exhibition of the label than any actual realisation.

Thus the ascent of the mountain is a convincing representation of Ransom's personal quest, and the mother-figure at the peak corresponds. But between the ascent and the summit lies the twin brother, and here the key changes, and he is the Dragon, with appropriate fairy-tale appurtenances. But he is more, he is imperialism; and F6 is political power. And in the political exploitation of the ascent—its transformation to commercial heroism—appears the theme of the scapegoat: the hero who vanquishes alike despair, and the varieties of desperation which are suburbanism: (here enters the clerk).

One is, of course, asked to believe that these are not different themes and different levels, but have an essential unity. The authors work with cross-reference to confirm this; but in the end it is perhaps only clever juggling. The tone of the work as a whole is strangely uncertain, even at times defensive. It is not easy to be certain whether one is watching a Dance of the Seven Veils or simple commercial strip-tease.

The popular parts of the play are clearly the comic verses, which are still interesting, although inferior to the comic invention of *The Dog Beneath the Skin*. The successful parts are a few isolated scenes; the early soliloquy of Ransom; the death of Gunn; the meeting of Ransom and the Abbot. It is perhaps significant that two of these are in prose.

Ransom's soliloquy, on the summit of Pillar Rock, is the first scene, and sets the substance of the tragedy:

"Deny not, to this brief vigil of your senses that remains, experience of the unpeopled. world behind the Sun". . . . One can picture

Ulysses' audience . . .; glad they must have been to believe it, during the long uneventful voyage westward: yes, even up to the very end, when the last deceptions were choked from each in turn by the strangling Atlantic.

This is the context of the quest, and the prophecy of its end, as again:

> Friends whom the world honours shall lament their eternal losses in the profoundest of crevasses, while he on the green mountains converses gently with his unapproachable love.

But the apparent search for Virtue and Knowledge can be represented as a mere search for power. With Ransom, this leads to a kind of reversal of rôles between himself and his political brother, so that in their final exchanges on the mountain each speaks the words the other had spoken at the beginning of the quest. Similarly, the mother had sought by withholding love to give Ransom the "power to stand alone." She won, but must ask herself—

> Was the victory real?

In the chess-game on the mountain, the Liberation provokes the same question:

> Was the victory real?

In the trial, Ransom and his mother seem identified, and are accused of spiritual pride and found guilty. With the verdict comes release:

> At last his journey ended
> Forgiven and befriended
> See him to his salvation come.

The various identifications only convince in their own right on one or two occasions: the rest receive merely abstract support. There is also a disturbing "knowingness", briefly represented in such *jeux* as the "psychrometer" which the climbers consult, and the mountain flowers with such names as Frustrax Abominum. This is all very much on the level of:

> The croquet matches in summer, the handshake, the cough, the kiss,
> There is always a wicked secret, a private reason for this.

DRAMA FROM IBSEN TO ELIOT

These general weaknesses are correspondingly revealed in much of the verse. The suburban couple chant:

> Moments of happiness do not come often,
> Opportunity's easy to miss.
> O, let us seize them, of all their joy squeeze them,
> For Monday returns when none may kiss;

and the passage slips by, amid the customary defensive irony, without much question. More seriously, at a climax of the play, there is this kind of bathos:

> Do you think that it was easy
> To shut you out? I who yearned to make
> My heart the cosiest nook in all the world
> And warm you there for ever, so to leave you
> Stark to the indifferent blizzard and the lightning?

Once again, the edges between distinct elements in the play become blurred; and just as fairy-tales or political satire are mixed with a serious individual theme, so are contrasting levels of poetry. It is not that the play is a welding of these diverse elements, which might well be to its credit; but that they seem to run together, each affecting the other, because of some fundamental uncertainty of control. So that in the serious statement of the mother, around the substance of which the play pivots, such a phrase as "my heart the cosiest nook in all the world", which would slip naturally into one of the comic lyrics or the satiric diversions, intrudes and destroys. It is the local indication of the more general failure.

Individual salvation, at the end of the quest, was at least conceivable to Auden and Isherwood; and according to the rules of their attitude this would imply social salvation also. What, in detail, this might be was less certain. Perhaps the choice was made when the first version of *On the Frontier*, which ended in a revolution and "the seizure of power by the people", was re-drafted into the inconclusiveness of a protracted civil war, and the lament:

> Will people never stop killing each other?
> There is no place in the world
> For those who love.

There have been many who have criticised this development on political grounds, and I do not wish to be involved in a complaint of that kind. More to the literary point is the implied

SOME VERSE DRAMATISTS

complaint of Mr. John Lehmann, in his *New Writing in Europe*.
He is writing of the period between *The Ascent of F6* and *On the
Frontier*:

> Auden and Isherwood seem to have felt the weight of criticism
> that gathered against their private allusions and the mystical
> High Church note of some of their speeches. . . . The next play at
> any rate is free of them.[1]

Mr. Lehmann, in this concealed judgment, is the spokesman
for "democratic simplicity." The judgment is in part justified:
there are obviously many private allusions in the earlier plays,
some of which are intractable to the uninitiated reader. But
when the complaint is bracketed with a complaint against the
"mystical High Church . . . speeches" one begins to see the
substance of Mr. Lehmann's opposition more clearly. For the
unmistakable implication is a complaint against allusions and
obscure poetry as such: it is the commonplace of complaint
against modern poetry, and particularly against the work of
Eliot. These things were to be purged in favour of the new
realism. Mr. Lehmann's attitude—and he is a representative
figure—is clear from his complaint elsewhere against the soliloquies of Ransom in *The Ascent of F6*, from which he concludes
that the "character" is a "super-prig whose solemn soliloquies
are a match for even the most elevated sermons of Bishops."
But if there is anything in the play which has the full assent of
the authors, it is surely the initial soliloquy of Ransom. But this
mystical business is not wanted: it introduces diversions from
the straightforward political exposition.

Mr. Lehmann is, of course, right in saying that *On the
Frontier* is simpler. The play is made up of political satire and a
minor descant on Love; it is the dullest work which the
collaboration produced. The substance is war and high
politics: it may be interestingly compared to "C. K. Munro's"
The Rumour. There are two or three lively episodes, but the
general interest seems to have gone, and we approach the
flatness of the living newspaper.

The phrase "living newspaper" leads us back to the important critical problem. The contribution which Auden and
Isherwood made was definite. They set a certain lively achievement against the monotony of character-revelation with which
the ordinary playwrights were concerned, and against the
constricting influence of naturalist stage practice. But what they

[1] *New Writing in Europe*, p. 70 (Penguin).

offered in its place, when the dust of the high jinks had cleared, was subject to limitations which, though different from those of orthodox naturalism, were equally fatal. By means of conventions which corresponded to the techniques of mass mechanical culture—the radio announcer, the loud-speaker, the pair of commentators, the headline, the slogan, the jazz-song—certain points about society could be forcibly made. A substantial part of each of the three plays could thus be described in the narrow sense as a living newspaper; certainly these parts share with newspapers their impermanence of interest. In *The Ascent of F6* the dramatic issue was joined, and the possibility of handling more serious experience in a fully dramatic way was apparent in one or two scenes. But the other interest appears to have been stronger. It is in the achievement of any adequate dramatic *integrity* that Auden and Isherwood failed. Whether or not this integrity would have been achieved, in the maturing of their collaboration, we cannot now say. But it is a matter for regret that such bold experiments, and such lively dramatic talents, should have been so limited in success, not only by the absence of adequate conventions, but also by the extraneous preoccupations of a strange decade.

(ii) *The Faber Dramatists*

The public movement in verse drama in recent years has been under the direction of Mr. Martin Browne at the Mercury Theatre; so that there is both a personal and an organisational link between these recent plays and the productions of Mr. Eliot's two works. Even if this were not so, the relation of plays like Mrs. Ridler's *Shadow Factory*, Mr. Nicholson's *Old Man of the Mountains*, and Mr. Duncan's *This Way to the Tomb* to what Mr. Eliot has written, and particularly to *Murder in the Cathedral*, would be clear. There are other affiliations, but this one, re-inforced by the Christian orthodoxy of the group, is dominant. It would not be just to assess the vitality of the new kind of drama which Mr. Eliot has fashioned by the work of these later writers. An author's responsibility for his imitators is rarely large; and significant influence does not often appear at such short notice as the recent movement has arisen. But the plays deserve analysis in their own right, as some partial estimate of an aspect of contemporary dramatic development.

It may often happen that a writer, encouraged to attempt

a verse play by the example of the achievement of some major poet, will, when he comes to that complex of technical difficulties which the theatrical form involves, draw, perhaps unconsciously, on quite different examples from those which he would formally acknowledge. In the present situation, naturalist prose drama, although discredited among a minority, remains the dominant theatrical form; and ideas of effect and content—fundamental issues of method—are more likely to be influenced by naturalist practices than by more isolated examples, unless the dramatic impulse of the writer is quite certain and first-hand. For of course it is quite possible to write a naturalist play in verse, even a play embodying the most advanced devices. The function of speech in some forms of verse seems to remain representational; even more important, the object of a play may be representational, and this will determine its texture, particularly its emotional texture, however formal its pattern may appear.

Now the first of the Mercury plays, Mr. Nicholson's *The Old Man of the Mountains*, is, as it happens, the most obviously naturalist of the three plays in question. For Mr. Nicholson, dramatic verse is limited to two functions: the setting of a scene; and direct address. The first is a natural and perhaps conscious consequence of what appears to be his main quality as a writer, a talent for the picturesque:

> The tarns lie black and still
> As pools of tar, with not a thread of weed,
> To blur the edges. Even the turf
> Is tight and brown as hide.

The landscape is Cumberland—a profitable comparison may be made with parts of *The Ascent of F6*—and the function of these scenes in the play is clear. Mr. Nicholson's other main employment of verse is in the speeches of the Raven, who, besides his part in the action, serves as a kind of prologue and chorus. Here, his debt to Mr. Eliot is most clear:

> Forgiveness does not mean
> Escape from consequence, but grace to face the consequence.
> You must learn slowly, with bony fingers
> Grubbing the soil. . . .

But there is perhaps no need to quote further; these rhythms are well enough known.

The body of Mr. Nicholson's play is a retelling of the story of Elijah in terms of a modern dale-farming community. At the heart of the play are the characteristic metaphors of water and rock: Elijah, the servant of God, brings water to parched land where the servant of Baal—Squire Ahab—had failed. What is interesting is that Mr. Nicholson builds on this framework a naturalist portrait of Cumberland dalesfolk. This seems his normal concern whether in the long intervals of prose dialogue:

> Mr. Obadiah or no Mr. Obadiah, don't you come and throw all *my* washing in the dirt like that. I'll give you one under the lug-hole if you do;

or in such passages as this:

> AHAB: That orchard now, behind Ruth's garden yonder, that is good land let waste. I'll have the bushes cleared and the dykes thrown down and the soil well ploughed again. We'll have a rare crop next year.
>
> RUTH: But Squire Ahab . . .
>
> AHAB: Soft fruit clogs the market like mud on cartwheels, and damsons are not worth the labour of picking.
>
> RUTH: But, sir, my apple trees . . . .
>
> AHAB: You can have them for firewood. I'll send you a barrel of apples—you'll not miss them.

The interesting thing is that this latter passage appears in the text as verse. And it is not only that the verse is flaccid, the arrangement in lines in a sense an affectation; but that the substance of the language is representational, as in any naturalist play. My own judgment is that this is true of the play as a whole. The inherited devices of verse drama, and the dominating legend, seem external to the actual content of the play. There is perhaps a refinement of prose drama, by the use of verse at some points; but there is little important development of the drama towards the *status* of poetry. And it is such development which seems necessary, and which is the importance of Mr. Eliot's work.

Mrs. Ridler's *The Shadow Factory* is described as a Nativity play. Its crisis is contained in a nativity performance in the canteen of a factory, the elements of which the writer has elsewhere in the play been concerned to analyse. The work is not naturalist in the sense that it represents a "life section", but its ancestry in the specifically twentieth-century problem play is clear. It is perhaps a personal preference, for which one must make allowance, that I find the matter of Mrs. Ridler's play more at ease with her formal pretensions and ancestry than I find the work of Mr. Nicholson or—as will appear—Mr. Duncan. Mrs. Ridler's play is almost entirely concerned with abstractions, but certain of the abstractions seem to have been directly felt. As a dramatic writer, however, her range as yet is extremely narrow. She has decided to use verse, but this does not lead to, does not follow from, any *dramatic* conception where the special functions of verse can be justified. The construction, the unmistakable atmosphere, of every scene is naturalist and representational. For long intervals she uses prose. She has written elsewhere:

> We are still far from having a tradition secure enough to lift the burden of perpetual choice of style from the poet's shoulders: a tradition in which he can deal with any kind of subject-matter without having recourse to prose.

But an important dramatic tradition is more likely to confer a choice of *subject-matter* than of style (from this fundamental selection the body of style is created). Mrs. Ridler sees that certain kinds of subject-matter have to go into a play; she selects her material according to particular preconceptions. The process then adopted, it appears, is the fitting of these varieties, where possible, to verse. It is in this sense that I would describe Mrs. Ridler's dramatic experiment as the versification of naturalist drama, just as Auden's experiments were. (I am using naturalist in what I take to be its basic sense of a root attitude to experience: in theatrical terms the models one would instance would be the expressionists.) Verse drama ought not to be, indeed cannot be, confined to the institution of verse dialogue. What demands dramatic speech at its highest intensity and control is a particular dramatic attitude which we can characterise as poetic. Mrs. Ridler's play might be related to the moralities; but it is nearer Galsworthy than *The Castell of Perseverance*, and not only because of its date. The first three scenes of *The Shadow Factory* amount to scientific naturalism with certain abstract ethical reservations. They are written in a mixture of loose verse and conversational prose, between which there seem only formal distinctions:

> "It's my wife, sir;
> She's—that is—we're having a child;
> Not just yet, but all the same
> It'll mean a lot of extra expenses.
> Next year I shall be due for a rise:
> I wondered if . . ."

I've been letting the batches accumulate and now Progress are chasing me. What I'd really like to do is to change the lay-out and make it Op. 2, but O.D. won't have that, so perhaps you . . .

The unfinished, the tentative, the inarticulate; these are the characteristics alike of Mrs. Ridler's prose and of much of her verse. One can see the difficulty she has recorded—the difficulty of "perpetual choice of style"; in such instances there is indeed nothing to choose. A dramatist will cease to have recourse to representational prose—or similar verse—when his material ceases to be representational. It is on the dominant naturalist tradition that Mrs. Ridler is still borne. In opposing this tradition Yeats and Eliot made experiment possible. But these fundamental aspects of the older poets' work are generally ignored; while the superficial achievements are everywhere imitated. As if by dogged conviction Mrs. Ridler attempts one scene—the last—of which parts might be poetic drama. In its context, the scene fails, because it is unattached, and because we are unprepared. In its substance it fails also, because Mrs. Ridler seems unprepared for writing of this kind, remaining constricted by the preconceptions of her dominant inheritance.

Of the three plays here discussed, Mr. Duncan's *This Way to the Tomb* is clearly the least original, although it has qualities of showmanship which have brought it a merited commercial success. The work is described as "a masque and anti-masque", with a reference to Jonson. I do not know that Mr. Duncan has anywhere claimed that he has in fact written a masque, although there has been the usual reviewers' gossip about "the revival of an ancient form." At all events, Mr. Duncan's masque has as little to do with that form as it is generally known as Mrs. Ridler's play with a morality or miracle. His experiment must be judged, that is to say, in its own terms.

Mr. Duncan's debt to Eliot is the kind of debt that jars. There has, of course, been a great deal of loose talk about the "followers of Eliot", which is often a stupid description. It is virtually certain, for instance, that any considerable poet for many years will be, in a real sense, a follower of Eliot; he will have learned from him where to begin. But in another sense, the suspected opprobrium in the term comes near to justification:

To live is to remember,
to die is to forget,

Present existence
      is all reminiscence,
            memory
Of our imperishable soul's past journey,
      woven in and out of time
As strands which never sever,
      we thread death to birth and get
New feet for the old dance.

Mr. Duncan's very respectable philosophy might even, obliquely, justify his borrowings; but even its orthodoxy would fail to make his verse interesting. The positive elements of Mr. Duncan's work—primarily the masque—are all of this nature and quality, and would seem likely to be successful only to those persons for whom the intoned recital of half-remembered phrases represents a kind of emotion, often as overwhelming as it is vague. Yet in the performance of the work it seems likely that the success resides in the negative elements—the comic verse and the theatrical high jinks. There are "chants quasi blues", boogie-woogie expositions, semi-private jokes and hellzapoppin-revelry in the audience. So devout an exponent of the play as Mr. Robert Speaight admits that "one can see how Auden and Isherwood would have done it better"; the point is rather that they have already done it. Mr. Duncan is as Valiant-for-Humility as Mr. Auden was valiant in his earlier, political, ways; and there is a bouncing, spiritually appeased, complacency about Mr. Duncan's demolition of his abstractions that makes for good entertainment, however ill it accords with the formal emotion of the work. But as literature the play has little importance except that in emphasising the loneliness of Mr. Eliot's achievement in the drama, it requires us constantly to assess the nature of our difficulties, the tenuity of the general achievement. The failures of Mr. Nicholson and Mrs. Ridler do not teach us much that we could not have learned from a study of the naturalist drama in prose. Mr. Duncan's attempt at a formal drama, however, and its notable failure, asserts the importance of constantly reconsidering whether Mr. Eliot's achievement will in fact prove a fruitful point of departure for the drama. The failures also provide a certain necessary context within which one may realise again the unique achievement which Mr. Eliot's successful experiments represent.

(iii) *Christopher Fry*

The brilliant success, in the last five years, of the productions of Christopher Fry's plays in verse, has been well deserved; and the success has been a very good thing for the theatre. Mr. Fry's plays reveal a consistent and pleasant personality, and have a distinctive and interesting tone. To estimate the success accurately, however, we must see the plays, not so much as an achievement in poetic drama, as an original application of verse to familiar theatrical ends. Mr. Fry's work, that is to say, is not really a part of the revived tradition of poetic drama. It is to be related, not so much to the poetic drama of Yeats and Eliot, as to a particular tradition of comedy in which, in our own century, the most successful practitioners have been writers in prose. Mr. Fry's masters in comedy are not Jonson or Massinger, nor the Synge of *The Playboy of the Western World*, but Oscar Wilde, Shaw, Chekhov, and, indirectly, Pirandello.

One specific way of stating this distinction would be to say that Mr. Fry's plays are not comedies of theme, but comedies of mood. The comedy is not a matter of the drama as a whole, but rather of local incident and attitude, and, more commonly, of a self-dedicated verbal humour—pun, epigram, burlesque— which is given point (its own point, rather than any general end in the drama) by the verse. Thomas Mendip, in *The Lady's not for Burning*, is a direct descendant of the protagonist of *The Devil's Disciple*, and Jennet Jourdemayne, in the same play, has more than a casual relation to Saint Joan. The Chaplain is a typical minor character out of Chekhov; Bates, in *Venus Observed*—

> There are faces
> As can be mauled about wiv, and there are faces
> As can't be mauled about wiv. Mine can't
> Be mauled about wiv.

—is in the tradition of the comic uneducated of Shaw and Gilbert and popular twentieth-century prose comedy. The Duke, also in *Venus Observed*, is primarily the "mature" figure of the dramatic world of Shaw. As for Wilde, such phrases as these—

> RICHARD: All I can claim as my flesh and blood
> Is what I stand up in. I wasn't born,
> I was come-across.

and

> THOMAS: Your innocence is on at such a rakish angle
> It gives you quite an air of iniquity.

—leave us in very little doubt of this part of Mr. Fry's ancestry.
But I do not cite these relations in an effort to prove Mr. Fry
unoriginal; this would, in any case, be a point not worth
making. The real point is the kind of drama which the plays
represent, and I am arguing that this kind is, essentially,
familiar naturalist comedy—a comedy of incident and phrase;
and that the fact that the plays are written in verse represents
not an innovation in dramatic method but an embellishment
of a method with which this century is already familiar. The
verse is not the form of the drama, but its polish.

Now it is true that from such plays as *The Lady's not for
Burning* and *Venus Observed* it is possible to construct a kind of
theme. This theme—it would be more accurate to call it a
familiar attitude—appears in such speeches as these:

> Over all the world
> Men move unhoming, and eternally
> Concerned: a swarm of bees who have lost their queen.

> . . . this great orphanage
> Where no one knows his origin and no one
> Comes to claim him.

> . . . the question is a man's
> Estrangement in a world
> Where everything else conforms.

> And of course you're right.
> I have to see you home, though neither of us
> Knows where on earth it is.

But it would be a very limited response to the plays which
offered us such sentiments as the essence of the dramatic
creation. They are persistent moods, but the plays do not, in
their substance, either concentrate on or embody them. The
sense of loss of origin is genuine, but as an element of the drama
it is offered diffidently, almost casually. There is a certain
concern with death, but Mr. Fry's is an essentially genteel
eschatology. He is frequently surprised by the nature of
existence, but he keeps his surprises well under control, and

263

permits himself only a few well-bred and perfectly unexceptionable doubts. The apprehensions fall:

> as airily as lime flowers, intermittently,
> Uninterrupting, scarcely troubling
> The mild and fragile progress of the sense.

These general critical questions have not, in the properly wide attention to Mr. Fry's work, been much canvassed. They have been ignored in the general congratulation on the felicities of his verse. But the most important point about the verse is the nature of its dramatic function, and Mr. Fry's position in the development of modern drama can only be seen when it is realised that his verse is not, in the traditional sense of poetic drama, dramatic at all. I do not mean that it is a different kind of dramatic verse, inadmissible because of its lack of reference to some orthodox canon. I mean that the drama is not in the verse as verse; its root is in characters and in moods and in phrases, which the verse certainly bears, but which it does not embody. In discussions of the quality of Mr. Fry's verse, it is usually phrases which are cited, and this is characteristic. One can make such an anthology at random:

> The lanterns, Rosabel. They'll be very pale
> Compared with the foment of wild flamboyant rose
> We have in the sky tonight.

> Horses . . . the caves of their nostrils blowing
> Bright clouds of breath

> . . . I, as unlaborious
> As a laburnum tree, hang in caresses of gold.

> . . . the river
> Where the water gives those girlish giggles around
> The ford.

> Our English sun, convalescent after passing
> Through the valley of the shadow of the moon.

> I, the little heretic as he thinks,
> The all unhallows Eve to his poor Adam.

> Such white doves were paddling in the sunshine
> And the trees were as bright as a shower of broken glass.

> . . . I've an April blindness.
> You're hidden in a cloud of crimson catherine-wheels.

Now it is very easy to say that such writing is the very stuff of poetry, that "Mr. Fry . . . can let down his bucket into a sea of dazzling verbal invention where he wishes, and bring it up brimming." [1] The language clearly invites the kind of comment that is made on the language of Sean O'Casey: "colourful, rich, exuberant." But surely one comes to feel, as one does with O'Casey, that rather tóo much of the colour and the richness is *external*, and that the exuberance is not so much intensification as a defect of precise imagination. The *cloud of crimson catherine-wheels*, the doves *paddling* in the sunshine, the *girlish giggles* of the water, the *caves* . . . *blowing* bright clouds, the *foment* of *wild flamboyant rose:* these are surely a kind of straining after effect which is seen as straining precisely because no real balance of imagination is achieved in the language. They have the air of contrivance because they add so little but a vague diffusion of fancy. The *caresses of gold* and the *shower of broken glass* are commonplace romantic incidentals; the *valley of the shadow of the moon* is a reminiscence of profundity which the image as a whole not only does not sustain, but to which it has no reference. *All unhallows Eve* is a different kind of phrase, in a manner in which Mr. Fry is more often successful than the manner of romantic fancy. It is not very successful here, but it is seen pleasantly enough in:

> The Society for the Desecration
> Of Ancient and Modern Monumental Errors

in

> An occasional signpost of extreme prejudice
> Marked "No Thoroughfare"

and in Jennet Jourdemayne's mathematical biography of her father. The reference here is not to romantic poetry, but to Auden and—

> Give us our trespassers as trespassers will be prosecuted for us

—to Joyce. This kind of interest is seen again in the playing with unfamiliar terms:

> God give me a few
> Lithontriptical words

—which is very apt when the meaning can be taken. A similar

---

[1] From a review in the *New Statesman and Nation*.

interest serves the many phrases of abuse (one is again reminded of O'Casey); but in

You spigoted, bigoted, operculated prig

operculated is noisy rather than telling, is rather less happy than *O blastoderm of injustice*. The best abuse is in the familiar O'Casey style:

You bubble-mouthing, fog-blathering, Chin-chuntering, chap-flapping, liturgical, Turgidical, base old man

—where the sound and fury is allowed to have its own way. This scattering of verbal jokes is responsible for much of the incidental success of the plays, but there is a dogged persistence about it which occasionally becomes tedious, and which reaches such sad ends as when Perpetua, in *Venus Observed*, remarks after having shot the apple:

To please, I always aim.

It is not a bad epitaph for Mr. Fry, but his own ambiguity on *aim* is worth pondering.

One aspect of Mr. Fry's verse may be seen very well by a concentration on phrases, but for a full understanding one needs also some examples of extended speech. Of the phrases, one's feeling is that too often the apparently significant word turns out, on examination, to be either numb or commonplace.

The word is an arrow
Of larksong, short from the earth's bow, and falling
In a stillborn sunrise.

The inevitability of *stillborn* is not a matter of the image, in which it is no more than a gesture, but a matter of what one might call "adjectival rhythm." This may be seen more clearly in a somewhat longer passage:

There it is,
The interminable tumbling of the great grey
Main of moonlight, washing over
The little oyster-shell of this month of April:
Among the raven-quills of the shadows
And on the white pillows of men asleep:
The night's a pale pastureland of peace,
And something condones the world, incorrigibly,
But what, in fact, *is* this vaporous charm?

SOME VERSE DRAMATISTS

The movement of this passage, if studied closely, is based on what one might call a refusal of the noun. At every point, adjectives, or adjectival phrases, are used to usher in the objects; and their cumulative effect is a relaxed, almost careless rhythm, moving always on the outside of statement. Whether the adjectives are "striking" or not, the effect of this dulling rhythm is an unmistakable vagueness. This vagueness cannot then be redeemed by a phrase, even by so striking an effort as:

> that sappy upshot of self-centred vegetabilism
> The trees of the garden.

Now this is Mr. Fry's predominant rhythm. Its main variant is the curiously persistent

> Anyone would think I had made some extraordinary
> Suggestion.

or again,

> Which were excellent and bright and much to be
> Remembered.

At times there is a momentary tightening, accompanied always by a closer approximation to speech:

> He tries to be a copy of all his kind.
> How can he be? He is Roderic-phenomenon,
> Roderic only, and at present Roderic in pain.

But the general measure is a loose sliding away from speech, a monotone of seeming, with slow, wide meanders into adjective and adjectival phrase. There is hardly any variety in the movement of the plays, so that even the felicities come to be blurred. It can be said that *The Lady's not for Burning* is an April mood, and *Venus Observed* the mood of November (Mr. Fry, I believe, has said something like this), but the strange thing is that both moods *sound* very much the same:

> I can see
> The sky's pale belly glowing and growing big,
> Soon to deliver the moon. And I can see
> A glittering smear, the snail-trail of the sun
> Where it crawled with its golden shell into the hills.

> Branches and boughs,
> Brown hills, the valley faint with brume,
> A burnish on the lake; mile by mile
> It's all a unison of ageing,
> The landscape's all in tune, in a falling cadence,
> All decaying.

The result, both of the rhythms and of the method of the phrases, is the exact opposite of what Mr. Eliot had in mind for poetic drama, when he spoke of a poetry which is such that one does not look at the poetry, but at the drama which the poetry embodies. Certainly, because of his methods of language, one is always "looking at" the poetry in Mr. Fry's plays, except that, as a result of the lulling rhythm, "looking at" may be a less accurate description than "acquiescence." But it is not, it seems to me, the kind of acquiescence which the best poetic drama creates; it is not the perception of embodiment, in speech and image and movement, of the total dramatic experience. One's response, in the end, is a recognition of Mr. Fry's tone for what it is, so that we do not expect poetic drama, but rather an embellished kind of minor comedy, incidentally brilliant, often verbally exasperating: a tone summed up in lines like these:

> Surely she knows
> If she is true to herself, the moon is nothing
> But a circumambulating aphrodisiac
> Divinely subsidised to provoke the world
> Into a rising birthrate—a veneer
> Of sheerest Venus on the planks of Time.

There is a definite place in modern English drama for Mr. Fry's comedies, but, in the resonance of his success, it is important to emphasise that this place is neither innovating nor directive.

4

Criticism Into Drama

IN 1950, now that an American actress visiting *The Cocktail Party* has told American playwrights to go home and smash their typewriters, a phase of the modern poetic drama may be said to have ended. Several plays in verse have emerged from a studio and little theatre existence into the commercial theatre of Broadway and the West End; and although the emergences are relatively isolated, the entrance into a new situation is clear. My purpose here is to review the phase that has ended, with particular emphasis on one element in it that has a general and continuing importance. The rise of the modern poetic drama presents a case of a body of successful criticism preceding, and largely assisting, the creation of a body of successful drama. To those who believe that criticism is a primary agent in the development of a literature, this particular history has an obvious importance. At a time when the dominant public view of criticism (which it scarcely distinguishes from reviewing) is of an "after-the-event", almost parasitic activity, the part which criticism played in the development of a new dramatic form deserves emphasis.

Much of the important dramatic criticism of the last seventy years has been what is usually called destructive; and this, too, is worth emphasising. There are many categories of criticism, but in the popular view two categories predominate: "constructive" and "destructive." And it is commonly assumed that constructive criticism is good, and destructive criticism bad. The current prospectus of a monthly review, for example, promises, with some show of satisfaction, "constructive criticism only." Yet there is an essential place, in the development of a literature, for criticism of the kind that is usually called destructive. The large body of destructive criticism of the last seventy years was fundamentally necessary to the reform of the drama. The energy of its revolt was the moving power; and its intelligence ensured that it should pass, at the proper time, into construction and into creative development. The history, indeed, is of criticism into drama.

The reform of modern English drama has two main phases:

first, the development of naturalism; and, second, the establish-ment of verse plays in the theatre. In the phase of naturalism, English drama was on the periphery of a large European move-ment. In the case of the poetic drama, although there have been European influences, the product is largely native, and draws much of its strength from traditional English drama. In both phases, however, English criticism has played an active, and at times a determining part. It is the continuity of criticism, in fact, which allows us to see these apparently contrasting phases as necessary and interdependent elements in a general reform. Although my main interest here is in the verse play, a brief account of naturalism, in its relation to criticism, is necessary to the subsequent analysis.

The roots of naturalism, as a dramatic method, lie much further back than the nineteenth century, but it was in the second half of that century that it became a distinctive and major European form. One of the landmarks in criticism is Herman Hettner's *Das Moderne Drama* (1851), in which, at a time when the dominant European form was the intrigue drama of Scribe, the related ideas were put forward of "a serious mission" in drama, and of the major importance of *burgerliche Tragödie*. But Hettner was not widely influential, and the leading European dramatic critic of the half-century was a man of very different views, Francisque Sarcey, the most important theorist of the *pièce bien faite*.[1] Ibsen, the master builder of the naturalist drama, was influenced by both of these apparently contradictory schools; it is this double influence which has misled so many of his critics. In the series of plays from *Pillars of Society* (1877) to *Hedda Gabler* (1890), Ibsen created the type of modern naturalist drama, but he created it from his own inheritance and apprenticeship to the play of romantic intrigue. Seriousness was achieved, if not "a serious mission." Romantic characters gave place to "everyday, insignificant people." But Ibsen's situations, even in this series of plays, were hardly, as Shaw described them, "everyday"; and many of his technical devices, as I have shown elsewhere,[2] were those of the *pièce bien faite*. To these plays of Ibsen there were two immediate critical reactions, both of seminal im-portance: Strindberg's *Preface to Lady Julie* (1888), and Shaw's *The Quintessence of Ibsenism* (1891). Strindberg was the first great destructive critic of romantic intrigue drama, in his

[1] See especially *Essai d'une ésthetique de théâtre* (1876).
[2] See Part One, 1; *Henrik Ibsen*.

attack on its "patent-leather themes played in patent-leather shoes on Brussels carpets." But Strindberg, with Ibsen obviously in mind, did not think it possible to reform the intrigue drama from within:

> In other countries it has been thought possible to create a new drama by filling the old forms with the contents of a newer age; but . . . we have not got the new form for the new contents, and the new wine has burst the old bottles.

Strindberg's criticism of the drama was, in fact, more radical than that of the naturalist critics (the method which he calls "naturalism" in the *Preface* is very different from naturalism as generally understood, and confusion between the terms must be avoided).[1] It led, in the first instance, to his own dramatic experiments, from *Lady Julie* to *The Road to Damascus*, *Dreamplay* and *The Ghost Sonata*. It led also to the method which was to be defined as expressionism, and had a real, if indirect, influence on the development of English verse drama.

It is interesting that several of Strindberg's dramatic techniques were more advanced in his criticism than in his current plays. His idea of "contrapuntal dialogue", for example, is proposed in association with *Lady Julie*, but one does not find the method really in practice until the first part of *The Road to Damascus*, written ten years later. This dialogue, "providing itself in the earlier scenes with material which is afterwards worked up, admitted, repeated, developed, and built up, like the theme in a musical composition", was of great positive importance for future drama, for it re-established *theme* as the centre of a play, rather than plot or character; and it conceived this theme not so much in ideas (the "message", the "serious mission") as in words.

Shaw's criticism, although Strindberg is usually classed with him as one of the naturalist innovators, is of a very different kind. He is more generally destructive than Strindberg, and only his initial targets—the "old drama", the romantic intrigue play, the *pièce bien faite*—coincide. Shaw's real concern is with the "serious mission" of drama, and he has his own definition of seriousness:

> The worst convention of the criticism of the theatre current at that time was that intellectual seriousness is out of place on the stage; that the theatre is a place of shallow amusement, that people go

[1] See my discussion of this point, in the chapter on Strindberg.

there to be soothed after the enormous intellectual strain of a day in the City; in short, that a playwright is a person whose business it is to make unwholesome confectionery out of cheap emotions.

The "unwholesome" is a telling adjective, and it indicates Shaw's preoccupation; for him the reform of the drama was a matter of subjects of social importance, and of a framework for moral teaching. The methods of his own plays show this very well. He accepts and exploits, for his own purposes, almost all the devices of the old romantic drama. To these he adds one element of his own (an element which he claimed that Ibsen invented) : the discussion. His whole drama is certainly a case of "new wine in the old bottles."

Shaw's career, of course, is an obvious example of the making of criticism into drama. He was a critic before he seems to have thought of writing plays, and it was a situation largely created by his own criticism which led him to write his first play, for an experimental theatre—Mr. J. T. Grein's *Independent Theatre*; for the theatre had been a result of enthusiasm for the new drama, but it found itself at the outset without any new plays.

It was a critical judgment, also, which led Shaw into a practice which was to have great symptomatic importance. By the time when he was beginning to write, the novel was the dominant literary form in England. Most writers of the time, including most of the dramatists, were far more affected by the methods of fiction than they seem to have realised. It was this domination by the technique of fiction which led Shaw to his notorious misunderstanding of Elizabethan drama, and thence to the inclusion in his printed plays of descriptions of scenery and characters and modes of speech, as well as prefaces on the subject of the play as a whole. The practice has spread so widely that it is difficult now to realise its eccentricity, but the fact that plays had to be dressed up into a kind of novel in order to be read is indicative of the central dramatic problem which the writers of our century have had to face.

It is one of the ironies of dramatic history, and yet at the same time serves to remind us of the common origin of the two phases of drama which we are considering, that in the first programme of the *Independent Theatre* should be plays both by Shaw and by W. B. Yeats. The plays were far apart in method, and the divergence between the two dramatists was certainly to widen. Yet there was more common ground than is usually realised. Yeats, for example, accepted the idea of a "People's Theatre", and recognised the "liberation of mind" and the growth of "intellectual excitement" which the new naturalist drama had brought about in the theatre. Again, he rejected the old romantic drama as absolutely as Strindberg or Shaw (indeed more definitely than Shaw); but his rejection, characteristically, was in literary terms. He saw that it was impossible to found good drama on "dead words", and insisted on the use of "words that have the only thing that gives literary quality— the breath of men's mouths." His emphasis on a living speech, however, did not lead him, as it had led Ibsen and Strindberg, to naturalism. He wanted to evolve capable dramatic *forms*, to restore "ritual"; and the purpose of this evolution was that living speech should be able to bear a greater weight of experience, should be able to "become impassioned", rather than be confined to the representation of actuality. The consequence of this critical decision was far-reaching, for it led Yeats to reject both the "fictional drama", and the "visual theatre." The rejection of fictional methods was based on the belief that the centre of drama is not character, but speech. The rejection of the visual theatre was based on the consequent belief that the purpose of acting was the communication of a pattern of speech, rather than the projection of character or actuality. Thus Yeats came wholly to reject the contemporary theatre, and to work in creating a new theatre which should answer to the literary need. The Abbey Theatre, like the "new theatres" everywhere in Europe, was essentially created in response to certain decisions in criticism; and it can be said of it before 1914, as it can be said of the criticism of Yeats which inspired it, that it created the necessary confidence that verse plays could again be written for the public stage.

But the Irish theatre before 1914 had an advantage which the English theatre lacked and still lacks: the existence of a native speech which had direct and obvious possibilities for poetry. For T. S. Eliot, considering the possibility of an English poetic drama in the early twenties, conditions were very different, and the whole problem of speech had to be faced as if there had been no beginning. The problem, as Eliot defined it, was "to find out how people of the present day would speak, if they spoke poetry." It is a problem that cannot yet be said to be solved.

The main point of that large part of Eliot's criticism which precedes his experiments in the drama is an insistence that the problem of speech, like all related problems of the new drama, can only be adequately negotiated by a concentration on form. The speaker E in his *Dialogue on Dramatic Poetry* says this:

> Let me for a moment transfer the discussion to the question of form. A few years ago I . . . was delighted by the Russian ballet. Here seemed to be everything that we wanted in drama, except the poetry. It did not teach any "lesson", but it had form. It seemed to revive the more formal element in drama for which we craved. . . . If there is a future for drama, and particularly for poetic drama, will it not be in the direction indicated by the ballet? Is it not a question of form rather than ethics? And is not the question of verse drama versus prose drama a question of degree of form?

More explicitly, in his own voice, Eliot wrote:

> We must find some form to restrict, as it were, the flow of spirit, before it expands into that desert of exact likeness to reality which is perceived by the most commonplace mind.

The question of form is, of course, very largely the question of the establishment of conventions. And the essential fact of a convention is that it must be agreed. Agreement on a dramatic convention, between writer, actors, and audience, is the essential preliminary to form. And when one says "agreement", it is not so much a deliberate consent that one has in mind— for the very deliberateness might hamper adequate communication. What is required is a full consent, a consent both of the intellect and the emotions, and it is probable that the drama will always be the greater where the consent is virtually unconscious.

It is in this light that Eliot's plays must be judged, for the whole series of his experiments seems directed towards a creation of the conditions for such consent. In his early plays, of course, Eliot deliberately deprived himself of the most widely consented convention of the day: that of the representation of actuality. In doing so, he was of course aware of the necessary sacrifice of communication. But "wherever you have a form, you make some sacrifice against some gain." In *Sweeney Agonistes* the form is a matter of language: the deliberate stylisation of contemporary speech in terms of a skilful mechanical rhythm. The danger, of course, was a restriction of communication to the limits of the caricature; and Eliot proposed to avoid this danger by the use of a central character whose "sensibility and intelligence should be on the plane of the most sensitive and intelligent members of the audience."

Sweeney himself, to an extent that one perhaps only realises in performance, very largely fulfils this function, and there is a great gain in communication because he is designed in this way. But the limitation of this device is the necessary integrity of the chosen verse-form. The gap between Sweeney and the rest cannot be allowed to widen too obviously; and while there is striking success within the fragments, it is open to question whether so difficult a balance could have been maintained throughout a full-length play.

The perfect integral form was found by Eliot in *Murder in the Cathedral*, where it grew naturally from the material of the play. The various difficulties of convention are met at once, in a perfectly convincing manner, because Eliot is able to avail himself of the one full, living convention of form and formal speech: the liturgy which is natural to a play of the death of an Archbishop. *Murder in the Cathedral*, for this reason, and for the unity of feeling which it makes possible, is the most completely satisfying play which Eliot has written. And a less bold writer would probably have been content to confine himself in future to similar material, where such conventions would always have been available. But Eliot went on with his search, attempting to establish dramatic conventions for the explicitly contemporary play. *The Family Reunion* and *The Cocktail Party* enable us to judge how successful he has been.

In these two plays, Eliot seems to have abandoned form in the sense in which he had originally defined it. Form now is less a question of deliberate pattern and stylisation of the material and characters of the play. Form, as parts again of his early criticism had foreshadowed, is primarily a question of verse. This is more noticeable in *The Cocktail Party* than in *The Family Reunion*, where devices like chorus and chant are still in occasional evidence. But it is true of both plays that the significant form is the verse itself; verse, moreover, written according to a convention which virtually excludes any of the more obvious conventions of formal dramatic pattern. For once again, but in different terms, Eliot is seeking to meet a popular audience on its own ground. The primary convention of both plays is a form of verse which should have sufficient flexibility to include, in the first place, naturalism—as the immediate point of contact with a contemporary audience, but to include also both formal dramatic statement and dramatic rhetoric (in the sense in which Eliot had defined this in his essay *Rhetoric and the Poetic Drama*).

Implicit in the question of the unity of form is the more difficult question of the unity of feeling. Insofar as *The Family Reunion* failed, it was at a point short of this final criterion: at the point, I have suggested, of the unity of form. *The Cocktail Party* does not repeat this failure—its success on this score is indeed triumphant; but if one still has doubts about the play, they may best be stated in relation to what Eliot has himself insisted on as ultimately important: unity of feeling. In a very interesting discussion of "meaning" in *The Use of Poetry* Eliot wrote of "the chief use of meaning in certain kinds of poetry" as "satisfying one habit of the reader, keeping his mind diverted and quiet, while the poem does its work upon him: much as the imaginary burglar is always provided with a bit of nice meat for the house-dog." It is an illuminating comparison; but burglars, one supposes, can, like everyone else, compromise too far; they might even become genuinely fond of the dog. In the surface comedy of *The Cocktail Party* Eliot is almost certainly engaged with his "bit of nice meat", and very quiet it keeps us. It is, once again, part of the persistent endeavour to gain the audience's assent: a very difficult endeavour for the poetic dramatist in the contemporary theatre, and one that demands sympathy. But one feels at times that what is really taking place is the supplying of "comic relief", not only for the audience, but perhaps also for the dramatist. The comment may come from Eliot himself:

> . . . I find the readjustments of mood required in this play very trying. . . . The desire for "comic relief" on the part of an audience is, I believe, a permanent craving of human nature; but that does not mean that it ought to be gratified. It springs from a lack of the capacity for concentration.

If this judgment (on *The Witch of Edmonton*) should have any relevance to *The Cocktail Party*—and I think myself that it has—the word to which we should return is "audience." As Eliot goes on to point out:

> The audience which can keep its attention fixed upon *pure* tragedy or *pure* comedy is much more highly developed.

The development of an audience is the point at which criticism and drama finally come together. Eliot's dramatic experiments are of too great an importance for us to forget their nature as experiments in our delight in their finished forms as plays. Where one makes reservations about success, it is not by comparison with the general level of the contemporary theatre —for then the successes would seem absolute—but in relation to what was intended to be achieved.

The contemporary English poetic dramâ is certainly not lacking in vitality, although its status must still rest primarily on the work of Eliot. Its revival, as I have tried to show, was very much dependent on good dramatic criticism. At the time, with Yeats's lonely controversies in *Samhain*, and with Eliot's *ex cathedra* pronouncements in his essays of the twenties, it probably looked to many as if criticism were off the main current, or supporting a lost cause. But this particular body of criticism has not followed out the parallel which some made between it and the work of Sidney and the school of the Countess of Pembroke. At least some poetic plays have become popular successes, as well as being the only new drama of any serious account. Yet we still cannot finally say that the poetic drama will be something more than a minority drama. "I believe that the theatre has reached a point at which a revolu- tion in principles should take place", wrote Eliot in 1924. There has been change, if not revolution, in the writing of plays; but in the theatre? For my own part I cannot see a performance of *The Family Reunion* or of *The Cocktail Party*, with all its revelation of uncertainty of form and inconsistency of convention, even alongside the brilliance, without feeling that the present is at best an uneasy passage between the old and the new. It is not perhaps that the poetic drama has taken command of the theatre, but that it has been absorbed by the theatre. And it is at this point that criticism is as necessary as it ever was. The most absolute critics, Yeats and Eliot, were willing to learn from the theatre, to use it as a workshop in which their dramatic experiments might be made. Such an attitude is proper and reasonable. But it is very easy, in the bustle of the workshop, to forget certain elements of the plan. In the confusion of success and failure, and amid the "*susurrus* of popular repetition", the continuity of standards which criticism can provide is indispensable if the best theatre is to prosper, and the best drama flourish.

Index

Figures in *italics* indicate principal references

INDEX

Johnston, Denis, 25, 234
Jonson, Ben, 155, 162-3, 260, 262
Joyce, James, 196

Kafka, Franz, 249
Kaiser, G., 179
King's Threshold, The, 214-15, 216
Knights, L. C., 12
Kongs-emnerne, 49

Lady from the Sea, 81-2, 85, 86, 87
Lady Inger of Ostraat, 47-8, 65
Lady Julie, 69, 74, 83, 99, 100-1, 104-9, 110, 122, 169, 271
Lady's not for Burning, The, 262-8
Lamm, M., 110 n
Land of Heart's Desire, The, 212-13
Lawrence, D. H., 18, 19, 63, 98, 103-4, 178
League of Youth, The, 45, 60, 66
Leavis, F. R., 12, 211-12, 223
Leavis, Q. D., 12
Lee, J., 73-4, 83
Lehmann, John, 255
Lillo, G., 46
Lind-af-Hageby, 110
Little Eyolf, 85, 86, 88-91, 92, 96, 97
London Merchant, The, 46
Long Mirror, The, 193
Love's Comedy, 49
Lucky Peter's Travels, 99-100, 120

Ma non e una Cosa Seria, 190
Macbeth, 46, 65, 166
Machera e il Volto, La, 188
Machine Infernale, La, 196
Machine Wreckers, The, 179
Maeterlinck, M., 120, 130
Mallarmé, 156
Mankowitz, W., 83
Marshall, N., 34
Martin-Browne, E., 244-6, 256
Masses and Man, 179, 183
Massinger, P., 262

Master Olof, 99
Masterbuilder Solness, 43, 73, 85, 86-8, 89
Maulnier, Thierry, 196
Medée, 196
Megarée, 196
Merchant of Venice, The, 34-5
Michael Kramer, 175
Miss Julie, see Lady Julie
Molière, 155, 162-3
Moon in the Yellow River, The, 25
Moore, George, 210-11
Mouches, Les, 196, 200
Munro, C. K., 255
Murder in the Cathedral, 198, 199, 200, 223, 226, 227-31, 232, 244, 256, 275
Murry, J. Middleton, 12, 50

Nicholson, N., 256-8
Nightingale in Wittenberg, The, 120

O'Casey, Sean, 26, 169-74, 177, 178, 265-6
O'Neill, Eugene, 196
Old Man of the Mountains, The, 256-8
Ollen, G., 110 n
On Baile's Strand, 216-17
On the Frontier, 247, 254-6
On the Vidda, 85
Only Jealousy of Emer, The, 219
Orphée, 196
Othello, 34

Paid on Both Sides, 247
Parisienne, La, 103
Peacock, R., 219-20, 230
Peer Gynt, 11, 43, 56-60, 62, 69, 78, 85, 86, 87, 92, 96-7, 99, 112, 122, 163, 249
Pensaci Giacomino, 190, 192
Peter Pan, 121
Philanderer, The, 142-4
Piacere dell' Onesta, Il, 190
Pillars of Society, 60, 66, 70, 72, 74, 270

INDEX

Printed in Great Britain
at Hopetoun Street, Edinburgh,
by T. and A. CONSTABLE LTD.
Printers to the University of Edinburgh